RANDOM HOUSE

LARGE PRINT

MY AMERICAN DREAM

MY AMERICAN DREAM

A LIFE OF LOVE, FAMILY, AND FOOD

>‹ ‹

Lidia Matticchio Bastianich

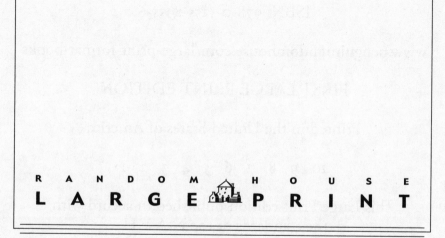

RANDOM HOUSE
LARGE PRINT

Front-of-jacket photograph by Melanie Dunea
Back-of-jacket photograph courtesy of the author
Cover design by Kelly Blair

The Library of Congress has established a Cataloging-in-
Publication record for this title.

ISBN: 978-0-5255-8955-6

www.penguinrandomhouse.com/large-print-format-books

FIRST LARGE PRINT EDITION

Printed in the United States of America

10 9 8 7 6 5 4 3 2 1

This Large Print edition published in accord with
the standards of the N.A.V.H.

To my five precious grandchildren,
Olivia, Lorenzo, Miles, Ethan, and Julia.
This book is the story of your great-grandparents and
their children. You are the products of my mother's
and father's hopes and dreams for a new beginning.
You have my unconditional love and blessings.
Go forth, flourish, and help keep this great country
of ours ever greater.
Our life here began as Italian immigrants but we are
now all proud Americans.

Contents

PART ONE

Giuliana

Few people outside of my immediate family know this, but for the first five years of my life, my name was not Lidia, it was Giuliana. My mother had chosen this name for me as a way to remember her homeland, which was then part of the Friuli–Venezia Giulia region of northern Italy. The Second World War had ended, and communism was coming to Pola, the small city on the southern tip of the Istrian Peninsula, overlooking the Adriatic Sea, where my family lived. The Yugoslav Partisans, who were communist-led, had fought as guerrillas against the Nazis and Fascists and had taken over the government of Yugoslavia when the Germans were defeated. As part of the 1947 Treaty of Paris, our city, and most of the Istrian Peninsula, which had become part of Italy after World War I, was given to communist Yugoslavia.

The redrawing of borders sparked a mass exodus from the area, with more than three hundred thousand people fleeing to Italy to reclaim their Italian citizenship. Many of them had deep Italian roots; they spoke Italian, and their families were Italian. Many of them migrated on to Australia, New Zealand, Canada, and the United States. My parents planned to join the migration, but my mother was pregnant with me, and they knew that travel would be difficult. There was also the question of where to go once we crossed the border. Refugees were being placed in camps, and my father was not comfortable with the idea of my mother's giving birth and caring for an infant in such a place. They also had my three-year-old brother, Franco, to consider. The war was still raging when my mother gave birth to him in July 1944. With the collapse of Fascist Italy in 1943, the Germans occupied the city and used it as a U-boat base, making it a target for Allied bombardments. The family had no money for clothing or food, much less furniture, so my mother fashioned a **cassetta,** a wooden cradle, for little Franco from a spaghetti box marked with the word "fragile" on two sides, and she fitted it with a mattress of corn leaves. When he was five months old, two bombs were dropped on Pola. The minute the siren sounded, alerting residents to the bombardment, my father assumed his role as driver of the fire truck for the Pola town arsenal, Cantiere Navale di Scoglio Olivi. My mother awoke to see pieces of the ceiling falling onto her baby's cradle, and she hurried to his side, grabbed the spaghetti box with Franco inside, and ran to the bomb shelter.

At the end of the war, Pola was under the Allied forces when my mother became pregnant with me. The exodus of the Italian Istrians was still open, and many of my mother's friends and relatives were moving to Italy, because Istria was soon to be under the Yugoslavian rule. Food was scarce, and jobs were scarcer.

Still, my mother was an Italian schoolteacher and had the possibility of finding a good job somewhere in Italy. Her supervisor had requested a teaching position for her in Brescia, a city at the foot of the Alps, between Milan and Venice. The position supposedly included housing, so my father loaded all of the family's furniture onto his truck and traveled there to set up what was going to be our new home. He was lucky he had a truck. Many of the **optanti**—opters, people who had opted to leave Istria—loaded their belongings, packed in crates and boxes, onto trains. Some would go toward Trieste, Italy, the Free Territory, their horse-drawn carts with piles of pots, pans, chairs, tables, and other furniture as high as the carts could handle. I recall the stories that my grandmother Nonna Rosa would tell me about how some of those **optanti** had even dug up the bones of their deceased from the cemeteries and took them along in boxes. They could not bear to leave their loved ones behind.

Port of Pola, c. 1950

When my father got to Brescia, he found that the promised "apartment" was nothing more than a single room, much too small to accommodate our growing family, and a search of the area for available housing turned up nothing suitable or affordable. My father could not bring his pregnant wife and small son there, so he returned home after one week; he still had all of our furniture loaded in the back of the truck. He told my mother the family would remain in Pola until after she gave birth.

That January, my parents went to the pier in Pola to bid farewell to friends boarding the **Toscana,** a ship full of **optanti,** for the short voyage to Italy across the Adriatic, headed for Venice and Ravenna; my mother, now eight months pregnant, was teary-eyed and shivering in a coat that barely covered her belly. One month later, on February 21, 1947, she gave birth to me at the hospital in Pola, and seven months after that, on the fifteenth of September, the day the provisions of the Treaty of Paris were put into place, the border between Italy and Yugoslavia was officially closed. My parents— and Franco and I—were now stuck in Yugoslavia.

≫·≪

Change came to Pola ("Pula" in Croatian) almost immediately under communism. The names of streets, towns, and monuments were changed to reflect the area's new official language. Everybody's last name was changed as the new documents and identification cards were issued. Ours was changed from the Italian "Matticchio" to the Slavic "Motika." Churches across the peninsula were ordered closed. Suddenly, people weren't allowed to go to church or even practice religion openly. It was a sharp blow to many—both Italian and Croatian— who lived in the city and had practiced Catholicism for generations. My mother wanted to have me baptized, but now even that seemed out of the question.

I was only a few days old when my mother's younger sister, Lidia, and her husband, Emilio, walked quietly into my mother's hospital room one evening. Lidia had secretly arranged to have me baptized, and the priest was waiting for her at

Aunt Lidia Fonio,
my unwitting namesake

the small stone church adjacent to the elementary school where my mother taught second grade. To prevent the authorities from discovering the baptism ceremony, my aunt intended to sneak me out of the hospital, meet with the priest who would perform the baptism, and then sneak me back into the hospital, all without arousing suspicion among any of the doctors, nurses, or other staff.

Of course, I was way too young to remember anything from that night. But, according to my mother, Aunt Lidia wrapped me in a blanket and then tucked me inside a small sack she'd brought with her to the hospital. No doubt, everyone prayed that I was quiet as she walked me out of my mother's hospital room and out into the cold night air. I can only imagine the anguish my mother felt, waiting for our return, and the joy she felt upon hearing her sister's voice declare, "Here is your Giuliana!"

Lidia told my mother that everything had gone off according to plan: the priest was at the church waiting when she arrived, and he performed the baptism without incident. There was just one small detail my aunt kept secret—she had ignored my mother's wish to name me after her homeland, Venezia Giulia, and instead directed the priest to christen me with her own name, Lidia, and Giuliana as my middle name. On the way out of the hospital, my aunt even stopped by the records desk to list "Lidia" officially as my first name. She told the clerk she was there at the request of her sister Erminia, the mother of the child, and the woman happily obliged.

It wasn't until my mother went to the city hall in Pola to obtain a copy of my birth certificate so she could register me for the first grade that she learned the truth. A clerk told her that there was no record of a "Giuliana Matticchio" born on February 21, 1947. "I have another baby girl Matticchio born to Vittorio and Erminia Matticchio **Motika** on that date, but her name is Lidia-Giuliana."

"Giuliana" had a deep meaning for my mother. Friuli–Venezia Giulia is still a region of Italy, and Istria before the war was part of that region. Istria was in the Giulia part of the region, and we were Giuliani, as the emigrants from this area were referred to.

In one of my life's more unusual twists, the switch to communist rule allowed my aunt to change my name. For the first five years of my life, I was known as Giuliana by everyone who knew me—friends, family, and everyone in town. I **was** Giuliana. Then, suddenly, I wasn't. Suddenly, I was Lidia.

In school, I had to go by the name shown on my birth certificate—Lidia. My teachers and fellow students all called me Lidia, a name that I associated with my aunt, but certainly not with me.

It was as if I was being asked to play two roles in life: Giuliana at home and Lidia at school. At first, I didn't even respond to the name Lidia and wondered whom people were calling. Eventually, I got used to responding to both names, much like some people respond to both their given name and a nickname.

My grandmother never really embraced my new name, and to this day, my mother and my brother still jump back and forth between the two, sometimes calling me Lidia but most of the time Giuliana. No matter what name people used, I remained true to myself. Deep down inside, I was still Giuliana from Pola, even if people called me Lidia. Over time, I learned to embrace both. It wouldn't be the last time that I had to find a way to embrace more than one "me."

❧ ❧

Life in Yugoslavia under the rule of Marshal Josip Broz Tito was not easy for the ethnic Italians who remained, my family included. My parents were watched closely by members of the UDBA, the secret police. My mother was tutored and forced to teach all of her classes in Croatian; she was also expected to indoctrinate all of the young and impressionable children in her classes on the new communist order. From a rather prosperous lifestyle under Italian rule, everything shifted to stringent living conditions under communist rule.

My time as a young child was divided between two very different settings. One was in the city of Pola, where I lived with my parents and brother in a beautiful house with parquet floors, a tiled kitchen, and a bathroom with its own water heater, a luxury back then, and a claw-foot tub. The other was Grandmother Rosa's home, three kilometers or about two miles away, in sleepy Busoler, a tiny village with just thirty homes along one narrow white stone road. Most of the people in Busoler were farmers, and my grandmother tended goats, pigs, and rabbits. She also labored over a large garden, which provided much of the food for my family.

In Pola, my parents owned a two-family house in a fashionable area of the city. The apartment was spacious, with a living room, dining room, two bedrooms, a kitchen, and a bathroom, with long

My official school photo, mid-1960s in Astoria; my mother was still calling me Giuliana.

hallways connecting some of the rooms.

The entire family was careful to protect the parquet wood floors from nicks and scuffs. We'd make **i pattini,** sliders, that allowed us to move—slide, actually—from room to room without worrying. They were sewn together in the shape of a large sole from pieces of old blankets or tattered clothes. We'd step on them and slide with the fabric under our shoes to prevent scuffing. As an extra benefit, they helped shine the floors, too.

My brother and I always had fun stepping on the sliders and racing down the long hallway leading into the kitchen. We'd get a running start, then slide the rest of the way and sometimes fall. Once, things didn't go quite as planned, and both of us wound up in trouble for the broken door glass in our wake.

My family shared the yard behind the house with the family that rented the other apartment in our house. My mother tended a small garden there, though she didn't grow much—at least not in comparison with my grandmother's garden. I remember two apricot trees, a walnut tree, a large fig tree, a small peach tree, and a loquat tree. I had a pet turtle I called **"la mia tartaruga,"** my little turtle, who would resurface every spring. She loved the apricots—and, yes, it was a she, because she laid eggs every season and would bury them underground. But there was no male turtle to fertilize them, and year after year she would resurface alone. I also had a black-and-white cat named Micia. I played with my pets during the school days, when I was not with Grandma Rosa in Busoler. We also had a **cantina,** or cellar, where my father stored his tools, and a laundry room with a cauldron that we filled with water and heated to wash our clothes. The windows at the back of the house overlooked the playground of my nursery school, which I attended when I was four. Sometimes I'd get homesick at school and miss my mother. During recess, I'd stand in the playground and stare up at the windows of our house and cry, wishing she would come pick me up. Today the two-story building sports a fresh coat of deep burgundy paint and a new number 7 by the front door. But otherwise the building looks unchanged.

Now when I go to visit Pola, I stay in the courtyard in Busoler. But I always pass by this house and recall my life as a young child, running up and down the street, playing hide-and-seek in and out of entrances and gardens, playing tag and skipping rope, and playing house in the old fortress, the Kaštel, on the hill, just behind the house and built on top of old Roman ruins.

My parents were considered well off by local standards. My father, a mechanic, had a small trucking firm with two vehicles that he used for making deliveries. Few people in Pola even owned a car, much less two trucks, which drew attention to him and prompted members of the local Communist Party to label him as a capitalist. People would hire him to haul their goods and other materials, sometimes locally and sometimes over long distances. He'd spend some nights on the road, doing deliveries to far-off locations. Occasionally, he would take the family with him. Sometimes the cargo he'd carry was wine, or fish, or bags of wheat, or even containers of olive oil. Other times, the truck would be loaded with furniture, as people moved from one town to another. Sometimes his truck would be used in lieu of a hearse, carrying both the deceased and the deceased person's family as they escorted the individual back to his or her birthplace for burial.

He did not always get paid with cash. Sometimes, his payment was a demijohn of wine, or bottles of olive oil, or some of whatever was in the back of the truck. On his way back to the shop, he would make a stop at home to drop off his latest treasure for the family to use.

My mother thrived in the city and drew joy and happiness from everything that Pola had to offer. One of her favorite pastimes was dressing up in a hat to meet friends at the café in the Giardini, the central square and main gathering place, that is bisected by a street of the same name. Our home was just a short walk from the square, and I have fond memories of running through it with my friends on my way to and from school each day. Today it draws many tourists who are eager to relax over a drink in one of the outdoor cafés that have served generation after generation of patrons, shaded by majestic, century-old hackberry trees, planted in four uniform rows. We would play hide-and-seek behind those trees. There are more people and cars there today, of course, than there were during my childhood. But in many ways, the area remains unchanged, the three- and four-story buildings looking much the same as they always did, and the cafés serving drinks, pastries, and ice cream for people who were watching passersby.

My mother liked to patronize the cafés of the Giardini in the late afternoon, and I'd sometimes spy her there, sipping coffee, as I raced by with my friends en route to the park or the narrow stone streets of old-town Pola. The most prominent entrance to the medieval town was just steps from the square and marked by the Triumphal Arch of the Sergii, an imposing Roman arch built at the end of the first century B.C. by Salvia Postuma Sergii with her own money, in honor of family members who took part in the Battle of Actium. It was one of the original gates into the city during Roman times, which even then was called "Pola." My friends and I would spend hours racing along the narrow streets, careful not to slip on the uneven stones that had been worn smooth over the centuries. Sometimes we'd play house in the old Roman arena on the outskirts of the old city, now in the center of Pola. We would have favorite corners of the ruins, making believe that the space was an oversized home for us, with "rooms" for our dolls and ourselves. We'd pretend that the massive pieces of stone that lay flat on the ground were our beds and the round fragments of fallen Roman columns were tables for our pretend meals. We often collected poppies and wildflowers from the nearby parks and gardens and arranged them in empty bottles and cans to decorate our spaces. And we draped fallen tree branches across the stones to serve as a roof. We played for hours, climbing up and down the stones that had been carved by our ancestors. Now, whenever I visit an archaeological site or a museum, I can't help but think back to my childhood days spent romping with friends amid these ancient structures. There was no need for my mother to worry, because she knew that the streets were safe—the most we could get was scuffs on our knees and elbows from climbing on the rocks.

My mother, Erminia, was well known around Pola. She'd been much appreciated as a teacher for years, and many knew her, because they either had once been in her class or currently had a child in her classroom. At the end of each school year, the

Me as a little girl, on the steps
above the Giardini in Pola, c. 1955

mothers would come bearing gifts of thanks to her:
a bouquet of flowers, four or five freshly laid eggs,
pieces of bacon, strudel, homemade prosciutto, or
sausage. I loved it when she brought home freshly
baked goodies. In retrospect, there was such an appreciation for teachers, scholars, and mentors then.
My mother still tells us stories of how she took particular care in teaching and aiding children who
had special needs and those whose parents needed
them to work in the fields during school hours; she
took extra time to tutor these children. Sometimes
they would even come to our house in the after-

noons and early evenings for special classes that my mother would hold free of charge. I was very proud to have a mother who was a teacher to students my age. She liked the prominence her position afforded her, and her salary allowed her to do some of the things she enjoyed. She'd proudly gone from wearing handmade shoes with soles made of recycled bicycle tires to stylish ladies' shoes and elegant hats, which were considered a symbol of class. It was, perhaps, a small touch—but an important one for someone who'd grown up without any luxuries. Her desire to dress well extended to her children. When Franco and I were young, she liked to dress us up in fancy outfits and bring us to the Giardini to show us off. One time, she outfitted us in matching sailor suits and put us on display.

"I didn't know you had twins," one of my mother's friends remarked.

I was growing so fast and was so strong that, although I was three and Franco was almost six, we were nearly the same height, and looked about the same age.

My mother also had a fancy bicycle, given to her by my father when she first began teaching at an elementary school in the town of Sissano (Šišan in Croatian), on the outskirts of Pola. He had surprised her with her very own Italian-made Bianchi to make her commute to Sissano easier. The two had moved in with my father's parents in Busoler until they could afford a house of their own, so getting to the schoolhouse each morning meant a vigorous forty-minute walk for my mother. She continued to ride the bike even after they moved to the city. More a work of art than mere two-wheeled transportation, the Bianchi was something to be treasured, and my mother truly did treasure it. My father had even customized it for her; he covered the back wheels with colorful netting to prevent her skirts from becoming ensnared in the spokes, and fastened a fancy basket to the handlebars for her books and other small items. She proudly tells the story of how the children would wait for her at the base of a hill so they could help push her while she pedaled, to make the climb easier for her, and then run alongside her as she pedaled up to the schoolhouse, eager to greet her and help carry her books to class.

Erminia had grown up in a two-room house, with no plumbing and an outhouse. She and her sister had shared the home's only bedroom with their parents and slept on a mattress made by hand, using materials found on the farm—cloth, sheep's wool, feathers, and corn husks. Every other year, the sheep's-wool mattresses would have to be rethatched, a process that usually took an entire summer. First came the gentle dismantling of the stitches that held the mattress together; then Grandma would wash the outer cloth in a tub of soapy water, scrubbing it well with a brush, before stretching it and putting it out in the sun to dry. It was a heavy task, and she would ask me to help her. Some of our relatives also came to lend a hand—family members served as a support system, and, in turn, Grandma was there when they needed her. The inside wool clusters were also washed and spread out on a canvas under the sun in the courtyard until the wool dried. My job was to flip the clusters of wool so they would dry on all sides. When they were dried, they were brushed with a steel brush until the wool became fluffy again. A professional mattress thatcher would then come to the house to sew the mattress back together. Until then, just the corn husks sufficed.

Aunt Lidia and my mother
in the courtyard in Pola

I loved that old corn-husk mattress and still remember cuddling next to my grandmother on it. The aroma of corn and the rattling of the dry leaves lulled me to sleep night after night. Sometimes the rattling husks, especially when I was sleeping alone, would feed my imagination. I heard all kinds of frightening noises—animal calls, the wolves, the bears—but if I stayed still, they would all go away. These handmade mattresses didn't hold the same fond memories for my mother. She was delighted to leave them behind when she married my father and eventually moved into the city.

Erminia felt she'd elevated her status when she married my father, Vittorio, who was nine years her senior and from a well-to-do family in Busoler. Her father-in-law—my paternal grandfather, Antonio Matticchio—operated a local construction business there and owned numerous properties in the small village.

She was nineteen and fresh out of school when my father asked for her hand in marriage. Vittorio had actually been engaged to a young woman named Maria from the neighboring town of Jadreški when he was twenty-one, but the two never married: Maria died from tuberculosis before the wedding took place. She was just twenty years old, and Vittorio was devastated. He lived with his family in the house at the other end of the village; every Sunday, my mother would see him walk by on his way to the cemetery to place flowers on Maria's grave. One afternoon, my mother asked if she could go with him, and, with Nonna Rosa's permission, he invited her along. Erminia was only fourteen at the time, but she understood my father's grief and wanted to offer him some company. That day, she helped Vittorio clean the weeds from Maria's grave, and after that the two became friends. My father didn't really date anyone after Maria, and as the years passed, his family worried that he might never marry. It wasn't until my mother was eighteen years old that he started to take an interest in her, which made his parents and siblings happy. He would wait at the gate to his house in the afternoons so that he could greet my mother as she walked home from school. Sometimes his mother, Francesca, was there, too. She liked Erminia and was heartened that her son might have someone to make a life with. On some days, Francesca would wait by the road alone for my mother to pass, so that she could give her a hunk of freshly baked bread or a pastry to enjoy. She knew that my mother's family struggled financially, and she wanted to provide my mother with a little extra nourishment.

It was customary for the bride's family to provide a dowry, but my maternal grandfather, Giovanni, had no money; he'd spent it all on Erminia's schooling. Giovanni worked in the **arsenale,** or shipyard, as a machinist, and his job had taken him all over the world—Africa, Asia, South America, even New

York. He began working on ships when he was in his early teens, and his travels were the reason he was so determined to provide his own children with an education. Though he had never gone past the elementary-school level, he wanted more for his two daughters. "There's a whole world out there beyond our little village," he'd tell them. Any extra money went to their education, and his efforts were rewarded when my mother graduated from the Scuole Superiori, a specialized and highly regarded high school where students trained to be teachers. My mother became the first teacher in Busoler; her sister, Lidia, became the town's first accountant and landed a job at the local post office.

Sadly, he told Erminia there was no money left for my mother's dowry. She'd have no choice but to turn down Vittorio's proposal and find a job so that she could earn sufficient money for her own wedding chest.

Vittorio's parents told him not to worry; that very day, they went into Pola, bought twelve sets of linens to create a dowry for my mother, and hired a woman to embroider all of them with the couple's initials. Few in Pola would have been able to afford such a large purchase, but my father's parents were among the more financially comfortable families in Busoler. One month later, they presented my mother with a beautiful trunk that contained her dowry and declared, "Now you can marry!" My

My father, Vittorio; his sister
Anna; his mother, Francesca; and
his father, Antonio (Pola, c. 1935)

mother cherished those linens. She even brought
a set of them with her to America when we immigrated, and we used them for years.

My parents' wedding was among the biggest and
most widely attended in Busoler; my grandmother
hosted more than eighty guests in her tiny courtyard. Both she and my grandfather came from big
families. Nonna Rosa had seven brothers and sisters, and Grandpa Giovanni was one of five. My
mother describes her wedding day in grand fashion, recounting the horse-drawn carriage that
brought her to the Cathedral of the Assumption of
the Blessed Mary in Pola, where she and my father
were married. Vittorio's parents provided much of

My parents' wedding,
September 21, 1940

the food served at the reception, and there was an accordionist and dancing, enjoyed by all.

Often, my mother nostalgically reminisces about her early days in Pola and tells me how even the simplest things in life had mattered so much more than they do to us now. It's a life view that I share at the deepest level. With all that we have and all that's going on around us, we don't take the time to appreciate the simple but still valuable things that life has to offer.

There was no doubt that my mother loved her new life in Pola and relished the joys of being in the city, including going to a café for coffee or shopping in a boutique. Yet she never lost the mind-set that she developed as a young girl in the country, where even little items were treasured and simplicity was appreciated. I often reflect on my mother's words: **"Does having more make us happy? Do all those things give us satisfaction?"** In this world, there are still many places like that courtyard in Busoler, where a little goes a long way.

As I grew and evolved from that courtyard, a lot of things changed in my life. I have been given many gifts over the years, but those simple sentiments and expectations remain deep in my heart and mind. I go forward, sharing them with my children and grandchildren because I want them to know, respect, and appreciate the simpler things in life that make the growing complexity of our present lives more meaningful. I express these emotions with food as well, the way I buy, the way I cook, the way I appreciate the earth, the sun, and the animals that feed us. I am so gratified when I can share this with others in my restaurants, in my cookbooks, and through my cooking show.

Even as a child, I knew that my mother wanted nothing more than to leave the courtyard in Busoler in favor of the hustle and bustle of city life in Pola. I enjoyed the creature comforts there, too, and certainly treasured my parents' love and compassion. Still, from my earliest visits there, my soul always seemed to be in Busoler with Nonna Rosa in her courtyard.

I continue to make my yearly pilgrimage to that courtyard. My grandparents have since passed, and the animal pens and coops are now empty. But I continue to find such comfort and strength in reliving my experiences in that space. I fill it now with my memories. At night, a descendant of the hooting owl that I was so afraid of when I was small still hoots today. The wind still hums through the pine trees in the **pineta**, the pine forest that abuts the property, and the fig trees, like big umbrellas, still shade the courtyard. In August, these fig trees, now like then, are full of ripe figs, and I do as I did then, pluck them off the branches and have my breakfast, sixty-plus years later. In the mornings, I now wake early to sweep the courtyard as Grandma Rosa once did, clearing the fallen figs and leaves from the stones.

I am forever drawn to living close to nature, to tending the animals, and to caring for the garden. Yes, it was a hard life on the farm, and Grandma had to work no matter what the elements, wind or rain or the blistering heat in the summer months. But somehow that was my true home, and the place that has forever centered me.

2

Life in Busoler

I would go to Busoler as often as I could, every weekend, every holiday, and to celebrate the first eight birthdays of my life. The town was on a seasonal clock, with all the work and labor dictated by nature. My grandfather Giovanni worked as a machinist to earn both an income and a pension. His passion was the **campagna,** the land in Busoler where he and my grandmother grew, raised, produced, vinified, and milled everything they needed to survive. They made wine, distilled grappa, cured prosciutto and pancetta from the pigs. They milled their wheat at the communal flour mill, and in the cold of November harvested the olives to make olive oil. The vegetable patch behind the courtyard produced all the vegetables and salads needed to feed us, and the surplus was jarred, dried, or cured, and saved for use in the winter. We had jarred tomatoes, pickled cabbage and turnips, dried shelled beans, ceci beans, corn, figs, grapes, and all kinds of herbs.

Braided shallots, garlic, and onions would hang in the **cantina** along with the prosciutto and slabs of pork-belly bacon. Apples were lined up like soldiers on a wooden plank in the cool **cantina,** and Seckel pears and quince would be tucked into the wheat berries to ripen. Anything that was left over after the family's basic needs were met was either sold at the **mercato,** market, in downtown Pola, about two miles away, or bartered; nothing was wasted, no matter how small or seemingly inconsequential. Even leftover breadcrumbs were saved, to feed to the chickens and pigeons.

My grandparents' house was one of three on the half-acre property; their relatives occupied the other two.

One of Grandpa Giovanni's sisters, Maria, whom we called Santola, godmother, lived in the house adjacent to my grandparents' in the courtyard. The two homes were almost identical: boxy one-story concrete-and-stucco buildings, with one small window in the back bedroom and another in the kitchen, at the front of the house. The windows and door were always open; we knew everyone in town, so there was no need to lock the house, even at night. Today the houses are freshly painted in bright hues that recall the flowers growing nearby. In my youth, the stucco was left in its original off-white color.

The third house on the property was not in the courtyard. It belonged to our cousins Matteo and Teodora, known as Toda, and now belongs to the family of their son, Renato, who recently passed, and was just to the left of the main entrance to the property. You had to pass it to get to the courtyard, which was closed off with a wrought-iron gate. Matteo and Teodora's home was somewhat larger than the others and looked out onto the large shared garden that was divided equally among the three families. Each family had its piece of the garden to tend. But we all did some of the work together.

To the north of the courtyard, leading into the **pineta,** were the pens for the animals. Nonna also had there a **casetta nera,** literally meaning a small black house. The structure earned its name because its walls were truly black from the smoke that came from its open hearth. Inside, bouquets of bay leaves and oregano hung from the walls. It was in the **casetta nera** that Nonna would do some of her food preparation—rendering fat, smoking prosciutto, sausages, and pancetta, and hanging braids of onions and garlic to dry in the winter. She'd cook for the pigs there, too, using potato peels, pumpkins, food scraps, and the bran left over after we milled the wheat into flour for our bread and pasta.

Beyond the **casetta nera** was the chicken coop, a small loft made of carefully spaced wooden planks complete with wooden stairs for the fowl to climb up to their elevated living area. Along the wall, there was space for the ducks and geese. Inside the chicken coop were wooden boxes filled with hay, where the chickens would lay their eggs. One of my chores was to place clean hay periodically in those boxes. We had some larger hay-filled boxes on the floor for the ducks and geese. But the geese tended to do as they pleased and sometimes laid their eggs under the bushes in the woods. I loved to collect the eggs, and over time I learned all their secret spots. During the day, they were free to roam the court-yard, and some of the chickens would even come inside the house, perhaps to see what Grandma was cooking.

The geese in particular were noisy and always protesting about something. They could be quite nasty, challenging and pecking me with their or-ange beaks as I rounded them up with a stick. But Grandma praised their large eggs, and used them for making fresh pasta. For holidays like Christ-mas, she would roast a whole goose for hours in a wood-burning oven, with rosemary, until the flesh fell from the bone. Meat was not a staple of our diet; it was saved for holidays and other special cel-ebrations. I just loved roast goose; maybe there was even a bit of revenge on my part as I savored the bird's tender, cooked flesh.

We always had two or three pens for the rabbits, which we kept separated by sex, united only when Grandma wanted to breed them. They demanded a lot of attention and food, eating the outer leaves of our lettuces and cabbages. They also ate the trim-mings from the vegetables that we cleaned and prepped for the market. Grandma and I would go to the fields with a sickle, especially in the spring-time, and harvest clover and flowers for them. In the wintertime, they would eat hay. Straw from the milled wheat was used to line their pens, along with those of the pigs and chickens. I loved playing with the young bunnies; they were like furry little balls and would tickle me as they tried to smell my face when I held them near.

There was also a pen for goats, and they were always a handful. Grandma would send them to pasture behind the house, where they would indis-criminately eat anything, although they preferred garden vegetables and fruits, particularly grapes. Thus, they had to be closely watched, and that often became my job. We'd tie the adult goats to a metal stake that had been pounded into the ground and allow them to graze in one small area at a time. The kids were allowed to roam free, since they would never go too far from their mom. My duty was to keep an eye on them and monitor how much grass they were eating. Once they were done grazing in one area, I'd pick up the stake and move them to another section, with fresh grass. Watching them was one of the many jobs that had once been per-formed by my mother when she was my age.

The kids were always lively and loved to play, run-ning and performing acrobatic jumps. We would get involved in their playtime, too, trying to catch them, or just laughing at their wild antics. I loved holding them and petting them, although they never stayed still for long. I especially loved caressing the young animals on their necks, where they had two white, furry puffs hanging. As they matured, the hanging puffs would retreat into the neck as glands. I remember tying shreds of colored cloth into bows to place around their necks. They looked so cute, as if they were dressed for a party. The brightly colored bows made such an eye-popping statement against the kids' pristine white fur.

The goats produced excellent milk, from which Grandma would make ricotta and other fresh cheeses. Sometimes we'd even drink the milk still warm from milking the goat; I especially liked the foam that was created during the milking. Never mind cappuccino—this foam was beautiful. Grandma would bring the milk to a boil to pasteurize it. When she let it cook, it formed a creamy crust that I liked to spoon onto my bread. That was one of my favorite meals, second only to the homemade fig jam we'd make from the fallen figs of the courtyard tree to spread on our morning toast.

I was okay with the goats, but I didn't particularly enjoy the pigsty, although Grandma and Grandpa deemed it very important to care for and raise our pigs properly. We would go to an animal fair once a year, usually in February or March, to buy piglets. I still have vivid memories of accompanying my grandparents to the fair, which was held in Dignano, today Vodnjan, an archetypal town of stone houses with red tile roofs some ten to fifteen kilometers away from Busoler; we used the horse-drawn cart to ride there, buy the baby pigs, and bring them home.

My grandparents had no choice but to buy suckling pigs at the fair, because they didn't mate pigs on the farm. That was another whole process. At the fair, the little pigs would be in pens often temporarily built around various trees, and Grandpa would go from one piglet to the next, picking each one up by the hind legs and carefully checking each animal's health. Ignoring the animal's squealing, he would examine its bone structure, and see how easy or difficult it was to stretch its legs. Everything he did was thoughtful and measured; his goal was to buy the piglets that had the best chance for growing big back on our farm. He wanted the animals to grow as big as possible and yield a lot of meat and fat. Usually, we would choose two or three of the sucklings to take back to the farm. If we needed it, we'd buy oils and cheeses at the fair, too.

My grandparents had a handmade basket to carry the piglets home in. It was fashioned of woven twigs, and sized to fit right under the seat of our cart. The two little pigs would squeal as the horses slowly pulled the cart along the rough road toward home. It was a long ride, some two or three hours, and I kept myself busy by feeding the pigs tiny pieces of an apple or two. They would stop their squealing for a little while to nibble on the apple— and then go right back to making noise. I could feel the warmth of their snouts and breath through the basket. We usually stopped at the **osteria** for lunch, where Grandpa would talk with his friends and Grandma would enjoy a glass of wine. There was always somebody playing the accordion. The trip provided a fun respite from the daily grind of farm life.

The piglets were cared for, cooked for, and fed until they were ready for slaughter, around November or December, when the traveling **macellai,** butchers, would come to town. The butchers moved from house to house, and town to town, slaughtering the pigs for one family at a time, until all the animals were killed and cut into pieces to be salted, cured, and preserved. The visit by the **macellai** became a festive event; all the neighbors were invited over to help with the work, and the host household provided a feast—food and wine—for everyone who participated. As the **macellai** traveled from one house to the next, we'd follow along to help our neighbors and celebrate the occasion. Every few days, it was another household and another celebration.

The butchers' visit meant that everyone was assured of having food for their families that would last for the whole year—prosciutto, sausage, bacon, confit, and cured pork meat. Most of the families in Busoler had at least one pig; Grandma Rosa raised two every year.

Everyone understood that the animals we cared

for would eventually be slaughtered and end up in a pot—food that sustained my family and innumerable others. There was no such thing as going to a butcher shop or supermarket to buy pork or chicken. It was understood that the meat came from the animals that we'd raised on the farm, and slaughtering was part of the cycle of life.

Once the pig was slaughtered, prepping and curing all the pieces would take another two days of hard work. The whole family was involved, and, as usual, nothing was wasted. Neighbors in Busoler routinely helped each other. They'd spend two days at our house, and then Grandpa and Grandma would go and help out other families, until, finally, all the work was done.

The morning of the slaughter, there was always a lot of activity in the courtyard. Big vats of water were put on the hearth to boil, a long plank of wood was balanced on two upside-down barrels, and the long thin butcher knives were sharpened. When the butchers put on their thick aprons, we'd know that it was time for them to begin their work. As children, we'd quickly run away as the men brought a squealing live pig from the barn and laid it on the plank of wood on the barrels. We all knew what was coming next, and none of us wanted to witness it. The pig was placed on its back, and Grandpa and three of the stronger male neighbors each grabbed a leg and held the wiggling animal as steady as they could. Grandma stood by with a large bucket ready to catch the flowing blood as the butchers pierced the pig right in the heart. The squealing ended, and slowly the pig's movement would ease and then stop. Next, the men turned the pig on its side with the cut toward Grandma and her bucket, so she could collect every drop of the pig's blood.

While the blood was still warm, Grandma would put it in a large pot on top of the wood-burning stove. She used a long wooden paddle to stir the mixture while it slowly came to a boil. She'd add cornmeal (polenta), raisins, cinnamon, salt, pepper, rice, lemon rind, sugar, chopped nuts, and small pieces of chocolate if she had any. Nonna would continue to cook the mixture until it was fairly dense, like porridge, and the rice was cooked. She would then cover it and let it rest in a warm place.

In the meantime, the men were shaving and washing the pig with hot water while it was still up on the plank. When the pig was clean and shaven, the breaking-down process began. The hind legs were very important—they became the prosciutto—while the front legs were cured like the prosciutto, and called **spalletta**. The front legs have less meat on them and cure faster than the thicker and more meaty hind legs. Next the head was cut off, and the cheeks became **guanciale**. The tongue was put in salt and water—a **salmistrare**—to cure; the ears were cut off, cured with salt, and hung to dry for future use. The pig's belly was carefully opened to avoid piercing the large and small intestines, and the stomach removed—a dirty job. The women, each with her bucket, cleaned sections of the digestive tract, the stomach, the small and large intestines. All those pieces of the animal had to be vigorously washed, rinsed repeatedly, and then soaked in water and vinegar before being used. The stomach cooked into **tripa,** and the rest turned into the casing for the **cacciatorini,** or sausages, that Grandpa made, and dried along with the prosciutto and **spalletta** hanging in the **cantina.**

Once they were soaked and cleaned, some of the small-intestine casings were filled with the cooked blood mixture and became delicious blood sausages that Grandma would pan-fry for us in the morning with some polenta—at least as long as they lasted. The inner organs were the first to be separated and eaten. The heart, lungs, kidneys, and sweetbreads were cut up and sautéed with lots of onions, bay leaves, white wine, and a splash of vinegar. Along with a mound of polenta, that was lunch for the **macellai** along with all the neighbors and family.

Usually, there were about twelve to fourteen of us eating the lunch, and the courtyard was as busy as a beehive when the food was being served. Some of Grandpa's wine was always saved for this event, as there had to be enough for the two days the **macellai** were working with him. The women cooked, the men worked, and tables were set up wherever there was room. For the kids, little pieces of meat from here and there were seared on a grill. With some bread, we were happy with our **porchetta** sandwiches.

The curing of the different cuts of meat continued after lunch. The fat of the chest and stomach with the skin still on was cut into rectangular pieces, rubbed with coarse salt, pepper, and bay leaves and hung to cure into **lardo;** a good pig lard was the thickness of about four fingers of fat; I recall Grandpa measuring it with his fingers. The piece of the belly slab that had some meat between the fat became pancetta, or bacon. This was the foundation of many **minestras**, or soups, and many pasta dishes for the rest of that year.

As the butchering continued, the smaller pieces

The all-important ritual in the courtyard in Busoler: slaughtering a pig that fed many people. Aunt Lidia is at the right, pouring the hot water to shave the pig.

of meat were put in one bucket while the fat was placed in another. The meat with some fat became the sausages, fresh and dry, while Grandma patiently rendered the fat into **strutto**, or lard, and the delicious cracklings we ate like popcorn. The pork butt on the shoulders would be cured with salt, pepper, and some bay leaves, then put into pieces of large intestine to cure and dry, to become **capocollo.** The slabs of ribs with some meat on them were cured with salt and pepper and dried, as was the filet. The trotters, or pigs' feet, were scrubbed and washed with boiling water, then cured with salt and pepper and hung to dry-cure.

As I look back, what strikes me most is how carefully we used every part of the animal and never wasted a bit. It was a sin to waste. Even the pig's bladder, the only piece of the animal we could not eat, was made into a soccer ball for the children to play with by rubbing it in sand until all the outside fat was rubbed away; then it was hung to dry in the sun, then it was inflated with a straw and tied. The slaughtering of animals was very much a part of life on any farm in Busoler—or elsewhere at the time. It was the life that we knew, understood, and respected.

We hear every day about hunger in the world, about food drives, and about children who don't have enough food. Yet so many of us eat only selective parts of the animals—chops, filets, hams, butts. The remains, those parts I so vividly remember being appreciated in the courtyard, aren't used for food these days. Instead, they are often sent to rendering plants, where they are turned into soap, toothpaste, mouthwash, hair dyes, nail polish, crayons, glue, solvents, shoe polish, toys, ornaments, pharmaceutical products, and cosmetics. For me, there is value in using as much of the animal as I can for nourishment and sustenance.

3

Nonna Rosa

My grandmother's face told a thousand stories of a life spent outdoors, laboring in the garden, tending the animals, cooking, washing, and caring for her family. My earliest memories were of Grandma Rosa when she was in her fifties. Even then, her skin was leathery-tough from years of exposure to sun, wind, and cold, and when she smiled, you could see she was missing a few of her back teeth. She was a petite woman, standing just over five feet tall, and she looked almost fragile in the black dress, apron, and kerchief that she wore almost every day. She was wiry, too—surprisingly strong and quick on her feet, from the hard work she'd done for most of her life. The deep wrinkles and creases around her eyes and across her forehead added at least ten years to her appearance. If I close my eyes, I can easily picture her darting around the courtyard as she gathered the fallen figs to feed to the animals from the tree that graced its center,

My favorite photo of
Nonna Rosa, late 1950s

cleaning the animal pens and coops, tending the garden, and washing and hanging the laundry on the clotheslines strewn across the courtyard.

There was little free time in her world, and always more demands for chores than hours to do the work. When she hoed the land in the summertime, she did it barefooted; I can still picture her callused feet in the red earth. In the wintertime, she smelled of smoke from the fire she kept going in the **casetta nera.** Sometimes, after dinner in the evenings, she would gather there with some of the ladies from the village, to relax and socialize. Like Grandma, these women were dressed in black with kerchiefs covering their heads. Grandma would make coffee, and she and some of the women would sniff tobacco. My friends and I wouldn't be far, usually playing somewhere nearby. I was curious, and would frequently return to listen in on what was being said. They'd complain about their husbands, wonder about whether there would be a good crop and if there would be enough food. They'd talk about making the olive oil, and even chatter about the pigs that some families were lucky enough to have.

The men kept to themselves in the evenings. Grandpa, who spent most of his days laboring in the fields, liked to station himself on the big rock out by the road and wave hello to the passersby, some of whom would stop to talk for a bit.

In the morning, Grandma was always up before the sun to begin her chores—and that meant that I was expected to be up early, too. I would find Grandma wherever she was working, and learn what my chores would be. Sometimes she'd hand me a plate of food for the chickens, or an empty metal pail to milk the goats. The pail always came with a simple message from Grandma Rosa: if I wanted milk with my dinner, I'd better help her and get to work. Other days, I was tasked with gathering pinecones from the state-owned forest behind the house; we'd store them away for the winter. They were great for lighting the fire in the fireplace to keep us warm. Anyone from Busoler and the surrounding villages could go into the forest and pick up pinecones, just as I did. But we had the luxury of having the forest as our backyard.

Milking the goats was always one of the first chores, and we would do it together. First I would position Grandma's stool. Then she would get hold of a goat by its hindquarters, hold one of the goat's rear legs with one hand, and milk the animal with the other; I would hold the pail. A delicious aroma came from the frothy milk in the metal pail, and I would sometimes take a sip of the rich liquid while it was still warm.

Usually, I'd have a simple breakfast that would include some goat milk. I'd take some with a touch of coffee and sugar, and shred pieces of day-old bread into it. **Pan e caffè latte,** it was called in local dialect. It remains my brother Franco's favorite breakfast. If there was no bread left over, polenta cut into snack cubes would do. I still enjoy it from time to time today, though I do miss that fresh goat milk. Sometimes, if there was a surplus of the goat milk, Grandma and I made ricotta from it; I loved ricotta on bread.

At 10:00 a.m., we'd have our **merenda,** or midmorning snack: some bread, a bit of cheese, or a freshly picked fig. Then it was back to work until lunchtime. In the summertime, I'd gently pull the ripe figs from the trees with a quick twist of the hand, and line them to dry in the sun, usually on a low cement wall. First I'd cover the cement with fig leaves to keep the fruit clean, then place the figs on top in a neat row. I had to make sure they didn't touch each other, so they'd dry uniformly. Once the figs had dried but were still somewhat soft, we would thread them on long sprigs of the bloom flower, packing them close, and placing one bay leaf between each fruit, before knotting them into what seemed like a necklace. We placed them in the sun and kept turning the figs until they were finally dried; then Grandpa would hang them in the **cantina** for the winter.

Grandpa and I would also put the grapes to dry, so we would have raisins. He would carefully cut the whole cluster with the stem connected to the vine, forming a T, then hang them one by one on nails in the wooden beams that supported the **cantina**'s soffit to let the clusters dry out. Depending on the season, some days I helped pick cherries, walnuts, almonds, or hazelnuts from the trees; other days I worked alongside Grandma in the garden, planting, hoeing, watering, and harvesting the vegetables. I still vividly recall the moments when I'd pull potatoes out of the dirt. They were always surprisingly warm in my hand and seemed full of life, a warm gift from the earth. Potatoes fresh from the field were bursting with flavor, too. We put some aside in a cool, dark place in the **cantina** for use during the cold winter months. Unfortunately, the ones that had been stored never seemed quite so flavorful.

Often, when the heat of day was too intense, we'd find things to do in the shade, sorting vegetables, shelling beans, braiding onions to store for the winter, or preserving fruits. At mealtime, I helped

Grandma in the kitchen, chopping the meat, rinsing the vegetables, putting together the salad, and setting the table. She'd bring a stool over to the sink for me, so that I could stand next to her as we prepared the potatoes and other vegetables for the pot. I especially loved kneading bread and making pasta or gnocchi with Grandma, getting my hands into the dough, shaping the pasta, or making the ridges on the gnocchi by rolling them down the tine of a fork. If it was nice outside, we'd carry the small wood table from the kitchen into the courtyard and enjoy our meal al fresco. On cold, damp, or rainy days, we'd eat inside. There was often not enough room for all of us at the table, so we kids would take our plates and sit on the steps leading into the house.

When I go back to the courtyard now and look at my old home, and that kitchen, I see that you can barely squeeze four people around the table. Somehow, everything is smaller than I remember from my childhood. And yet that's where we ate. Back then, we all seemed to fit just fine.

❧ ❧

Of course, everyone worked hard during the day, and it wasn't unusual to be ravenous by the time dinner was served. We always had enough food for everyone: to be sure, no one went hungry. But finding sufficient food for all could sometimes be a challenge, and it wasn't unusual for us to go foraging to supplement our cultivated vegetables.

Spring was the time for wild asparagus, **bruscandoli** (butcher's broom) shoots, dandelion greens, nettles, chamomile, violets, wild leeks, chives, and all kinds of mint. We also gathered **ovoli** (egg-shaped mushrooms), chanterelles, morels, **prataioli** (portobello-like), **chiodini** (little nails) and in the fall **grifola** (hen of the woods), porcini, and others.

My favorite thing was, and still is, foraging for wild asparagus. In Busoler, depending on the spring rain and the sunny days that follow, wild asparagus begins to sprout in mid-March and continues into April. **Asparagina** is what we called the plant. It flourishes in rather arid and rocky terrain, and the mature plant spreads out its prickly and surprisingly sharp fernlike branches. The older, tougher branches spread out close to the ground, and new skinny long shoots emerge each year; those new shoots—those green, tender spears—are wild asparagus. The treat of foraging is to harvest the skinny long spears poking through the soil every spring before they grow into feathery branches.

For the forager, the challenge is to pick those sprouts at their lowest point, closest to the earth, but tender nonetheless. I always carried a stick to push away the old prickly branches (and snakes) and help get to the tender sprouts unscathed. The mark of a good asparagus forager was hands that looked as if you'd been scratched by a cat. The wounds took days to heal. Still, they didn't seem to matter, because the flavor reward was so memorable. Today I bring my gardening gloves with me when I go foraging in Istria. Otherwise, I go about my work in the exact same way that I did so many years ago. And I still carry a stick with me, just as I did when I was a child.

We had our special places—we knew exactly where the asparagus plants were, and would walk for miles gathering them. In much the same way that you'd gather a bunch of wildflowers, we would forage for our wild asparagus and collect them in bunches until we couldn't hold any more. We always used one hand to hold our asparagus, and the other to gather. We took great care when gathering the bunches, careful to avoid knocking off the extra-tender tips. An asparagus without a tip simply wasn't an asparagus.

Sometimes we'd carry our asparagus under our arms, much as you might carry a basketball or football. Other times we'd carefully place them in a basket for the walk home. Most often, when we had an armful, we'd consider our work done and head back. As a child, I relished every spear—and do so even more now when I return for my annual wild-asparagus pilgrimage.

I can still savor the wild-asparagus frittata made with Grandma Rosa's extra-virgin olive oil, goose eggs that were so fresh they were still warm, my foraged asparagus, and a hunk of homemade bread to mop it all up. Gnocchi with olive oil, garlic, asparagus, and pecorino cheese was a Sunday treat. Salads of cooked asparagus with boiled eggs, soups of asparagus and spring peas and favas, asparagus as a condiment for pastas or a side dish for meats, risottos speckled with them—all delicious asparagus memories for me.

In season, wild asparagus were everywhere, on everybody's table in Busoler; children and adults alike enjoyed them. The wild asparagus is thin and fragile but intense in flavor; there is an initial underlying pleasant bitterness followed by the taste of the green fields, the brightness of the sun, and an appeasing sweetness at the finish. The texture is a bit resilient, but it all plays a role in this gustatory delight.

The places I recall from my childhood are places where the asparagus still grows. In today's changing world, where not much is constant, the flavor of those wild asparagus is still just as I remember from sixty years ago. What a relief to reaffirm that nature can remain constant if we give it a chance.

Through the passing years, in honor of my grandparents, we have maintained the house and the courtyard so the property is much the same as it was when I was a child. Where once there were fields of wheat, corn, and vegetables, we planted olive trees—those noble trees that can transcend several human life cycles, swaying their silvery leaves in the wind, bearing the fruit that gives the golden liquid, olive oil, so essential to life in the Mediterranean and so essential to that wild-asparagus frittata.

In late June came the **mietitura,** the harvest of the wheat, when the tiny green stalks of grain had grown tall and taken on a golden honey color, and a profusion of red poppies dotted the field. Just like the slaughter of the pigs, the **mietitura** was a town-wide event. But instead of the traveling butchers, families reserved a visit from **la mietitrice,** or thrasher, the big machine that separated the kernels from the hay.

My grandfather would assemble a team of men, usually comprised of relatives and neighbors, to go into the field with sickles and scythes to cut the stalks and tie them into big bundles; these were left standing like soldiers in the field for **la mietitrice.** Once the big, noisy, belching machine had done its work, the kernels were placed in burlap bags and stored in the **cantina.** The hay was built into a **coppa,** a tall cone-shaped pile around a long pole, covered with canvas held down with wire and stones to protect it from the elements, so that it could be used year-round for the animals. Wheat has a very particular smell, a sun-toasted aroma that I loved.

My job as a child was to bring the men lunch, which was served under one of the shade trees at the edge of the field. I would bring out the big bowl of dressed pasta topped with an inverted plate to keep it warm, all tied up neatly, including the bread—like a beggar's purse—in a large table-cloth. I'd untie the tablecloth, spread it out on the ground, and carefully arrange the plates and uten-sils. Then I would uncover the big bowl—usually a chicken stew, **guazzetto,** with some homemade pasta (fuzi, garganelli, or gnocchi) that Grandma had prepared—accompanied by some bread and cheese, and set out the glasses and the wine. The workers would sit on the grass around the table-cloth and have their lunch.

At the end of the day, Grandpa would bring the kernels home in their burlap bags and spread them on the floor of the **cantina** to aerate them. My brother and I loved to run through them in our bare feet, although sometimes we would get very itchy.

Once the harvest was complete, Grandpa would burn the wheat stubs that remained in the field, then hand-plow it with a horse-drawn plow. Some-times he'd rent a tractor to till the soil, with the stubs and ash, returning them to nurture the earth—and next year's crops.

The wheat from our fields had to last Grandma throughout the year. The kernels would stay in the **cantina** until she needed to make flour. Then she would take them to the mill in Pola, where they would be stone-ground into bags of fresh white flour, along with sacks of bran for the animals. We'd use the donkey-drawn cart to make the jour-ney, which was always fun for me. Grandma rarely

Busoler, main road, at the front entrance to the
courtyard: Santola Maria (Grandpa Giovanni's sister),
Aunt Lidia, Grandpa Giovanni, Nonna Rosa, Teodora
(Toda, wife of Matteo, Grandpa Giovanni's cousin)

paid for the milling, bartering in exchange some of
the kernels for the millwork.

My grandparents didn't have a bread oven, so they
would pay a small sum to use the one that belonged
to our neighbor across the street. Everybody had
to come with their own bundle of wood to bake
their bread. The oven was fired up twice a week,
and there was always a line of people waiting—
which gave the women a much-needed break to sit

and socialize. Sometimes I'd hold Grandma's place on line so that she could go and finish her chores. When her turn came, I'd shout to her across the street and she'd join me.

Grandma's routine was always the same. She'd place four risen loaves of bread on her wooden kneading board and cover them with a cloth. Next she'd roll another piece of cloth until it looked like a coiled serpent and place it on top of her head. Finally, she'd balance the kneading board atop it all, so that she could hold the load with just one hand. With practiced ease, she'd walk over to the bread oven when it was her turn. And so women from Busoler paraded back and forth from their homes with their loaves of unbaked and baked bread.

There always seemed to be a quiet competition between the women for baking the best-looking loaf. If they were pleased with the final product, the women would take their time covering it—giving their neighbors ample opportunity to admire the still-warm loaf. More important, there was something almost spiritual, a bonding moment, as the women came together to bake bread in a communal fashion around the single, shared oven. I always felt part of a community with a rich and deep heritage as we shared time together, performing a very simple yet essential task. We felt secure, too, knowing that, as a result of our efforts, the family would have bread to eat.

When my grandmother and I came home,

Grandma would lather a warm slice with some **strutto,** rendered pork fat, and sprinkle some sugar on top; that was my treat. But for an extra-special treat, there was nothing like the taste of freshly baked bread spread with homemade fig preserves from Nonna Rosa's courtyard tree.

4

By the Sea

There were quiet times in Busoler, too, when all the farmwork was done and we had time to go to the beach. For me, the white-pebbled beaches of Istria are among the most beautiful in the world. The coastline is dotted with quiet harbors and coves, and it's always possible to catch views of the Adriatic, no matter where you are in Pola. The Adriatic has its own special color, too, a translucent blue that is different from its close neighbor, the Mediterranean Sea. It's so clear you can see the bottom, even in water that is over your head. It isn't unusual to spot small baitfish swimming by, or little crabs climbing up the rocks looking for sea snails for lunch. The Adriatic is especially salty, so it's extraordinarily easy to swim there; the higher salt concentration allows you to stay afloat for long periods with little to no effort.

When I was young, I would go to the beach with my parents or one of my relatives. We'd pick our destination from among our personal favorites: some spots were protected from the waves, and at others it was easier to walk onto the beach. Many of the beaches were quite rocky, and a challenge even for us kids.

Stoja was a little promontory just outside of Pola covered with umbrella-pine trees, and it was here that we had our summer camp. There were wooden dormitories, communal boys' and girls' showers and bathrooms, and the **mensa,** the mess hall, with long wooden tables under the towering umbrella pines. This beach was special: it had a trampoline, a slide, and stretches of concrete where we could crawl like crabs from the sea and stretch in the sun like the lizards who shared the area with us. The lizards probably wished we had just left them alone. The boys would often play with them—catching one by the tail and watching with fascination as the animal would detach itself from its tail and scamper off to safety. I guessed the lizards regrew their tails, and rather quickly, because I don't recall seeing any tailless lizards running around.

As I got older, I preferred to go to the sea with my friends. We'd walk from Busoler together to the beach at Val Sabbion—today known as Pješčana Uvala—cutting across fields and gardens, and hiking through Bosco Rizzi, a beautiful pine forest, to get to the closest part of the shore. We knew we were close when we saw the two aboveground tanks that held the thousands of gallons of cooking gas used to fuel the stoves in nearby Pola. The tanks are still there—rusty and forgotten, but for me they are still a landmark, a marking point. It usually took us a little under an hour to make the trek, and once we were there, we'd spend the entire day. Our route wasn't flat, and coming home was harder, because we were tired and hungry—and it was mostly uphill.

We had jute bags to carry sandwiches, fruit, and drinks, usually water and, if we were lucky, lemonade. Most of the time, I'd bring water flavored with a little vinegar and some sugar, which was always refreshing. We'd find a spot beneath the Mediterranean pines to set up camp. Those towering trees served as our umbrellas, keeping us cool and protecting us from the sun, and the chattering of the cicadas provided our background music. To this day, the aroma of pine, no matter where I am, evokes a quick nostalgic mental trip back to my youth. Somebody always had an old blanket for us to sit on, and those who had a towel shared with those who did not.

We used the sea to chill some of the things we'd brought with us, anchoring them with rocks so they didn't float away. The sandwiches we would hang off the lower branches of the trees; otherwise, we would have had the ants to contend with, and, even so, many times we had to blow and shake them off our bread before we bit into our sandwiches. I'm sure we unknowingly swallowed some along the way. We'd spend hours running along the rocks, swimming, floating, splashing and dunking each other in the surf. The older kids loved diving off the big rocks cradling the shoreline in one area of the beach. Thankfully, my brother, Franco, was usually with us and acted as a lifeguard, especially to the younger kids like me.

❧ ❧

Being at the beach or on the sea always energized me, and I never turned down an opportunity for either one. Some of my fondest memories are of the nights I spent fishing with my uncle Emilio. He was married to my mother's sister, my aunt Lidia, and he'd been with her at the hospital the night of my "secret" baptism. He was an electrician by trade, but loved to fish and did it to make extra money on the side.

When his fishing buddies weren't available, Emilio would usually invite Franco and me along. He said he needed "company," which meant somebody to hold the fishing lines, or help with the fish traps. No matter what the chore, or how hard the labor, I didn't mind; I loved being out on the water with him. He'd usually come by to pick me up in the late afternoon, after work; he rode a motorcycle, so I'd always sit in front of him, and my brother in the back, for the short ride to the port in Pola where he kept his boat, a small wooden skiff with an oversized rudder at the stern. It was after dusk when we finally got out on the water. Sometimes we went out for just a few hours; other times, if the fish were biting, especially in the summer, we'd stay out all night. I sometimes fell asleep in the boat on the way home.

We'd go for big crabs, **granzi,** spider crabs, during all the months that had an "r" in their names, **febbraio, marzo, aprile, settembre, ottobre, novembre,** and **dicembre.** We used traps made from chicken wire. The traps had floaters that bobbed on the surface of the water to let us know it was time to pull them up. It was always exciting to see what was there.

One time, when I wasn't with him, he made a huge haul, but it was too early in the morning for him to take the crabs to **mercato,** the big market in the center of Pola, to sell them to the local fish vendors. Instead, he brought them to my parents' house in Pola where he dumped them into our bathtub for safekeeping. I was not expecting to see them when I went to use the toilet that morning. They were crawling out of the tub, and I had to knock them back in.

Emilio would often come by at four or five in the morning, and I'd wake up to find him in our kitchen, frying fish. (I guess he was hungry after a long night of fishing.) He'd always share some of his catch with my family. If he had caught a beautiful

branzino (sea bass) or **orata** (gilthead sea bream), both special fish of the area, he would bring it to the restaurants, where they would give him more money than the vendors at the **mercato**, who paid only wholesale prices.

I liked being there with my uncle for the big catches. I also enjoyed going out for the smaller bounties, such as calamari. Uncle Emilio would shine a light into the water, and I would wiggle strips of torn-up rags over the surface to attract the calamari to come to the top. When one would appear, Emilio and whoever else was in the boat would "lasso" it with a **puscia,** or squid jig, basically an inverted hook in the shape of a palm tree attached to a line. The lassoing didn't take long; the calamari would float quickly up to investigate the moving rag. I loved watching them extend and move their tentacles trying to catch the prey. Once the calamari was on board, I liked to play with its pigment spots, which moved, changed colors from pink to purple, and clustered wherever I put my finger.

The big fish, like the **branzino**, were sometimes brought in by line fishing, but most of the time were caught with nets. This was a big man's job, because the net needed to be coiled properly on the boat so it rolled out smoothly when tossed. Even though kids usually trampled the nets, Emilio would sometimes take me along. We'd go out in the

Uncle Emilio

evenings to cast them, and return in the mornings to pull them up, a job that required great strength. I was usually given a position by the rudder, and my uncle would tell me where to turn the boat. It was always fun to see what we'd caught—the fish were still jumping in the net—and I watched as my uncle selected them and put them in different containers, according to species and size. How happy we were when we got a big catch, and how low our morale sank when there weren't any fish in the nets!

What I liked most about going fishing with Emilio was being so much a part of nature. The salty smell of the sea and the glow of the moon reflecting on the water are sensations I look for now when I am by the sea. But sometimes the Bora, the northern wind, would surprise us, and I would sit low in the boat, cover myself with whatever we had on board, and hold tight and still until we made it to the dock. In those days, we were much closer to the elements; we respected and related to all the aspects of nature and understood how we were affected by them.

I think Emilio would be surprised by all the technology available to fishermen today—especially the fish finders that allow you to find schools of fish with far less effort (and knowledge of local waters) than we needed in the past. I got to experience some of this cutting-edge fishing equipment first-hand during a recent trip to Alaska with my grandson Miles. When he asked for a fishing trip as his graduation present, I jumped at the chance. Growing up, my time with Grandma Rosa in the Busoler countryside allowed me to create lifelong and treasured memories. Those memories are among the most important I carry with me. As I grew older and became a grandmother, I searched for ways to create special one-on-one time with my grandchildren, ways I could give them moments that they, too, would remember for years to come.

My plan was simple. For every special occasion or accomplishment, instead of presenting my grandchildren with a monetary gift, I'd let them pick a destination and plan a trip for us. Sometimes I'd take just one grandchild along, other times more than one. It would be our special time together. My grandson Ethan and granddaughter Julia chose London for their trip, and one of my grandsons, Lorenzo, picked Dubai for his graduation. I traveled with my three oldest grandchildren—Olivia, Lorenzo, and Miles—to Vienna, Austria. These trips were learning experiences, too—for both my grandchildren and me.

When it was Miles's turn, he chose fishing in Alaska. As luck would have it, I'd recently spent some time in Seattle, working on a fund-raising project, and was regaled with fabulous stories of fishing expeditions in Alaska.

It was recommended I visit the Glacier Bear Lodge in remote Yakutat, a tiny coastal village more than a thousand miles southeast of Anchorage—population 642—that was not possible to reach by road or commercial flights. At the time, Yakutat had a small general-aviation airport used mostly for mail delivery or by owners of small private planes. We decided to catch a ride on an Alaskan Airlines flight used by the U.S. Postal Service to make mail runs between Seattle, Juno/Anchorage, and Yakutat, as well.

A friendly woman wearing denim overalls met us at the airport and drove us to the lodge in her pickup. We stayed in a small cabin with two double beds and jaw-dropping views of snow-capped mountains. Our itinerary included three days of ocean fishing, followed by two days of salmon fishing on the Situk River. Our guides were former commercial fishermen who had the knowledge, attitude, and equipment to make our trip truly thrilling.

Only four of us were on the rugged, thirty-three-foot-long vessel as we left the dock that first day and headed out onto open waters: It was just Miles and me, joined by a father-son fishing duo. The son happened to be about Miles's age.

The boat seemed sturdily built for the harsh conditions in Alaska and able to handle any seas we might encounter. It was equipped with two powerful outboard engines; a variety of electronics, including radar for navigation and communication; and enough fishing rods for a party at least twice as big. The boat had a cabin up front that allowed us to get out of the weather or avoid the salt spray if need be. As we headed toward the fishing grounds, our captain and his mate described our surroundings, told us about the wildlife, and explained local catch-and-release rules. Each of us was permitted to keep only three of the fish we caught, and they had to meet certain weight requirements or be thrown back into the sea.

The highlight of our open-water adventure came when Miles hooked a forty-pound halibut that gave him a long and hard fight. The battle began almost immediately after the fish took the bait, and Miles struggled to hold the rod as its tip bent toward the dark-blue water. After about a half-hour of fighting, the fish showed no sign of giving up, and our guides strapped Miles into a belt that firmly held the butt of the rod and gave him more control. My grandson hung in there and, with a little help from the captain, won the fight, prompting high-fives from the crew and applause and laughter all around.

Back at the dock, the fish were hung from a wooden frame, and we were given the opportunity to pick the one we wanted prepared for dinner that evening. The others were filleted and flash-frozen for the trip home.

At the lodge that night, we marveled at the taste of the fresh-caught fish—which proved to be the highlight of the meal. Since there weren't any fresh vegetables available, we made do with frozen green beans. On the days we returned early from fishing, Miles and I did a little sightseeing, including one tour that suddenly put us face-to-face with a moose.

After our third day of open-water fishing, we turned to salmon fishing on the Situk. We took a small boat upriver in the morning and visited spots that were only accessible to our professional guides. The boat would slowly be run ashore, and we'd don waders and head out into areas selected by our guides. We'd cast our lines and wait for the first bite. The scenery around us was breathtaking, with tall cedar trees, and many bald eagles that would quietly observe our every move from high over our heads. We were competing for the same prey.

One of our days on the river had me engaged in one of the most exceptional fights I have ever had with a fish. It took about fifteen minutes, as the salmon dived in and out of the water, left and right, gradually reeling him closer and closer. Miles cheered me on, and I persevered until I finally reeled in my large sockeye salmon. The guide saved the day by snatching it out of the water with a net. Alaska also had rules governing the salmon we could catch and keep. By law, they had to meet minimum size requirements. We picked the fish we wanted to keep, and the guide gutted and cleaned it. The guide did not give even a hint of what would happen next. As he gutted the first salmon and swung the guts in the air, the eagles, like torpedoes, dived down and caught the food in midair. Their wings moved the air so powerfully, and their claws looked so sharp, that Miles and I ducked; the guide giggled. For the next eagle dive, we had our cameras ready.

Exhilarating moments came when we least expected them. One night, Miles and I were relaxing by the dock as one of the guides was cleaning the fresh-caught fish. Again, the guide would reach inside the fish, pull the guts out, and then toss them high into the sky. This time, when the eagles who'd been observing the work from afar swooped in and caught the remains in midair, Miles was fortunate enough to capture their lightning-fast move with his camera.

The eagles never went far while the guide worked on the fish. With a flap or two of their powerful wings, they'd soar aloft and continue to observe the activity from a safe distance. When the guide had completed his work, he'd place the cleaned fish on a ring to make it easier for us to carry back to the lodge.

Miles was delighted with his shots of the eagles' graceful moves. Deep down, I knew that this would be one of those times my grandson would remember for decades to come, much as I still remembered my nights on the water with Uncle Emilio.

As I walked back to the lodge with Miles, I was a world away, back on those nights on the water with my uncle, rejoicing over the countless fish that we'd brought home from our trips.

That night, we had our fish dinner and went to sleep, only to be awakened by the sound of a grizzly bear scrounging through the trash cans—probably looking for some of that salmon. I secured the cabin's wooden door shut with a chair as Miles peeked out at the animal through the window. Bears were not in our plan, at least not as middle-of-the-night guests in our cabin.

My uncle Emilio would have been amazed at the plentiful fish we saw in Alaska, as well as by the technology that we had at our fingertips during the trip. The only "tool" that Emilio had at his disposal was his deep knowledge of the area and memories of the various points on the dark Adriatic where he'd been successful in the past. It was all so different, and I couldn't help but wonder if all the changes were good.

I thought back to the beauty of fishing in a small open boat at night, the surprise when a fish takes the bait, the excitement that comes with bringing the catch on board. There was always that question, **Will they bite?** I treasured those moments with Emilio, and I treasured our catch as well. I never felt apprehensive about keeping the fish we caught.

On the contrary, I felt a sense of gratefulness to the sea, to nature, to God, that we had been given these gifts. Whether it was a net full of **branzini,** a trap filled with crabs, or even a handful of anchovies, everything given to us by nature was a gift.

5

Safety in the Courtyard

Starting at age five, when I entered kindergarten, I began to spend a lot more time with my parents in Pola. I attended the same elementary school where my mother was a teacher, so in the mornings we'd walk to class together. We'd often get up extra early to go to the **mercato** to buy provisions for our dinners, which would be delivered to the house while we were at school.

The market was held in Pola's central square, where a massive two-story iron-and-glass building—built at the turn of the century, during Austro-Hungarian rule—still serves as its centerpiece. Vendors manned stalls both inside the building and under the chestnut trees of the adjacent outdoor square. Most of the city's residents shopped here, and you could find almost everything you needed. Seasonal fresh fish, vegetables, and meats were all on display.

On one side of the indoor market were the **macellai,** butchers and meat vendors—the meats were mostly controlled and sold by three or four governmental co-ops—while on the other side was the **pescheria,** the fish market. In the fish market there were large marble slab tables; most of the big stalls were from government fishing co-ops. But there were also small mounds of privately caught fish on display on small tables, usually the overnight catch being sold by the wives or family of the fishermen. On the east side of the **mercato** building was the open-air farmers' market, about the same size as the enclosed market, and shaded by rows of wild chestnut trees. Here four long lines of stone tables faced each other in two rows, on which the farmers sold their products: vegetables, fruits in season, potatoes, onions, eggs, foraged greens, and mushrooms. It was mostly the women from the farms who gathered and prepared their goods for sale. For most, the amount was small; their goods could easily be displayed on a three-foot table. A mound of eggs, whatever the women had collected from their chickens for two to three days; bouquets of parsley, celery, and wild asparagus; a braid of onions; a kilo of garlic; six or eight heads of cabbage; bouquets of flowers—basically, whatever the garden yielded that day.

I recall going to the market with Nonna Rosa. She'd usually go twice a week to sell the surplus from the family garden. We would use a hand-pushed cart—one long wide plank of wood with two big wheels. We'd take turns grabbing the T handle, which we

used to push the cart as we walked the two kilometers, or about a mile and a quarter. Grandma would
share the cart with her neighbor, Giovanna, who
often accompanied us to the market.

We'd spend the night before the trip preparing
all the vegetables—washing and cleaning everything so it would look its best. The vegetables and
other things were all lined up in wooden boxes
covered with wet cloths. Then, at 6:00 a.m., we'd
load everything onto the cart and start making our
way from Busoler to Pola. It usually took us about
thirty minutes to make the walk. The rule for me
was "**Per su si spinge, per giù si mena,**" meaning
"Upward, you push; downward, you can ride."

Grandma Rosa had her regular spot on a table
in the middle, under the chestnut trees, where she
shared the brass balance scale with Giovanna. After
the vegetables were placed on display, she set up
a little money-box with a lid, and we began making cone-shaped bags out of newspapers, to put the
sold vegetables in. There were no plastic bags; each
shopper had her own jute string bag. The shopping
began by 6:30 a.m., and it all ended by 11:00 a.m.,
because the women had to return home to begin
cooking lunch. My pay was an ice-cream cone
when we were finished selling.

I loved being the **vendrigola,** the vendor who
would place the vegetables that the customer had
selected into one of the scale's brass scoops, and
then add the different weights to the matching brass

scoop until it balanced. It was fun, and the hours passed quickly. Around ten-thirty in the morning, Grandma would collect whatever hadn't been sold and walk to the restaurant Da Piero, now Kod Pjera, on the corner of the **mercato,** to barter unsold vegetables for old bread and any collected leftovers. She would bring these home to feed the chickens and pigs. Nothing was ever wasted.

Though Grandma provided my family with much of our produce and meats, we still visited the market on a regular basis to pick up additional things, such as salt or some inexpensive cuts of meat for our soups and stews. My mother would buy just what was needed for that night's meal. Our menus were much more planned in Pola than they were at Grandma's, where whatever was in season was what we cooked. On our trips to the market, my mother and I always included a stop at the bakery for a loaf of fresh bread, too. Sometimes my mother and I would see Nonna Rosa there when we made these trips before school.

We'd visit the butcher to buy inexpensive soup bones for my father's soups, which saved us money and allowed my mother to make some nice broth. If there was ever any soup left after a night's meal, she would store it overnight in a cool place to be reboiled the next day.

With no refrigerator, we were careful about what we bought, and careful about how it was stored once we brought it home. When we bought butter, we would keep it in water and store it in a cool corner of the kitchen. Lettuce was also kept in water, in the sink, as were fruits such as watermelon, and the water was changed periodically. Olive oil and potatoes were stored in a cool, dark place.

On the days my mother didn't make it to market, she'd send me to the **trattoria** by the market for some tripe or goulash, usually made from secondary cuts of meat and slowly braised with potatoes and carrots. Basically, I was allowed to roam the city freely; I just had to promise to be careful when crossing the street.

❧ ❧

My elementary school was in the same square as the Catholic church where I had been baptized, and on occasion I would see Grandma Rosa duck inside to say a prayer—ignoring the communist rule that forbade everyone from practicing religion. Authorities seemed less concerned about the small number of older men and women who went to church; they didn't hold official jobs or positions of authority in the community and didn't pose much of a risk. Still, my mother was worried that Grandma Rosa's visits to church could cause trouble for her at work and so she looked the other way and pretended not to know her.

The schoolhouse itself was nothing special, a three-story cement-and-stucco structure that lacked any architectural interest. But the windows in the front of the building looked out onto a beautiful fountain, and from the windows on the side we could see the impressive old building that had been converted into a military headquarters. My mother would sometimes be required to go there in the evenings to attend meetings with local officials of the ruling party.

Our lessons were all taught in Croatian; speaking Italian was strictly forbidden. The curriculum was rooted in a communist/socialist point of view. We learned that capitalism was the opposition, and those who were suspected of practicing it in Pola would be punished.

Tito had brought many of his officers from Serbia and Bosnia to Pola, and they lived in the houses that had been abandoned before the border was closed. His men were charged with keeping order, and uniformed officers were posted throughout the city, a constant reminder of Tito's presence and of the communist regime.

These were deeply troubling times. Farmers were especially concerned about the government's new efforts to take people's farmland away from them. Left with just a fraction of what they'd owned, farmers literally had just enough to feed their own families. Fortunately, no one came for my grandparents' land: the plot was too small for the government to bother with.

Acres and acres of farmland were turned into large government-run co-ops. Workers all wore the same bluish-gray shirts and pants. They were paid a low wage and expected to put in long days in the fields. It was on these cooperative farms that fertilizer was first introduced as a way to ensure better production. Some argued that it was just a sign of modernization. We preferred the more traditional farms and farming methods, and my mother made it a habit to patronize only the local farmers she'd known for years—while avoiding the stands where produce from the large government co-ops was sold.

❧·❧

As I got older, I began to sense my parents' frustration with life under Tito's regime. Sometimes, late at night, I'd hear them whispering about their discontent; they were worn down by all the restrictions imposed on them—along with everyone else in the city. But in the morning, they'd go to work and behave as if nothing were wrong, just like all the other people in the streets. It was very unsettling; as a child, I didn't know what was right and what was wrong. We Italians were forbidden to speak our language anywhere in Pola, and holidays such as Christmas and Easter could no longer be celebrated openly.

It was different at my grandmother's place in Busoler, where the army wasn't ever-present and we could get away with speaking Italian. We even had a tiny Christmas tree, a juniper bush, which Grandpa would cut down every year; Grandma kept it hidden behind closed shutters so officials would not see the holiday decorations. Since we didn't have tree ornaments, we used oranges, Seckel pears, and little cookies that we baked to adorn the tree. We'd also wrap small stones in the silver wrappers from **caramelle** candies, and tie the ends with sewing string, and we would stretch cotton balls to cover the tip of the branches to look like snow. We did not exchange gifts for Christmas—it was not the custom, and money was tight. Our gifts as kids were the decorations on the tree, the cookies, the candies, and the fruits. The custom was to dismantle the Christmas tree on January 6, the Feast of the Epiphany, also known as Three Kings' Day. Epiphany was the day the three kings brought their gifts to Jesus, and that was the day we would enjoy the goodies from our tree. I still recall the aroma when Grandma would put the peels of the oranges we had eaten on the stove, so the whole house smelled of the citrus fruit.

For Easter, we would color the eggs using natural dyes, such as grass and beets, and Grandma would bake her special Easter bread, called **pinze.** She'd braid the dough in three rows, with a colored egg in between. This would be our Easter doll representing baby Jesus, with the hard-boiled egg serving as its head and the braid as its body. I remember nibbling my doll's feet; it was a big treat. Grandma would bake it in advance. She would then place a piece of the bread, a few hard-boiled eggs, and some scallions into a beggar's purse, which she would carry with us to 6:00 a.m. mass at the little church just outside the village, where they did have quiet masses that the older folks attended. Not every Sunday, but on special holidays. At the end of the service, she and all the other ladies in the village would bring their purses to the altar, unfurl them, and present their gifts. The priest would bless the contents, which were the first things we would eat once we got home for **merenda**.

Grandma would place the purse with the blessed food on the table, open it up, and sprinkle the contents with salt and, if we were lucky, a little prosciutto; then everyone would eat. It was not unlike other pagan rituals—thanking God, and thanking spring. The salt was for wisdom, the egg for fertility. The scallions and wheat were for the yield of the land, and the prosciutto was so the animals might be healthy. These holiday celebrations could only happen in Busoler, never in Pola. Going against the rules of the governing party could bring unwanted consequences, as would voicing any opposition to those rules or even singing favorite Italian songs such as "**Vola colomba bianca vola**" and "**Lo said che I papaveri son alti, alti, alti.**"

Even as a child, I knew at some level that our living conditions weren't ideal. But I was too young to really understand what the impact was, or to appreciate how different things had been only a few years earlier. My parents had weathered life under Mussolini's rule before and during World War II, and now were being forced to conform to another kind of censorship and repression under Tito.

Despite the pressures facing the adult world, I enjoyed a childhood that felt easy and carefree. I had two best friends, one in Pola and one in Busoler. When I was at Grandma's, it was Silvia who had my attention. And in Pola, Lilliana, my next-door neighbor, was my go-to friend. We did everything together. We'd walk home from school in the afternoons with a group of friends—down the **corso**, as the street was called—and inevitably find all kinds of mischief, games, or sweets to oc-

In the courtyard in Busoler, c. 1960, Santola Maria, Aunt Lidia Fonio, Grandpa Giovanni, and Nonna Rosa

cupy us. We would play hide-and-seek along the way, run after each other, and play tag. There were two **pasticcerie-gelaterie,** pastry/ice-cream shops, on the way home; I especially loved their chestnut-whipped cream roulade.

On some days, those walks seemed to take forever, and my tiny legs grew tired as I climbed and descended the steep stone steps en route to and from the schoolhouse. Since we had no money for toys, we would play with whatever was available to us. My friends and I liked to hang the stems of cherries we'd picked from the trees from the tops of our ears, so that they dangled like earrings. For lipstick, we pressed moistened rose petals to our lips. We would rub crushed rose petals on our cheeks to make rouge, and stick them on our fingernails to imitate a manicure.

Music was the main form of entertainment in the city. There was no television, so local performances were always a big draw. My mother sent me for piano lessons, which I enjoyed. And it was not unusual to find performances going on around the city, mostly military and marine bands performing marches and odes to Tito.

My favorite musical events were the concerts and plays put on at the spectacular Arena di Pola, an old Roman amphitheater built in the first century A.D. The structure was made completely of local limestone, and had seating for seven thousand spectators and standing space for five thousand more, all originally gathered there to watch the gladiators fight. Its location, on a gentle rise overlooking the harbor, added to its majesty and glory. The arena was built into the hill, a unique design that saved a lot on construction. Today it is considered one of the best-preserved coliseums in the world; its outer walls are almost entirely intact.

My brother and I often accompanied our parents there, and they would treat us to an ice cream along the way. It was rare for us kids to actually pay for a seat inside the coliseum. Seating inside the huge arena was reserved for adults, and we'd usually meet up with friends and hang around outside, watching and listening to performances through the soaring archways, and, of course, engaging in a game of tag or hide-and-seek to keep occupied. A lot of the concerts were classical music, and the sounds of the orchestra could be heard throughout Pola. Music was often playing in the piazzas as well, where people liked to sit, sip coffee, and play games such as chess, checkers, and cards.

It was in one of those piazzas that I sat down and played my very first game of chess. I was very young—in the first or second grade. I enjoyed the game and had fun strategizing my moves on the board. Later, I started playing with my brother, and we would get into very heated and competitive matches. Board games and cards helped fuel the social interactions in the piazzas and brought together family and friends for conversation, food, fun, and, for some of us, healthy competition.

I still enjoy playing chess with my brother when he comes over for the holidays and am intent on continuing the tradition with my grandchildren. I play with them when the family gets together, and often challenge them when we travel with my little magnetic chess set, which measures about four inches square and is superbly easy to carry. We start a game on the plane and quickly become focused on the pieces, paying no attention to the passage of time. And, before you know it, we reach our destination. Sometimes, if we are not finished with the game, the kids take a photo of the board so we can continue—especially if they are winning.

Like many of our neighbors, my parents had a radio, and we could listen to music at home. In Grandma's town, only two people had radios. One of them was my aunt, who lived in the house adjacent to ours and just across the courtyard. The other belonged to a neighbor down the road. On Sundays, we'd all gather around to listen to Radio Capodistria. The station was located right on the border of Italy with Yugoslavia, and it featured Italian folk songs and other traditional Italian music. Everybody would sing along, and sometimes we'd even dance. This was not really permitted under Tito's regime: Italians were told they could not sing in Italian. But the soldiers didn't pay that much attention to what happened in the sleepy villages like Busoler; most of the senior officers spent their time in the bigger cities. During the Sunday-afternoon music program on Radio Capodistria, the two radio owners would raise their volume until it sounded like a stereophonic town concert.

Sundays were also when my grandfather went to meet friends at the **osteria** in the neighboring town of Sissano, now Šišan. The men would drink wine, play **bocce** and sing folk songs about lost love and being away from family. There were always lots of sailors there, and an accordionist to add to the action.

We kids would sometimes tag along. Children were not allowed in the **osteria,** so we would hang around outside and wait for Grandpa to bring us a treat, either something to drink or an ice cream.

Grandpa Giovanni was a stern man, but he had a soft spot for his grandchildren. He took his farm responsibilities seriously and didn't have much time to fool around. He expected the same focus and dedication from those around him, and didn't like it when people weren't getting things done. Invariably, there were moments when I found myself in trouble—usually when my friends and I were out playing, running through fields, and inadvertently trampling part of his crop along the way. We didn't mean any harm, but it was difficult for him to see it that way, especially when he was dependent on those crops for his livelihood.

In Grandpa's **campagna**, fields, two majestic fig trees grew exceptionally close to each other. Fig trees grow many low and wide branches with spread-out palmlike leaves, which were easy for us to climb, and in late August they were full of ripe figs. We would divide into teams, usually boys against girls, each team claiming one tree. After eating our fill of the ripest figs, we would engage in a fig fight. One afternoon, Grandpa caught us engaged in the midst of a particularly heated battle, and was dismayed to see smashed fruit on the ground, oozing fleshy red centers. We were covered in the fruit, too, with pieces of tasty ripe figs in our hair and all over our clothes. If you've ever gotten fig in your hair, you know you just can't get it out; it's sticky, like bubble gum, and just as impossible to extract. My mother used to get so annoyed, because she'd have to cut strands of my hair in order to get out the clumps of gooey fruit.

My grandfather was angry with me that day, but not as upset as he was when he found me perched on a branch high up in his cherry tree with a mouthful of sweet red cherries.

I knew when I set out that morning in late May that there was a possibility he might catch me, but the lure of those plump Bing cherries, whose flavor I adored, proved stronger than my fear of his wrath. It wasn't that he'd forbidden me from picking them. The problem was that reaching the tree meant crossing through his wheat field and potentially trampling the grain, which might cause permanent damage to some of the carefully tended plants. There was no doubt in my eight-year-old mind that he would be angry if he caught me, but it was a risk I was willing to take. The wheat would not be ready for harvesting for another month, and those cherries were ripe and ready now!

Like a spy, I skulked around the property until I located him near the animal pens, helping Grandma with the feeding chores. After monitoring him for a bit, I decided to make my move and sprinted across the road and into the field. My plan to tiptoe around the tall yellow stalks so as not to trample them was only moderately successful, and I was disheartened when I looked back at the path I had cut to see at least a handful of the plants on the ground, flattened. It was too late to worry; those beautiful plump cherries were now within reach, so I forged ahead, inhaling the toasty smell of the grains and marveling at the profusion of red poppies blooming amid them.

When I reached the tree, I hoisted myself up onto one of its limbs and began my ascent. The best way for me to stay hidden was to climb higher into the tree, using its thick green leaves as cover. The perfect perch was right near the top, so I made myself comfortable, peeked out through the leaves one last time for Grandpa, then seized a handful of cherries and shoved them into my mouth. Their tangy sweetness filled my senses, and for a moment I felt like a bird, soaring high in the sky, the fresh, oxygenated air magnifying the syrupy taste of those cherries. Until the sound of Grandpa's voice snapped me from my cherry-eating stupor.

"I see you in that tree!" he growled.

My mouth was so full of cherries I couldn't swallow them fast enough to utter a defense. I do not recall the exact punishment. My grandfather was not lenient, and I still vividly recall the fright of that moment, and how I ran to hide with Grandma Rosa—she was going to save me. But he did not let her take it easy on me, and I was not to go on that cherry tree ever again without his permission.

This was not the first time Grandpa caught me "raiding" one of his fruit trees. The apricot tree on the way to the wheat field was another of my targets. Seeing him coming always sent me into a panic, which only made matters worse, since all I could think was to run and hide; this usually led me deeper into the wheat field, where I would cause even more damage to the crops.

When I see children playing now, I always wonder, **Do they feel the freedom I did, do they have the space in their mind that I had?** Sometimes, I would just lie back in the field and look at the sky and the falling stars. It seemed I had a lot of space, a lot of color, a lot of beautiful smells, and a lot of love. There was a kind of security in that courtyard. When I was there, I never felt afraid.

I had begun to experience moments of fright when

I was at the house down in Pola. We'd hear stories of people, mostly ethnic Italians, being pulled from their homes in the middle of the night by members of the secret police. Their hands and feet were bound and they were dropped into **foibe,** deep limestone pits in the area near Trieste, often while they were still alive. Others were shot or thrown into jail, never to be heard from again. They were rounded up and murdered, first by Tito's Partisans, and then, after the war, by members of the Yugoslav secret police. These mass killings, which have come to be known as the Foibe Massacres, occurred during and after World War II in Istria and in nearby areas in Friuli–Venezia Giulia and Dalmatia. Surprisingly little is known about the massacres. Even an approximate death toll has eluded historians; estimates range from hundreds to twenty thousand. It wasn't until the early 1990s that an investigation into the killings was commenced, with a commission of historians from both Italy and Slovenia working jointly to piece together what had occurred. Their research could not put a number to the casualties, and thus concluded that "hundreds of people," primarily ethnic Italians, died in the **foibe** and in mines and pits in the area.

My great-aunt Nina had lost one of her sons, Ferruccio, in 1942, when the communists arrived in Pola. Nina was Grandpa Giovanni's sister. She was a great cook and worked as a chef for Giovanni Benussi, one of the principals in a shipbuilding company, Cantiere Scoglio Olivi, now Uljanik. Nina's husband, my great-uncle Nicola Rapetti, who we all called Zio Rapetti, was a **carabiniere,** a policeman. The family lived with their two sons, Ferruccio and Corrado, in Benussi's villa. Ferruccio was around nineteen years old when he went out one evening with friends and was picked up by the opposing forces—either Germans or Yugoslavians. We never saw him again. Nina tried desperately to find him. She heard he was somewhere in the Velebit Mountains, near Fiume (now Rijeka), and she traveled there to search for him. But her efforts proved fruitless, and she returned home to Pola in despair. The war showed no sign of ending, and Nina and Nicola worried for their younger son, Corrado.

By the time the war was over, Nina's employer, Signore Benussi, was a widower and had lost two daughters. The shipyard had been taken over by the Germans, so he decided to move to Trieste. Zia Nina and her remaining family decided to go with him. They were heartbroken at the loss of Ferruccio, and with the communists coming to Istria; they wanted to keep their younger son safe. Nina returned to Busoler about once a year to visit her brother, Giovanni, and their sister, Maria, who lived in the courtyard. I looked forward to her arrival, as she would always bring us **caramelle, mandorlato** (nougat), oranges and fresh fruits, and sheer stockings for my mother. Stockings were scarce and expensive in Yugoslavia. During her visits, she would often lament about the loss of Ferruccio and the agony she felt at not knowing what had happened to him. Years later, she learned that he had been shot and killed by military forces.

Stories like these created an environment of fear, and there was always deep-rooted concern that one day the authorities might come for my father.

6

Midnight Visitor

It was after midnight when I heard somebody knocking on the front door of my parents' home in Pola. The person knocked again, this time louder, and I heard my mother stir. She put on a bathrobe and made her way to the front door. I sneaked a peek from inside my bedroom as she grabbed the door handle, turned it, and slowly pulled it toward her. Three men in uniform stood outside.

"Where is your husband?" one of them demanded.

"He's asleep in bed," my mother replied.

"Wake him up! He has to come with us."

"Why? He's not a capitalist," she said.

For months, the secret police had been slowly rounding up suspected capitalists in Pola. Friends and neighbors would suddenly disappear in the middle of the night. My parents knew that UDBA had been watching my father for a while. They suspected him of being a capitalist because he owned two trucks and had three or four men regularly

My mother,
Erminia, a teacher
in Pola, c. 1952

My father,
Vittorio, in Pola,
c. 1940

making deliveries for his trucking company. He was the boss, and everybody knew it. But under communist law, there could not be a "boss." He was even accused of exploiting the people, because he was financially well off and often did work for Italian businessmen.

The secret police asked my mother again where her husband was, and I could hear my father getting out of bed and making his way to the front door. He was still in his pajamas, and the officers ordered him to get dressed and come with them.

"Why are you doing this?" my mother pleaded. "Why are you taking him? What did he do? What's going on? Why are you here?"

The officers refused to answer and said only that my father was being taken to the police station.

We watched through the front window as a tow truck backed into place in front of my father's truck, hooked it up, and hauled it away. My mother was alarmed; she had no idea why they would take him. The only explanation that made any sense to her was that maybe something had happened involving one of my father's trucks, but that didn't make much sense, either.

The next morning, my mother went to the police station to see what she could learn. When she got back to the house, about an hour later, she told my brother and me that she'd been unable to find out anything about our dad, only that he was still in jail. The police told her that if it turned out he hadn't done anything wrong, he'd be released in thirty days. But if he was guilty of something, then the police could hold him for an additional, and much longer, period of time.

My father had been working on a paving project at the Pola airport, about six kilometers from the city center, delivering asphalt for a new runway that was under construction and making multiple trips each day. He also had people making additional deliveries for him. The airport project was government work, and we couldn't imagine what would prompt the secret police to arrest and detain him. It turned out that my father had been accused of conducting his business in a manner that was contrary to communist work protocols.

I was just eight years old when I accompanied my mother to the Prigione di Pola, the prison where my father was being held. Located at the top of a hill, the four-story stone building looked like it was more than a century old. It dated back to the period of the Austro-Hungarian Empire and was encircled by a tall stone wall and a metal gate. Guards brought my mother and me inside. We were led down a wide hallway to a plain-looking office, where another guard confirmed that my father was still being held at the jail. But we were not allowed to see him, and officials refused to tell us anything about why he was there, what if anything he might have done wrong, or when we might be able to see him again. Though my mother tried to put on a brave face, I could tell that she was fighting back tears; I was, too. This was the second time that the authorities had stonewalled my mother, and she didn't know what to do next, or whom to see.

We went home with no answers, only more questions. When I lay down in my bed that night, I couldn't fall asleep. I kept wondering about my father and what was happening to him in that cold and frightening-looking prison. Was he safe? Was he getting food and water? I wondered if he was warm enough. All of us—my mother, my brother, and I—were desperately worried about my father. But there was nothing we could do except try to make it through each day and hope he'd be home soon.

For twenty-nine days, we waited with no word. Even the rest of the family was afraid to comfort us or give us support for fear they might be considered accomplices to some unknown cause. We felt isolated and abandoned; my friends shied away from me, I recall, as if contact might cause their families to be next. The only place that offered me refuge was my grandmother's courtyard, playing and feeding the animals. Nothing stopped Grandma from showing us affection and love. But I feared that my mother and father were in the claws of predators, and I had no idea what would happen to them or to me. My mother was stoic, and continued her daily work at the elementary school. Though I was too young to know much about the politics of the regime, I was old enough to see that she was deeply worried about our future and my father's life.

On the thirtieth day, my father arrived home, tired but otherwise okay. He didn't tell us much about what had happened during his detention, but it was clear that he was shaken. I was so thankful to have him back with us; for the first few days, I watched his every move, I suppose because I feared he might be taken from me again. He was a chain smoker, just as he liked his café mocha, drinking at least four to five cups a day. As soon as he finished one cigarette, he was lighting up another. His habit was so strong that the tips of his fingers had begun to yellow from the nicotine. I had never liked the smell of cigarette smoke, but suddenly it was bringing me great comfort.

The authorities never returned my father's truck, telling him only that one was enough for him. This was deeply troubling to my father. He was constantly wondering what would happen next, what else they would confiscate.

Meanwhile, members of the local Communist Party were aggressively pursuing my mother, asking her to pronounce her commitment to communism and encouraging her to get more actively involved. They believed her position as a schoolteacher was key to helping inculcate the city's youth in communist ideology. When the communists first came to Pola, my mother and four other ethnic Italian schoolteachers had been required to participate in a special educational program held on the island of Brioni, just off the coast of Pola.

The program spanned an entire summer. Every morning at seven, she and the others were loaded into a car and driven to the small coastal town of Fažana, where they boarded a boat for Brioni. Tito had made the island his official summer residence and enlisted a Slovenian architect to design a pavilion just for him. During his tenure, countless heads of state visited him there, as well as a number of Hollywood stars, among them Elizabeth Taylor, Richard Burton, and Sophia Loren. Power is a strong magnet.

Tito was on the island during the time my mother was attending classes there, and she would often see him on her way to and from the schoolhouse. She and the other teachers were there to learn the country's primary official language of Serbo-Croatian. (Croatian and Serbian are very similar in spoken form, but Croatian is written in Roman script, like Italian and English, and Serbian in Cyrillic, like Russian.) She, like all of the students, had to learn the Cyrillic alphabet as well. My mother already spoke a Croatian dialect, as did her own mother, Nonna Rosa. But as educators, she and the others were expected to learn "proper" Croatian in order to educate their young students.

Istria is located where Western Europe meets Eastern Europe, and throughout the centuries there have been many invasions, occupations, and changes of government. In a border territory such as the Italian, Austrian, Slovenian, Croatian, or Istrian areas, it is common to have people of different ethnicities speaking different languages and practicing different religions. It was also common for people to speak three or four languages—their maternal language, and then the governing language and the language of their neighbors. In Istria, now divided between Croatia and Slovenia, the official language is Croatian in the Croatian part and Slovenian in the Slovenian part, yet Italian and some German are still spoken today.

My mother was suspicious of the teaching methods being employed by the new regime. The classes were infused with political lessons and discussions of important communist figures, such as Vladimir Lenin and Joseph Stalin. In class, my mother appeared genuinely interested; in private, she and the other teachers spoke of wanting to run away and escape this new regime.

My mother took her Croatian studies seriously, and for the next three or four years, she practiced every night, studying each word and speaking it aloud—she did not want to be wrong when teaching the language in her classrooms. She was also taught political songs, which she had to be able to recite and eventually teach to her second-graders. She and the other teachers at the school were ex-

Me, in Yugoslavia, with a second-grade schoolmate, as official representatives to a political celebration in the school's office

pected to bring their students to the airport whenever Tito was in town, to help welcome him. Each of us had to wear a **titolka,** a pointed hat with a **zvezda petokraka,** a five-pointed red star, sewn on the front, and to wave as he emerged from the plane.

Tito would come to town often on his way to his private resort in Brioni, and there were always organized celebrations along the roads of the city, with bands playing patriotic music and the local children participating in marches to commemorate visits from our leader, who was usually accompanied by a host of foreign dignitaries. As Mali Pioniri, Tito's Young Pioneers, we would have to line up alongside Pola's main road in our uniforms—white shirts and dark-colored skirts for the girls, dark slacks and white shirts for the boys—waving our little Yugoslavian flags as motorcades rode by.

Over the years, I waved my flag and smiled as Emperor Haile Selassie of Ethiopia, President Gamal Abdel Nasser of Egypt, Nikita Khrushchev of Russia, and Jawaharlal Nehru, the first prime minister of India, passed in front of me. I vividly remember the way they looked in their traditional dress. Tito, of course, was always dressed in his spotless white military uniform.

During her time as a teacher, my mother's performance in the school was graded annually, and she consistently received excellent reviews. She was not a political person and did not have much interest in politics, so she simply did what was expected of her.

On her tenth anniversary at the school, the director approached her to praise her ongoing performance in the classroom and to make her an offer. He told her the commander in chief of the school wanted to elevate her to the role of inspector for all of Istria. She would be given a car and many other benefits, and tasked with traveling the peninsula, visiting the local schools to make sure that everybody was doing his or her job properly.

That night, my mother told my father about the impending promotion, and he voiced skepticism. "What is it you really have to do for them?"

The next day, my mother went to see the director to question him further about what her new role would entail. "I am not a communist, and I am not in the party," she told him. "And I don't want to be."

The director explained that, to start, she would need to attend a meeting of the local ruling party. When my father heard this, he blew up in anger. "We are not communists!" he railed. Staring at my mother, he asked, "Do you want them, or do you want me?"

The job offer was immediately refused.

Not long after, my mother informed me that my brother and I would be joining her for a trip to Trieste, Italy, in the winter of 1956. She had received a telegram from my great-aunt Nina, who was terminally ill and wanted to see us before she died. The telegram was accompanied by a letter, signed by an Italian doctor, which affirmed my aunt's dire diagnosis.

I had no idea that both the telegram and the doctor's note were all part of an elaborate ruse my aunt had created to help us escape across the border to Italy. My mother never hinted to either my brother or me that the health crisis was all a pretext. We believed the story to be 100 percent true.

My mother had already attempted to get passports for all four of us, but she was turned down by local authorities. She'd gone to the police station to seek travel papers so that we could visit her "sick" aunt in Trieste. Officials didn't believe the story and rejected her request. Zia Nina was known to authorities in Pola, because she and her family had fled the city more than ten years earlier in 1945, before the border with Italy had officially closed.

"They are not communists," the police told my mother. "We will not let you go."

It was that denial from the authorities that had prompted my aunt to come up with the idea of providing the letter from the doctor saying she was terminally ill. This time, when my mother returned to the police station to present the officers with the "proof," she put on quite the show.

Between sobs, she pleaded with them, "I want to see my aunt before she dies."

The authorities agreed to issue three passports, one for my mother, and two more for my brother and me. There was none for my father: he would have to remain behind in Pola to ensure our return. She did tell us that Zia Nina was sick, but my brother and I still considered it a special treat to go to Trieste on holiday. I do not recall being worried about the severity of Zia Nina's illness, or that Zia Nina might die.

I had never been out of the country, and I was excited at the prospect of taking a train for the very first time. We each packed a single suitcase for what my mother said would be a ten-day excursion. We planned to leave on an evening train on January 23, 1956—which also happened to be the day of my mother's birthday.

On the night of our departure, my father loaded us into his truck for the short drive to the train station near the waterfront in downtown Pola. I was dressed up for the occasion in a green-and-yellow pleated skirt paired with a yellow sweater and white knee socks. My long reddish-blond hair was tied in two braids, with a big, colorful bow at the bottom of each.

My last memories of being in the city were those few minutes at the station with my parents, buying our tickets, and then waiting by the track for our train to pull in. Today the two-story stucco building still looks much the way it did all those years ago. Even the simple wooden benches in the ticketing area are unchanged, although the building now sports a fresh coat of coral-colored paint, and the harbor across the way is far more commercial than it was back then.

My mother was unusually quiet that brisk winter evening as we waited on the platform. I pulled my coat tight to guard against the cold wind. Though it was still early—around 7:00 p.m.—it was already quite dark, and there wasn't much of a view of the harbor. Boat traffic was light during the dead of winter, especially at night.

The first leg of our seven-hour train trip would be from Pola to Divaccia, now the Slovenian town of Divača, near the Italian border; we would have to disembark there to pass through a checkpoint. When our train arrived, I was surprised to see that my father was boarding with us—he was going as far as the border. Once we were settled in our seats and our luggage was stowed, my brother and I jumped up to explore the train, elatedly running from one carriage to another, waving as we ran past our parents. I noticed that my mother couldn't stop crying, and I wondered why: our journey to Trieste didn't seem like that big a deal. I figured she was just upset that my father was not making the trip with us.

I was too excited to understand the emotional turmoil my parents were experiencing that evening. But I did notice that my father's eyes were wet with tears when he signaled my brother and me to return to our seats for a hug goodbye. Divaccia was still a few stops away, but he was going to hop off at the next station and catch a southbound train back to Pola.

I watched as he reached into his front pocket and pulled out some chocolates, which he presented to my mother; they were for all of us to enjoy during the rest of the journey. "Happy birthday," he told her, smiling, placing the sweets in her hand.

My father leaned in and whispered quietly into my mother's ear. It was hard to make out what he was saying, but I thought I heard, "Don't worry about me. I will take care of myself. I will escape by walking." At the time, I thought I hadn't heard him correctly, or somehow misunderstood. We were supposed to be traveling to my aunt's house for a short visit—and then going back home. I briefly wondered what he meant. But then my mother handed my brother and me some chocolate, and I didn't think about it anymore. Only later did I realize that I'd heard him perfectly.

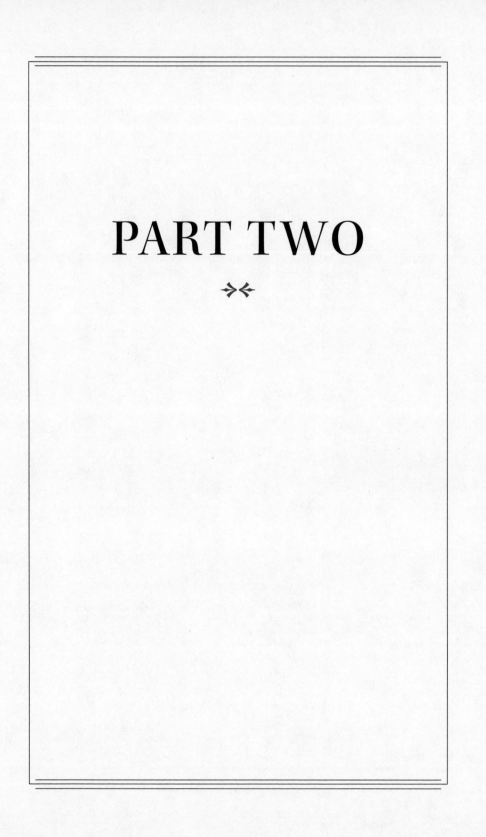

PART TWO

7

A New Chapter Begins

A light snow was falling when our train pulled into the railway station in Divaccia, sometime after midnight on January 24, 1956. It was deep winter, and the air was so cold I could see my breath as I hurried beside my mother, brother, and some of the other passengers to the first checkpoint, where uniformed officers from the Yugoslavian Border Patrol asked to see our papers. My mother had secured all the necessary documents and visas for our trip, so it didn't take long for us to be waved on. Once we were cleared, we were directed to walk with our luggage to a second checkpoint, a few hundred feet away, on the Italian side of the border, where Italian border police were waiting to check us once again. Eventually, the Italians waved us ahead, too, and we headed into the station to wait for the Italian train.

We spent nearly two hours in that cold, smoke-filled waiting area. There were some stiff wooden benches inside, and my mother, brother, and I did our best to make ourselves comfortable. Mom shared more of the chocolates my father had given us, and I drifted in and out of sleep while we waited for the train to arrive. It was after 4:00 a.m. when we finally boarded. I spent much of the two-hour ride to Trieste staring out the window into the darkness, imagining what this new city would be like. The idea of having a vacation in a "free" port excited me—a town that was not under communist rule. But something was clearly upsetting my mother. Though she did her best to hide it, I could tell that she was on the verge of tears for much of the ride into Trieste. I wondered if she was scared of traveling so far without my father, or if she was just worried about her aunt. My mother had told us that she was sick, although she did not impress upon us that Nina was in grave health, as she had told officials back in Pola.

The train station in Trieste was one of the biggest and most imposing buildings I'd ever seen. It had soaring, tall ceilings, polished marble floors, Corinthian columns, and arched entryways. Even at this early hour, dozens of people were moving rapidly through the building, some of them carrying large pieces of luggage and a few of them holding on to young children. People were going in all different directions, some headed for the exits and others for the tracks for outbound trains. It was dawn when we arrived, so there was no one to meet us—

relatively few people owned cars in Trieste at the time. My aunt's home was only a few blocks away, in the Centro-Stazione section of the city, but it was cold and windy as we left the station and set off on foot. Trieste is known for its strong northern wind, the Bora; sometimes it would howl for two or three days straight, with gusts so powerful that on some days we had to cling to ropes stretched along the streets and on the windiest corners to keep from blowing away. Squalls can reach in excess of a hundred miles per hour, ripping trees from the soil and tossing fish from the sea. Every so often, a bicycle or a Vespa would be swept into the sea.

On the morning of our arrival, the Bora was blowing with such force I had to lean my upper body forward to counteract the lashing wind and still maintain my footing. It was fun to wrestle with this unseen force, at least for a while, but I was tired and longed to get to someplace warm where I could finally go to sleep. It had already been a very long night. Even though my mother had packed just the essentials, my little suitcase felt increasingly heavy as we neared our destination, on Via Cecilia de Rittmeyer. Number 6 was a five-story corner building with lofty arched windows, dark-brown wooden shutters, and a massive timber front door.

Mom rang the bell, and we waited for Zia Nina to buzz us in. Her apartment was on the third floor, and there was no elevator, so we began our climb. The sound of our footsteps resounded in the cav-

Zia Nina Rapetti,
who took us into
her house in Trieste

ernous hallways as we scaled
the wide stone steps. Each floor
had three apartments with tall
wooden doors that stretched
almost to the ceiling. I was exhausted, so I grabbed the polished wood handrail for support
and pulled myself up.

Zia Nina was standing in the
doorway in her robe and slippers when we finally reached
the third-floor landing. Her
long braid, which she usually
wore clustered and pinned to the back of her head,
hung loose, and although she looked half awake,
she let out a shriek of joy as she pulled us in for
a big hug. Soon everyone was in tears. Zia Nina
was a beautiful woman, with powdery, peachy skin.
She always wore her favorite pair of earrings—gold,
shaped like flowers, with small round diamonds set
in a circle to resemble the petals. She also wore a
long, thick gold chain necklace with a hexagonal
locket in which she kept a photo of Ferruccio, her
lost son. I would ask her to open it for me now and
then, and she always obliged gladly; it was a moment when she could reminisce and share with me
stories of Ferruccio's life. That night, my aunt didn't
seem sick, and at eight years old I didn't really know
what to make of it. There was a lot of excitement
at our arrival, and I just followed everybody inside.

The layout of Nina's apartment was railroad-style, long and narrow, with a series of rooms off a lengthy hallway. The rooms had vaulted ceilings and glossy parquet floors. We followed her down the hall to a large kitchen, where a plate of cookies and three cups of hot caffè latte were waiting for us on a big wooden table with a marble top in the center of the room.

I'd never seen a kitchen big enough to accommodate a table surrounded by eight chairs and plenty of extra seating, with three or four chairs at the ready along the walls of the room.

The caffè latte tasted especially good after our brisk walk, and I hungrily gobbled up the cookies. Although I was curious to see the rest of the apartment, I was too tired for exploration, and contentedly followed Zia Nina to the last room off the hallway, to the left of the entrance door, where we would stay. There was a double bed for my mother, and two **brande**, army-type cots, for my brother and me. Franco took the one under the window, leaving me the one by the door. I didn't even bother changing into my pajamas; I just collapsed onto the little cot and fell right to sleep.

I awoke to the smell of freshly brewed coffee and the deep, throaty voice of Zio Rapetti, who was in the kitchen, catching up with my mother. My great-uncle was a quiet, reserved man who adored his wife, Nina. He was tall and skinny and good-hearted. He embraced me the minute I entered the room, then turned his attention back to my mother. Zia Nina had set out a tasty breakfast of fresh bread, butter, and jam, so I climbed onto a chair and helped myself to a plate. The kitchen looked even bigger in the daylight. Sun poured in through two double-hung windows on the south wall, just above a stone double sink. From the window, past the terra-cotta rooftops of the neighboring buildings, I could see the rooftops of the houses framing the Ponterosso Market, where we'd soon walk with Nina in the mornings to shop for produce. And if I looked to the right, I could glimpse rooftops giving way to the coastline of Trieste, the **riva.**

Not only was the kitchen big, it was well equipped. There was a wood-burning stove to keep us warm, and a flame gas stove with a hood that hung vertically from the corner of the ceiling. Encircling the hood, or **napa,** was a shelf where Zia Nina kept salt, pepper, dried herbs, coffee mugs, toothpicks, a coffee grinder, and the sugar bowl. The wood and coal were stored next to the stove, where there was also a **scagnetto,** a small stool (where I would later sit to stoke the fire; I also began to use it as a kind of ladder to help me reach things in the kitchen that were in high places).

A **credenza,** cupboard, next to the stove was where Nina kept the bread, glasses, and pots and pans. On the wall facing the west was another long piece of furniture, where she kept the provisions, although the potatoes, onions, and garlic were stored in containers under the sink. The cabinet on the north wall was for the kitchen linens—tablecloths, napkins, and such. A small radio sat atop this cabinet and was our main source of information and entertainment. It was always on, broadcasting the news and playing music, except at mealtimes, when Nina turned it off.

My mother and Zio Rapetti were still talking when I left the kitchen to explore the rest of the apartment. I started with the big bathroom with the tub, just to the left of the kitchen. This was where we all bathed and freshened up. Next to the bathroom was a small laundry room filled with metal tubs of various sizes and wood-and-metal washboards that we used to clean our clothes. Zia Nina did not have an ironing board. Instead, she used the kitchen table, which she covered with a big blanket, doubled for extra thickness and topped with a linen cloth.

My aunt and uncle used a clothesline outside one of the apartment windows to dry their clothes. Technically, it wasn't really theirs: they shared the line with a family who lived in a third-floor apartment in an adjoining building. The line ran on two pulleys, high above the courtyard that separated the structures.

My exploration led me to the long hallway, which circled back to the main entrance to the apartment. On the north side of this hallway were four large rooms. The first was a big and formal dining-and-living-room area that the family rarely used. This room contained all the items the family had brought with them from Pola, their best pieces of furniture, china, silver, and linen. We were not allowed in this room, which was kept locked and treated almost like a museum. The next room was where my aunt and uncle slept, on a great big carved wooden bed flanked on either side by matching wooden dressers. The windows on this side of the apartment faced south. In the springtime, Zia Nina would move all of her houseplants there for the light; geraniums and asparagus ferns were her favorites. I liked to watch the neighborhood cats jump from one rooftop to another, and the pigeons and seagulls that perched on the red terra-cotta tiles and chimneys across the way.

On the right side of the hallway, just past the window with all the plants, was a second, smaller hallway off of which were two little rooms that Zia Nina rented out to tenants.

The first belonged to an older woman from Vienna, whom I knew only as "La Professoressa," because she had once taught German at the University of Trieste. She was a slight woman in her late seventies with long gray hair that she always wore parted in the middle and tied in two braids, which were twisted into each other and then into a bun in the back of her head, just above the neck. She spoke many languages, including German, Italian, and English, and, like my mother, she was educated.

She had come to Italy during the war and found refuge with Zia Nina and her family.

Her quarters were small, but adequate. The space was furnished with a twin bed, a nightstand, and a wooden armoire where she kept her clothes. Beneath the room's only window was a desk; here she taught private lessons in English and German, so Franco and I had to be quiet if a student was visiting. Above the desk was her "library," two shelves filled with books, photographs, and a few mementos from her life in Vienna before the war. She had no family in Trieste, although she had a son in Vienna, who was a doctor.

Even though she was a tenant, Zia Nina still considered La Professoressa part of the family, and often invited her to join us for meals. I had never met anyone with dentures before, so I was surprised at how noisy they were. They made a clickety-clack sound whenever she chewed.

La Professoressa was quite a few years older than Nonna Rosa, but somehow she reminded me of my grandmother, and I liked spending time with her. The woman loved to eat, especially at night, so I'd keep her company in the evenings as she sipped on tea and munched on rectangular butter cookies. She'd make them into tiny sandwiches by spreading fresh butter on the inside of one and topping it with another, kind of like an Oreo. She liked to dunk the cookie sandwiches in her tea, perhaps to soften them and make them easier to bite. It was fun to watch rounds of melted butter float to the top of the tea, and the way she gulped them down, along with any cookie crumbs that may have drifted to the bottom of the cup when she took her last sip. These cookie sandwiches were often what she ate for her supper, and I could tell she enjoyed them immensely.

The second bedroom, off that same narrow hallway, was occupied by an elderly Italian woman and her daughter. They shared the bathroom with La Professoressa. I don't recall their names, only that they were very quiet and kept to themselves, although I would sometimes see them in the kitchen, cooking a small pot of food for themselves. Sometimes they would share their meals with La Professoressa, and sometimes they would eat with us.

Having these three women in the house provided an extra income and a nice distraction for Zia Nina. Her only living son, Corrado, whose room we now occupied, had moved to Australia with his girlfriend, a young woman from Trieste named Elda. Her family had decided to leave Italy to make a new life in Australia, and Nina had encouraged Corrado to go with them, believing he would be safer there. But she missed him terribly and would often speak of him.

Our days in Trieste passed quickly, and no one spoke of Zia Nina's health. My great-aunt continued to look fine, and there was no indication from my mother or brother that there was any reason for concern. My brother and I had always been close, and I could tell if something was bothering him. He seemed unconcerned, and, at almost nine years old, I had no reason to worry. As far as I knew, we were basically away on vacation. Looking back at it, I realize that my mother was likely having a very difficult time, trying to appear happy and keep us busy—all the while not letting on that Zia Nina was fine, and that this trip to visit our "ailing aunt" was a cover story for something quite different indeed.

Most everything we needed could be reached on foot, so we spent a good deal of time walking around. Trieste was an embracing, cosmopolitan city, reflecting its polyglot past. It had been the principal port for the Austro-Hungarian Empire, and the city reflected not just its Italian and Slovenian background, but also its imperial past. Its heterogeneous history was evident in the blend of architecture and the variety of houses of worship—not just Catholic, but Protestant, Jewish, Greek Orthodox, and Muslim.

A port city that embraced individuals of all religions and ethnicities, Trieste was a gateway for travelers, a very avant-garde and literary city, a place of poets and writers. At its heart, Trieste represented the meeting of the minds of different cultures, of East and West, of the liberation from communist thinking. It did not have the bustle that is commonly associated with Italian cities; to me, the Italian city most like Trieste was Torino. Both were places where the intelligentsia would meet and talk in cafés and stroll through art galleries.

The Italian contemporary-art movement actually started in Trieste, and I always find it interesting to think about the literati from all across Europe who came there, including James Joyce. Joyce actually first came to Pola, to teach for Berlitz, when the city was still an Italian territory, but he stayed there only a short time before relocating to Trieste. Trieste's architecture is also unique, a blend of Middle European influences from Vienna to Paris. Istria and Trieste were under the control of Austria for most of the eighteenth and nineteenth centuries, and under Italy from 1919 until Trieste was separated from the rest of Istria in 1947.

I had my first surprise the morning we accompanied Zia Nina to the produce market in the Piazza Ponterosso, a beautiful old square just off the Canale Grande, a waterway that had been dug in the mid-eighteenth century to allow cargo ships to offload inside the city. Here locals did their daily shopping, much as we did at the **mercato** back in Pola. Located in the center of the city, halfway between the Trieste railway station and the majestic Piazza Unità d'Italia, the largest sea-facing square in all of Europe, the Canale Grande is still used today. Three turntable bridges had once allowed sailing ships into the center of the city to offload their goods, but only one of those bridges, the Ponte Rosso (Red Bridge), remains. At the end

of the canal stands the Church of Sant'Antonio
Nuovo, the largest church in Trieste. The majestic neoclassical structure, fronted by six ionic columns and topped by a domed roof, holds special
memories for me: it was here that my brother and
I would eventually take Communion and Confirmation, something we had been forbidden to do
in Yugoslavia.

Colorful wooden boats bobbed up and down
in the channel below us as we followed Zia Nina
across the Ponte Rosso to the beautiful Piazza Ponterosso, where the Fontana del Giovanni, known

My Communion and Confirmation
in Trieste, at the Church of
Sant'Antonio Nuovo, 1957

locally as del Ponterosso, a historic fountain fed by water from a spring in the nearby neighborhood of San Giovanni, served as its centerpiece, and colorful four- and five-story neoclassical buildings built between the nineteenth and twentieth centuries created its borders. Dozens of **vendrigole**, local vendors, awaited us. I could hardly believe the abundance of produce on display. Back in Pola, we had a very limited selection, but here I found myself exploring a market full of fruits and vegetables, including some I'd never seen before. Blood oranges and dates were two fruits I had never tasted, and I excitedly sampled both. Oranges and tangerines were a "special event" fruit back in Pola: we would only get them as gifts when our cousins came to visit from Italy for the holidays. But this was the first time I tasted blood oranges, and I was amazed by their color when I first peeled them; they reminded me of the brilliant red cherries I had left behind in Busoler—intense, juicy, and sweet. The dried dates were expensive, but Zia Nina bought a few for Franco and me to sample, explaining that these were the fruit of the palm tree. They had a different texture from anything I had tasted before, and the pit reminded me of the bright orange **nespole**, loquats, that I so loved from our backyard in Pola.

Everywhere we went, the smell of coffee permeated the air. Historically, Trieste had been an important port for importing coffee duty-free for the famous coffeehouses of Vienna, and coffeehouses operated on almost every street of Trieste. The world-famous Illy Coffee Company was founded in Trieste in 1933 by Dr. Ernesto Illy, who developed the modern espresso machine that is now ubiquitous in Italy and elsewhere.

Coffee was a precious commodity back home in Yugoslavia. If you wanted to give somebody a gift, two or three ounces of ground coffee would be a generous offering. Here in Trieste, the streets literally smelled of coffee! And gelato, icy cold and flavorful, was available everywhere! Zia Nina would always stop at the café after going to the market to meet her friends for coffee, and she'd treat me to something special, usually an **aranciata**, orange soda, or an ice cream. When it was time to go, I would help her carry the bags the four blocks back to her apartment.

I sensed lightness here in Trieste that I had not experienced before. People seemed to smile at one another when they passed on the street, and everyone was so stylish. Men donned well-tailored suits and polished leather shoes, and women wore bright, figure-flattering Italian dresses, skirts, and suits, all paired with high heels and matching pocketbooks. The styles were much different from the drab, proletarian look in Yugoslavia. The fabrics were more refined and finished with elegant details, such as buttons and designs on the cuffs and collars. The fur stoles that many of the women wore over their suits and dresses were of particular interest to my mother. They were made out of the whole animal, usually a fox or mink, including the head, and had a clip by the animal's mouth that attached to one by its tail. When worn around the shoulders, it looked as if the fox was biting its tail.

Even the buildings were painted in colorful hues and were free of the soot, bullet scars, and propaganda writings that coated so many of the façades back home in Pola. But what I remember most is the wonderful aroma of coffee wafting around the city.

I was enjoying all of the new foods that were available to us, and I loved that the fashions were unique and so colorful. There was a joy in the way people communicated and socialized, gathering at cafés and bars and offering each other **un caffè**. The stores sparkled with merchandise, books, toys, chocolates, and other candies. It seemed as if everybody deeply celebrated life in a way that I'd never experienced before. Amid all the excitement, I didn't give much thought to not being in contact with my father. I knew, even at the age of eight, that there was no easy way to communicate with people in a distant place. Most families didn't have phones in their homes, which meant you had to use the phone in the local post office. That was true back in Istria, too. When you wanted to make a call, you had to arrange a date and time with the post office and get word to the people you were trying to reach to go to the post office near them at a preset time to receive the call. It often took one or more telegrams or letters to make the needed arrangements. Calls were expensive, too.

Spending time with Zia Nina in the kitchen was great fun. She was still working as a personal chef, and I got to assist her with some of her food purchases and preparations. I'd accompany her in the mornings to the market as she picked out the fruits, vegetables, and meats she would carefully prepare for her employer, and I'd help her clean and ready them once we were back at her home. When pheasants were on the menu for the evening, I'd help her pluck them. Much of the work we did in the kitchen was similar to what I did at Grandma Rosa's, but more refined, and I really enjoyed it. Zia Nina added a thoughtfully selected combination of herbs and spices, wines, and sometimes even Cognac to her dishes. Grandma sometimes hacked the chicken, rabbit, and vegetables without paying much attention to the joints and the bones; her time was limited, and there was always more work to be done around the house and the farm. Zia Nina, who didn't have the same time constraints, would look for the joints of the chicken, pheasants, and rabbits. She would carefully cut all the potatoes into pieces the same size, and all the vegetables into the same shapes. Plating the foods was more important to my aunt as well. Zia Nina always decorated with chopped parsley, leeks, or chives whenever they were in season. She also used citrus rinds and the juice of lemons and oranges—scarce commodities in Busoler. Nina was also a great risotto maker—rice was more available in Trieste than in Pola—and she would cook a lot with lemons and other citrus fruits that were rare and expensive back home.

Looking back, I realize I was learning so much about cooking from her. It was here in Trieste that I graduated from Grandma Rosa's delicious, simple, seasonal cooking to more elegant preparations and presentations suitable for dinner parties. I loved being in the kitchen with Zia Nina. She was my culinary transition from Nonna Rosa. She would season and taste a lot, and always extended the wooden spoon with something for me to taste. Many of the spices she used were not available to us in Yugoslavia: we had access only to what we could grow in our gardens. But here in Trieste, you could find many exotic spices such as cloves, cinnamon, and black pepper that were not indigenous to the area, and these had become part of Nina's culinary repertoire; even at eight years old, I found myself excited by all these new flavors.

As I later evolved in my culinary life, I always wondered about the different spices—cloves, cinnamon, black pepper—used in the northeastern regions of Italy, where I come from. Spices are indigenous to the tropical belt, whereas Italy is in the temperate zone, where fresh herbs such as rosemary, bay leaves, sage, basil, oregano, and marjoram are indigenous and used in the cuisine. It is evident not only how climate plays a role in a cuisine, but history as well.

For more than one thousand years, from the eighth century to 1797, the area of northeastern Italy was a sovereign state known as La Serenissima, the Republic of Venice, a maritime republic whose wealth came from its domination of trade in the Mediterranean Sea and on into Europe, North Africa, and Asia. Venice's trade strength was due in part to its location, exactly halfway between Constantinople and the West, so it controlled and profited from the trade routes it dominated. The main source of wealth, hence strength, for La Serenissima was spice trading, so much so that the Venetian Republic's currency was backed up by black pepper. The spices were initially delicacies that were used in the cooking and festivities of the courts and royal households of Europe, but they slowly seeped into the local culinary traditions and are still evident in today's recipes and cooking in that area. The taste of cinnamon and cloves evokes in me the memory of holidays and of the food Zia Nina would cook.

When we went to the market, she carefully selected her products and would coax me to smell and examine the color of the fruit, the crispness of the vegetables, and the shining eyes of the fish. She loved cooking game birds—pheasants, quails, squabs, and partridges. She meticulously cleaned and butchered them once we were home, then plucked every plume and burned off any remaining hairs on the birds. The innards made the base for the sauce, and the head, legs, and wings were used to make basic stock. Like a great maestro, she pulled everything together to create stunning masterpieces. I still recall the flavors of her cooking, and still have a soft spot for preparing game birds.

As the end of our visit neared, I noticed my mother becoming more and more agitated. Sometimes she would even break into tears for no apparent reason. I imagined she was probably just missing my father, and maybe she was also feeling a little sad about leaving Zia Nina. I had no inkling of what was really troubling her, and, given that I was just eight years old, it was probably better that way.

❧ ❦

Well after midnight on February 17, 1956, the sound of the doorbell startled me awake. No one had come to the apartment in the middle of the night during our entire stay, so I couldn't imagine who it could be. Back home in Pola, I wouldn't have been that surprised, especially after the night when the secret police came to imprison my father, but we were in Italy, a free country; a late-night visitor did not hold the same ominous connotation. I heard a lot of commotion coming from the entryway, and got up to find out what was happening. I walked out of my room to see my mother crying loudly, staring down at my father, who had collapsed on the floor. He was caked with dirt, pale, and bleeding. I had no idea what was going on.

My mother seemed to be showing a blend of fear and relief. She was clearly ecstatic to see my father, although I couldn't figure out why he was here. My aunt and uncle stood over him, hugging each other and thanking God that he was okay. Even my brother was smiling and looking relieved. It appeared they all knew he was coming, and I was the only one who hadn't been informed.

That morning, I learned that my father's arrival in Trieste meant that our family would not be returning to Istria—ever.

Our trip to Trieste to visit "sick" Aunt Nina had been a ruse; Aunt Nina was not really sick or dying. She and my mother had concocted the whole story so that we could obtain visas to travel out of Yugoslavia, but the plan had always been for us not to return. My father's parting words to my mother at the train station were now beginning to make sense. He would escape on foot, he had told my mother. And he had done just that.

The story my father told of his journey across the border was terrifying to me. I sat riveted as he recounted the harrowing escape he had made through the woods, on his own, under the cover of darkness—unsure if he would be caught and arrested, or even killed. My father and mother had been crafting his plan to flee Pola for many weeks. Even my brother knew that our father intended to escape on his own. After the rest of us were safely in Trieste, my father moved ahead with his scheme.

He knew that he couldn't take anything with him, not even a change of clothes, for fear of raising the suspicions of soldiers, border guards, or others that he might come into contact with. He had to make it look as if he were out for a hike, and nothing more.

He described how he'd paid a friend to drive him to a heavily wooded area on the outskirts of Capodistria, now the Slovenian city of Koper, about ten miles from the Italian border. From there, he would walk—quietly making his way through the woods and crossing the border at a remote spot that was infrequently patrolled. The friend who'd given him the ride counseled him on the route he should take and warned him to beware of the armed soldiers, accompanied by dogs, patrolling the forest in search of those trying to cross the border illegally. My father knew the journey ahead would be both arduous and perilous, and he had to be on constant lookout for anyone in the area. If he made even the slightest sound, it could raise alarm.

It was just after 8:00 p.m. when my father entered the forest. He told us he had been walking for a while when he spotted a dog approaching. Fearing it was a scent dog dispatched to sniff out border crossers, he crouched low to the ground to avoid being seen, then slowly lowered himself until he was flat on his stomach, with his face pressed against the cold earth. To mask his scent, he covered himself with mud. Bits of dirt and pebbles stuck to his lips, and the chill of night was in his limbs; he lay motionless for nearly four hours, until the dog finally lost interest and disappeared into the darkness. Wet, caked in mud, and numb from the cold, my father pulled himself upright and continued his frightening trek through the forest.

He knew he was getting close to the border when he spotted the uniformed soldiers patrolling the area just ahead of him. Just beyond them was the neutral zone, and then Italy. He was close, but the most difficult part still lay ahead. Once again, he hid, staying as still as he could, until the men dispersed. He watched them long enough to learn the timing of their patrols and figure out when he could make a quick dash toward the border. The guards followed a synchronized patrol pattern, marching in opposite directions for a certain distance before rejoining at a halfway point, at which time "code words" were exchanged, likely a signal that all was clear.

When my father determined the time was right, he just started running, and he didn't stop until he reached a clearing in the trees and saw the lights of Trieste in the distance. He had been on his feet for nearly eight hours when he heard a man's voice yell out to him in Italian.

"Did you escape tonight?"

He turned to see he was being addressed by an older man in work clothes, holding some tools. "Yes, I escaped tonight!" my father told him. "Where am I?"

"You are in the hills around Trieste," he replied. "Don't be afraid. I am not a soldier. You are in a free country. You are in Italy."

The people living close to the border had grown used to encountering asylum seekers who were escaping across the Yugoslavian border into Italy, and were usually generous and kind. It occurred almost daily, starting in the aftermath of World War II and continuing well into the 1960s.

The man instructed my father to continue walking until he reached the road, where he could board a bus for town. "Raise your hand and the bus will stop for you," the man explained. "It will drive you into the city of Trieste."

Even the Italian bus drivers understood the plight of the refugees. My father had no money to pay for the ride—the money from back home was worthless in Italy. But the bus driver did not make a fuss when he saw the bone-tired man in clothes soiled with dried mud flagging him down. He just let my father board, and said nothing as he quickly and quietly grabbed a seat in the back.

My father was so weak from the journey and all the anxiety and tension surrounding it that he fainted almost the second my aunt opened the apartment door. We managed to carry him to the bed, but he was not well. His whole body was shaking. "Where am I?" he asked over and over. When we told him he was in Trieste, he didn't seem to comprehend. Instead, he grew agitated.

"They will come to pick me up," he cried. "They will come to pick me up!"

But no one came. My father was safe, and his family was together in a free land. We'd left virtually everything we had behind—our home, furniture, clothes, and possessions. Our lifelong friends, too. We'd left behind the fields we'd lovingly tilled, the fig and cherry trees that I cherished, and the farm animals that were once so important to us. My father had nothing to show for the business that he'd worked so hard to establish and grow. His truck was now on the other side of the border, and there was no way to retrieve it, or anything else we'd left behind. Still, my father did carry two very small and precious reminders of home along with him the night he escaped across the border. One was a small stone that he had found inside the old Roman arena in Pola, where we'd often gone for concerts. It was a tiny bit of Istria, a vestige of his home, and something to help him remember the city—and everyone who lived there. He also brought a religious memento with him, a picture of the Sacred Heart of Jesus that his mother had given him before she died. He carried the image in his shirt pocket as he made the border crossing. They held more meaning to him than perhaps any of us could understand today.

We were now in a new land, and we would have to start over, from scratch. Maybe that explained why my mother had been crying for hours as we rode the train toward Trieste; maybe it was more than just nerves about my father's well-being. Maybe she was contemplating what lay ahead for us as a family. We had our health and our freedom. We were together as a family, and we had a roof over our heads and food to eat. Certainly, things could be worse. Still, the road ahead of us was unknown and filled with questions and uncertainty. Both of my parents had to be strong to keep the family together and create a new home for us . . . somewhere.

8

"Apolidi"

The reality of our situation was slowing sinking in. There was an undeniable excitement in knowing that we were starting a new life outside of communist Yugoslavia. But we also felt tremendous uncertainty about our future and where we would ultimately settle. My parents weren't sure what to do next. We knew that we could seek to stay in Italy and ask for citizenship here. But, even more than a decade after the war, Italy was still very unstable. Jobs were scarce, and not everyone was happy about the thousands of people who continued to pour over the nation's borders and compete for what few jobs were available. Italy functioned as a "country of first asylum," meaning that immigrants were welcomed—but they were not supposed to integrate. Instead, immigrants were expected to wait to eventually be resettled somewhere else. As a result, the immigrants' stay was merely a stop on a much longer journey to find a permanent home—a journey that often took years.

We'd heard great things about the United States from Grandpa Giovanni. He had been to the States, and New York City in particular, having been on the crew of the **Carpathia,** the ship famous for being the first to come to the aid of passengers of the **Titanic** after it struck an iceberg and sank on the morning of April 15, 1912. My grandfather had even considered jumping ship and remaining in New York. But, in the end, he returned home, though he always praised America and all it had to offer.

Grandpa and others described it as a nation of great opportunity, where jobs and education were available and easy to come by—all you needed to do was work hard. He had long encouraged my parents to flee communist Yugoslavia and take us to America, convinced we would find a life of opportunity and personal freedom. The United States was one of several countries that were taking war refugees, along with Australia, New Zealand, and Canada, among others.

My parents had a limited amount of time to consider our options, and the decision weighed heavily on them. The afternoon of my father's arrival in Trieste, Zia Nina had called a doctor to come to her home and check on him. Then she went to the police station to alert authorities to our plight. Police had counseled her to have my whole family report to them as soon as my father was well enough.

My parents knew that we had to act quickly: our visas limited our stay in Italy, and the police were strict and insisted that people comply with the travel restrictions. If we overstayed our entry permit by as little as one day, we would be at risk of arrest by local authorities in Trieste and possible repatriation to Yugoslavia. My father had crossed the border illegally, had no travel documents, and was in imminent risk of arrest—unless he told the authorities that he was seeking asylum in Italy.

My parents decided to wait as long as we could, so we stayed with Zia Nina for another three days, while my father took the medicine prescribed to him by the doctor who had visited the house and tried to regain his strength. He still wasn't feeling well on the day our visas were set to expire, but we had run out of time and could wait no longer. We had to report to the police or risk being arrested. Or worse.

❧ ❦

February is one of the coldest months in Italy; temperatures drop below the freezing mark, and snow falls in some parts of the country. In Trieste, icy currents sometimes struck the Adriatic and the Bora pounded the city. Winds were whipping the morning my brother and I went with our parents to police headquarters. Zia Nina and Zio Rapetti accompanied us to the station, but they didn't dare come inside. I'm sure that my great-uncle wanted to help us at the police station, but he was now retired from the force, and he didn't want to be seen helping our family when he knew that we would be treated as illegal immigrants.

The Questura di Trieste, the main police headquarters, was on Via di Tor Bandena, a narrow side street in the center of the city, not far from the Ponterosso Market. I remember walking into a smoky office with my parents and my brother and waiting on hard wooden benches for someone to speak with us. I was very frightened—and my parents were, too. They feared we would be expelled over the border to Yugoslavia, where my father would surely be sent to Goli Otok, or Isola Calva—the small, barren island off the Dalmatian coast that housed political and war dissidents.

We were finally escorted to a small interview room, where an officer barked questions at us. "Where are you from?" he demanded. "What led you to leave Yugoslavia?" "How did you get to Trieste?" "Why are you refusing your Yugoslavian citizenship?" His stern tone unnerved me and seemed to rattle my parents and my brother.

My mother and father answered the questions as best they could. My mother even presented the officer with the travel documents we had used to come to Trieste for our "visit" with Zia Nina. She then explained the circumstances under which my father had entered the country.

Our papers were collected, and after several long hours, new ones were prepared for us. Because we were refusing our Yugoslavian citizenship, we were now **apolidi,** without a nation, and would need to be processed and vetted to determine our eligibility for refugee status. This meant we were no longer permitted to move freely about the country and would have to be placed in a refugee camp until a determination could be made. I could see how relieved my parents were, but I didn't understand why we couldn't just stay with Zia Nina. I kept my thoughts to myself, however.

As soon as our interview was finished, we were loaded into a **camionetta,** a blue-and-white police van typically used to transport prisoners. Tears streamed down my mother's cheeks as she climbed onto one of the bench seats in the back, where steel grates covered all the windows. My parents were silent for much of the thirty-minute ride, punctuated by an occasional whimper from my mother. The magnitude of our situation was lost on me that day.

At almost nine years old, I was unable to appreciate the sacrifice my parents had just made . . . or the fear and uncertainty they were now experiencing. We were now refugees without any identification papers, without a home: we were **apolidi.** I knew that my mother was upset, and her distress heightened when the van turned onto Via Giovanni Palatucci and we got our first look at San Sabba refugee camp, a red-brick compound reminiscent of one of the long-standing brick factory buildings that dot older cities across New England. The unwelcoming complex consisted of two five-story buildings encircled by a spiky barbed-wire fence. A massive steel gate that stretched from one building to the other marked the entry, where a uniformed guard was posted twenty-four hours a day.

As I stepped out of the van, I, too, suddenly felt like crying. But I fought back my tears, wanting to be strong for my mother. One of the officers who had driven us there directed us to follow him into the complex, a former rice mill that had operated on the site since the turn of the century. Not until many years later would I learn its dark, macabre history. Less than thirteen years earlier, the complex had been taken over by the Nazis, who converted it into a concentration camp—the only one in Italy—that included a crematorium. The facility, now the Civico Museo della Risiera di San Sabba, had also served as a transit depot for the Nazis to house tens of thousands of people en route to concentration camps in Germany and Poland.

Remarkably, the San Sabba concentration camp has largely escaped the level of public awareness and visibility associated with other Nazi-run camps, such as Auschwitz. At the end of World War II, the Nazis destroyed the crematorium and sought to remove evidence of what had taken place there, but the outline of the crematorium remains on the floor of the interior courtyard. We were told only that the facility was a former rice mill; there wasn't even a whisper about its days as a Nazi concentration camp.

I grabbed for my mother's hand as we followed the officer down a cavernous covered brick walkway. It was dark and echo-y, and there was an odd, unpleasant smell that I couldn't place. The man directed us to a small office just at the end of the walkway, where we were told to wait while camp officials processed our paperwork. From there, we were taken to the second floor of an adjacent building, to a holding area where at least twenty other families were gathered. Up to this point, I had been able to contain my anxiety. But panic set in when I learned that we could no longer stay together as a family. Suddenly, my family was being divided. Other families, too, were being divided by gender. The men and boys were ordered to go into one area, and all the women and girls were ordered into another. I had no idea what was going to happen next, and I didn't know when I was going to see my father and brother again.

The area we were now in was a quarantine station for all the incoming refugees. We would have to submit to a lengthy medical examination and be deloused and sanitized. Officials ordered us to remove our clothes and shoes so that we could be thoroughly washed and sprayed with disinfectant—our bodies, our hair, even our clothes. I was deeply frightened; I did not know what they were doing or why they were doing this to us, and I was worried about what was going to happen to us. As a young girl, I was ashamed and felt violated, having to undress in front of other women.

Why were they handling us in this manner? I wondered. We were good, hardworking, **clean** people—ethnic Italians who had left our homeland in search of a better life in a free country. Yet we were being treated with suspicion. Everything around us felt cold and rough. Nothing there gave us any sense of comfort; no touchstone of home, no friends or relatives to make casual conversation with. We were forced to fend for ourselves in an alien environment. It was a period of near terror that I will never be able to forget, no matter how much I want to.

In retrospect, I now realize that there were thousands of refugees escaping into Italy, and, yes, though we were an honest family looking for freedom, hidden among those refugees were political criminals, and lawbreakers trying to escape their illicit pasts; we all had to go through this rigorous vetting system.

I can still remember looking out the window onto the large interior courtyard below us. It was filled with people—men, women, children—some huddled in small groups, others sitting alone. I scanned their faces, desperately hoping to recognize my father amid the strangers. But he was not there, and neither was my brother. Where were they? And what were the authorities doing to them?

We were given loose-fitting, pajamalike garments to wear—much like the ones that prison inmates spend their days in. Next we were brought to an area filled with rows of dark, prisonlike cells. We were assigned one of the small spaces, outfitted with one bunk bed and a small wooden table. This is where we would be kept for the next forty-eight hours, until we were thoroughly vetted, satisfactorily disinfected, and cleared of any criminal history. My mother and I barely spoke; I could see that she was struggling to keep her tears at bay, and I could think of no way to lift her mood—or mine, for that matter.

Sometime late in the afternoon, my mother and I were brought to a small room where we were finally reunited with my father and brother.

"Papa!" I cried, throwing myself into his arms.

Even Franco and I shared a long embrace. Throughout this ordeal, my brother would become ever more protective of me, especially as we moved on in search of a new life. After all, we had left our friends behind when we left Istria, and it was not easy for us to start new friendships as we moved from place to place, from situation to situation. As children in Pola and Busoler, we both had our own sets of friends. But here in Trieste, we grew ever closer as we sought to protect and comfort each other. Together, in our own little world, we would discuss our situation, how our parents seemed to be doing, and how we could help strengthen their spirits.

Children take on responsibilities of their own when they know the family unit is at risk and in need. This feeling of staying close as a family would continue as we moved to America and our parents needed us even more. My brother and I have continued to keep a close bond and make sure that our families, our children and grandchildren, understand the track that our family took in our quest to be free and have the opportunity for a new life. We make every effort to spend our holidays together, for this closeness is what helps pull us through tough times. Even those early days in the refugee camp were somehow more bearable knowing that my brother was there with me.

Our first meeting with immigration officials was particularly difficult for my mother. She could not understand why we were being held under such conditions. "We have done nothing," she told them. "We don't steal, we don't fight. We are good people. Why are you holding us here like this?"

The interrogator explained that the Italian government had no way of differentiating between innocent people fleeing communism, and criminals, even murderers, who were fleeing prosecution in their native countries. His answer seemed to make sense to my mother; still, I could tell that she hated our situation, and nothing could stop the flow of her tears.

We underwent two days of intense questioning before officials were convinced that my parents were not communist infiltrators, and we were cleared to enter the camp.

9

"Profughi"

No matter what the time or season, the San Sabba refugee camp always felt dark, gray, and inhospitable. It was bitter cold and rainy for the entire first week we were there. Our family was assigned a small cubiclelike space in the barracks on the other side of the complex from where we'd been quarantined.

More than two thousand **profughi**, refugees crowded the camp when we arrived there that winter day, people of all ages and nationalities. They included immigrants from Poland, Hungary, Czechoslovakia, Serbia, Bulgaria, and, of course, Istria.

Our search for freedom forced my family to leave behind a comfortable apartment in Pola. My parents also left their secure jobs. Gone, too, were all of our possessions—the furniture, clothing, bicycles, even my mother's hats, which she so cherished. My father, in hopes of salvaging his life's work and not letting it go into the hands of the communists, had handed over the keys to his truck to a relative; we learned that, eventually, the regime did take the truck anyway. He also had secretly transferred ownership of our apartment in Pola to my mother's sister, Lidia, to prevent the government from snatching it away. So one consolation was that Aunt Lidia, my fisherman buddy Uncle Emilio, and their one-year-old daughter, Sonia, had moved into the apartment; at least family was living in it. My father always held out hope that he'd be able to go back someday. Our belongings now consisted of the contents of the three suitcases my mother, Franco, and I had brought from Pola, delivered to us by Zia Nina once we had settled in.

The three-story barracks to which we were assigned was divided into distinct sections to accommodate all of the camp's inhabitants. The middle floor, where we were located, was reserved for families and the relatively few single women. The ground floor was the **mensa,** or mess hall, where we went for our meals. And the top floor was for the hundreds of single men who dominated the facility.

The people who ran the camp took my mother, father, Franco, and me up to the second floor—a large, open area with a long wooden plank floor that had been hastily and cheaply converted into a series of small "rooms," one for each family. Authorities used a mix of wooden boards and sheets to create walls that separated one family from another.

The walls were open at the top and bottom, and noise traveled freely among the twenty or so other families around us. Talk and other sounds echoed off the structure's old brick walls, and we could hear everything that everyone else said and did— including the babies, who cried at all hours of the night, and the parents, who angrily feuded with each other. You could never escape the noise. Our fourteen-by-sixteen-foot cubicle had a makeshift wooden door in front, not that it would have prevented anyone from entering if they'd wanted to.

It was frightening. During the night, when the various noises woke me up, I would lie in bed and listen, trying to paint mental pictures of what I was hearing. Where did these people come from? I wondered. Did they have a grandma like I did? Did they have baby goats and rabbits, like I'd had, to play with? Did they yearn like I did for the ripe figs and cherry trees filled with delicious ripe fruit? Did they have a sea where they would go to swim? Did they miss it all ever so much?

On some nights, the echoing voices and noises of people arguing, guards commanding, would come from the courtyard below. Sometimes **sotto voce** songs of lament would lull me to sleep. Most of the time, I did not understand the words, but the whining melodies told of the sadness in the singers' hearts.

Guards watched everyone at the camp twenty-four hours a day. I no longer had a home, a bed, a place to call my own; I felt vulnerable, and the only security I found was when we were huddled together as a family, just like my cat and her kittens back home in Pola. I used to love to pet them as they were huddling in a warm, furry cluster with their mother. Now I could no longer go for long walks through the forest or play with the animals in Grandma's courtyard. And I didn't have my grandmother. In a way, I didn't have an identity; I was neither Yugoslavian nor Italian. I was like a leaf in the wind.

We were at San Sabba for more than two years, and it seemed as if winter never ended. I expected that I would feel different in the camp, maybe just a bit better, as the seasons changed and the weather grew warmer. But in the courtyard the earth was always humid, with scattered patches of flat stones and puddles of mud in between the stones. The cavernous indoors always seemed dark; there was never enough light. No matter what we did inside our little corner of the gloomy barracks, it was always chilly, raw, and uninviting; the only consolations were the rays of sunlight that would come and visit us on sunny days through the tall window that separated the beds.

As many as eight hundred people a day were crossing the border into Italy from Eastern Europe. The mass exodus would continue for nearly twenty years after World War II, putting tremendous strain on the Italian government and its economy, especially since Italy was recovering in the aftermath of the war and trying to build infrastructure and jobs for its people. Italian authorities did the best they could to house and accommodate all the freedom seekers, many of whom were able to realize their dreams for safer and more productive lives. As ethnic Italian immigrants from Istria, we were treated more kindly than many others, and my parents were given the opportunity to find part-time jobs. We children were eventually allowed to go out of the camp, to school. We owe a lot to the Italians who accepted and cared for us during those times. No doubt, it was a struggle for everyone—the Italians who tried to be accommodating with very limited resources, and the refugees who had to endure difficult and oftentimes frightening conditions in San Sabba and elsewhere.

Our tiny "room" near the middle of the second floor was outfitted with two sets of metal bunk beds for the four of us, one pushed up against the makeshift wall on the left, and the other pushed up against the makeshift wall on the right. A table sat between the beds. My mother obtained a small hot plate we used for making coffee, tea, or hot milk for my brother and me. There was one chair at the table; usually, we sat on the lower beds to eat. We had no dressers to store our clothes, but there were nails pounded in the wooden wallboards around the room, and wherever there was some space, that is where we hung whatever clothes we owned.

Since we had only the clothes that we had brought with us in our small valises, we had to make do with whatever bedding and garments the authorities provided. I recall heavy army blankets and rough dingy towels. Periodically, the camp administrators would announce that they had received a shipment of used clothes—mostly from the United States, sent by the Red Cross and the Salvation Army. They'd open the boxes on tables in the big courtyard, and people went out and picked through things for whatever they needed. There was an odd assortment of dresses, undergarments, men's shirts and slacks, jackets, black and white "bowling-style" shoes, and things for children, too.

My mother struggled with the process, because she'd been accustomed to going to little shops back home and selecting precisely the fashions she wanted to wear; now she was picking through garments donated by others. Still, she was very appreciative, and was excited about some of the American styles. She found one dress in particular that she cherished and wore often—black, with a square collar embellished with green, yellow, and red accents, a design matched on the cuffs and hem. And I found a green-checked pleated skirt and a yellow woolen sweater, which I loved and wore regularly. I even brought the outfit to the States with me when we came.

The shipments sometimes included big boxes of crackers, peanut butter (which I had never tasted before), chocolates and chewing gum, cans of Spam (which I thought was a super treat), and packaged yellow American cheese that we could take back to our rooms. It was the first time I'd ever had American cheese, and I loved it. It was all rationed, and Mom would be parsimonious with the goodies so they would last longer. The chewing gum and chocolates brought back fond memories of my father surprising Franco and me with little treats he'd pull from his pockets after long days on the road.

There were communal showers and bathrooms on each floor, one for men and the other for women, at least on our floor—as I never dared venture to the other floors. The toilets were in stalls with wooden doors, and showers were separated with tiled walls and enclosed with plastic screens. My mother kept a bar of soap in our room, which we used to wash ourselves as well as for the clothes and linens. We used the same piece of soap to wash our body and our hair; there was no shampoo to be found. Still, we did what we could to look our best. My mother would rinse my hair with a potful of water and vinegar to wash out the soap and to help give my hair some shine. I always had to keep my eyes tightly shut so the vinegar wouldn't burn my eyes. Another advantage of the vinegar: it disinfected everything. There were times when I just didn't want to deal with it, but my mother just told me to "grin and bear it."

Our meals were all served in the mess hall on

the ground floor. It was one big room broken up
only by the heavy wooden columns that supported
the two floors above. Between the columns were
long wooden tables and benches made with long
wooden planks. Everyone was provided with one
plate; we were expected to keep it clean and bring
it to every meal.

We cleaned the dishes and utensils in the large
stone sinks in the courtyard just outside the mess
hall, the same sinks we used to wash our clothes.
There were long cement sinks along one wall of the
courtyard, and on nice days, everyone would be
out there doing laundry. We'd wash our garments
by hand, and then hang them to dry on clotheslines that were strung around the massive brick en-
closure.

There was an open section to the kitchen, which
was against the north wall, and at mealtimes we
would stand in line with our plates to get our food.
Often dinner was a small serving of spaghetti or
some other pasta, usually with tomato sauce, and,
as I recall, it was good. The spaghetti would sometimes alternate with soup. We would also get a piece
of bread and a **formaggino,** a triangle of soft cheese
wrapped in foil, much like the Laughing Cow
cheese that you find in U.S. supermarkets today.
From what we could tell, the Italian police force was
in charge of running the camp, but the Americans
supplied much of our food. There was always some
fresh fruit at every meal, most often apples. Water

was the usual beverage—though for breakfast there was milk, and a dry cookie.

Extra helpings of food were available in the mess hall, but they came at a price. A sign announced that people who wanted a second helping could get one, if they came in and cleaned potatoes or otherwise lent a hand with the food preparation. My mother helped out on a regular basis, spending a minimum of two hours in the kitchen, so that Franco and I could have an extra slice of bread or ration of spaghetti.

Growing up in Pola, we were used to meals being fun family affairs, full of chatter and banter. But life in the camp was far different, and we tended to rush through all of our meals. We'd find a spot at one of the communal tables that was big enough for the four of us, and then we'd eat dinner quietly, as a family. When we were done, we'd all head outside to wash our plates and utensils before returning to our room.

None of us ever felt comfortable in San Sabba. It was never a "home," just a place where we had to stay. There was rarely any joy or laughter. Everyone kept to himself or herself. But in every one of those dim faces and sad hearts there was hope: hope for a new life, for freedom and education. Everybody knew that San Sabba was a transitional place, though no one knew when we would be on the move again, and to where. The only excitement in the camp population came when someone got called to the offices and was told of a visa possibility, of a moving-on opportunity. In everyone's mind were the questions: Will I pass? Am I the person? Will our family be the one to be offered this opportunity for a new beginning?

I hardly spoke to anyone during our time there, and I didn't make any friends. People would hang around the courtyard in clusters, speaking in different languages. I heard lots of different languages that I did not understand, and by then I spoke Italian and Croatian. There must have been at least ten different languages being spoken in the courtyard, from Bulgarian to Czech to Albanian to Polish. Even at my young age, I could see the uncertainty and pain on people's faces, the grimness. Many of the men were unshaven. They'd cluster in groups, away from the women, sharing cigarettes. Some of the women would also gather together to talk and help pass the time, and a few brought their children along. But, for the most part, people tended to stick with a small group of family and friends; few were interested in expanding their circles of friends to those who spoke other languages.

There were some really tough people in the camp. Quite a few had crossed the Adriatic from other parts of Yugoslavia and from Albania. A lot of the young men had attempted their voyage to freedom using small fishing boats that plied local waters.

The physical journey was dangerous, and they also risked getting shot on sight if caught before they reached Italian waters.

When we were in Istria, I would sometimes hear whisperings about people who'd left by boat and never made it. Except for my father, we had come to Trieste with regular passports, but there was one young man at the camp who didn't have any papers when he crossed the border. To avoid detection, he hid in the undercarriage of a train—and lost a leg. He was just eighteen years old. Others hid in trucks, much like those that we see today crossing into the United States from Mexico. Travel across the border for undocumented people was always risky, and the consequences could be severe. And not just from the trip itself. Even though we had safely crossed into Italy, we still had tremendous fear that we might be sent back home.

A never-ending sense of insecurity pervaded San Sabba, which kept the socializing between the different ethnic groups to a minimum. People tended to huddle together with refugees from their old country, speaking their own language and sometimes singing their own national songs. There were no activities to bring everyone together.

No one completely trusted anyone else, no matter where they were from. We had all escaped from communist countries, and we all worried that there may have been spies planted among us in the camp. Rumors circulated that there were suspicious characters in San Sabba who would leave the premises at night to cross the border, ostensibly to visit their families, and then return, fueling concerns that the identities of those in the camp were being reported back to government officials in their respective countries. There were also rumors of refugees being kidnapped outside the camp and taken back to their respective countries by communist operatives.

My mother and father kept to themselves and only socialized with other Italian-speaking immigrants who had also escaped from Istria. Arguments between the different groups of refugees would erupt now and then, so my parents tried to keep us isolated and protected. But children did play together from time to time; my brother joined boys from everywhere to play soccer in the courtyard.

Some of the refugees worked their way up through the ranks to move into roles of authority in the camp. They'd start by helping out in the kitchen, then organize others, and eventually be promoted to more official roles, such as camp monitors, who would make sure there were no thefts or fights. They were sometimes more strict and authoritarian than the official guards and workers.

The first month in San Sabba was the hardest. My mother never stopped crying. My ninth birthday had passed that February while we were still in quarantine, but even after we were settled in the camp, we had no celebration. My father was nervous and unhappy and lost a lot of weight. He was despondent, missing his homeland and the life that he and my mother had built together. For my parents, there was nothing but uncertainty and fear of the unknown. They stayed awake at night, fretting about what they'd done and where we would finally settle. They wondered if they'd made the right choice, or if they'd created a nightmare scenario from which the family would never recover.

For Franco and me, there was fear of the unknown, too, but, there was also excitement and wonderment; we were on something of an adventure. That we didn't know what was going to come next didn't bother us too much. We were too young to worry about the future in the same way our parents did. Understanding that our parents were struggling and worried, Franco and I bonded together and resolved to try to cheer them up and give them more of a sense of hope. We believed that they might feel better if they saw that we were happy and willing to make the best of a rough situation.

There are critical times when children rise to a challenge and try to guide and bring strength to a family in peril. Children understand that what makes their parents content and gives them a source of hope is to see that their children are at peace, are well fed and happy, that the situation they are so concerned about is not desperate or unbearable for the children. And so my brother and I took on that role; we stayed positive, happy in the anticipation of what our new life was going to be. It was all so transitory, so unstable. But, throughout it all, we remained united as a family. The fact that today my mother, at ninety-seven, is still with me in my home is testament to the bond we forged. Only now can I look back and analyze and comprehend all that we endured; back then, I focused only on what each day brought.

Each one of us had our own personal struggles at San Sabba. For me, my time there represented a sharp break from an idyllic childhood. My greatest despair was that I had never been able to say good-bye to my beloved grandmother.

Even though I lived during an oppressive time in Yugoslavia, I still felt a sense of freedom as a child. Authorities there told me when I had to march in parades to celebrate the arrival of Tito and his men, and they told me when I had to wear the **titolka,** the pointed hat with the red star. But sometimes I could get away to play in the forest, or frolic on the beach and enjoy the crystal-clear waters with my friends. I was still a child, and I felt free in Istria, as long as I had access to nature. That ability to get out and enjoy the outdoors was taken away while we were at San Sabba. All of us were under lock and key, at least at the beginning of our time there. My freedom, my ability to enjoy the forests and the waters that had nourished my spirit for years, was now gone.

10

Finding My Spirituality

It was hard for my family to be in Italy yet not be Italian citizens. But if we wanted to be considered for legal immigration, this was the only way. Once we were settled in at the San Sabba refugee camp, authorities provided us with the necessary papers and permits. Then they asked my parents where they wanted our family to immigrate. America was our first choice, my parents said.

I knew very little about America. I'd seen picture postcards of New York City, with its skyscrapers and enormous bridges. And sometimes Franco and I would go to the **osteria** in Trieste with Zio Rapetti to watch sporting events on television—mostly soccer matches—and catch glimpses of New York City.

I'd also heard great things about the country from some of the seamen back home in Yugoslavia, who'd sailed there and returned with stories about job opportunities, massive and thriving cities, and streets full of cars.

Grandpa Giovanni had long advocated for my parents to take us there. Canada was also on our radar, but America was at the top of the list. I knew there was no turning back for us. In a way, we were already on our own voyage, and I was eager to take the next step. I was deeply anxious about where our journey would take us, but I was excited, too, and wanted to move forward. It was as if the dark and cold San Sabba was a tunnel—a step on a path that would ultimately take us to America. I could imagine a light at the end of the tunnel, and I hoped that my brother and parents had the same sense of hope that I did.

Gaining acceptance to the United States was unpredictable. There was no telling when the country would open up its borders to immigrants, and no one knew how many refugees the nation would take. When a nation did open its border, there was always a quota. America and other nations were looking for immigrants who could be good citizens. We were told by camp authorities that we were worthy candidates because my parents were both educated and skilled. People in the camps who had relatives living abroad willing to sponsor them had a greater chance of gaining admittance than those who didn't—and the process was faster, too.

Not long after our arrival at San Sabba, camp officials summoned my parents to a meeting and asked whether we had any relatives living anywhere in the world who might be willing to sponsor us.

My mother told them about her aunt Anna, Nonna Rosa's older sister. She had left Istria in the 1930s, when she was just eighteen, to join a young man she had dated before he left to work in the mines of Pennsylvania. He was a few years older than she, and so he waited until her eighteenth birthday to return to Istria to ask for her hand in marriage. No one in the family had been in contact with Anna since then. All anybody knew was that she was living somewhere in Pennsylvania.

Camp officials reached out to the FBI for help in locating Anna and found that she was living near the Susquehanna River. Her husband had died, and she was now widowed and close to seventy years old. Unfortunately, she was also in poor health and in no position, physically or financially, to sponsor us. Therefore, she would be of no help in moving forward our application for entry to the United States.

Our newly issued ID cards allowed us to leave the camp, but for no more than a day at a time. They gave Franco and me the ability to leave San Sabba to attend school and enabled our parents to find part-time work. They were both anxious to earn some pocket money that could be used to buy better, more nutritious food for the family. The ID cards also meant that we could leave the camp to visit Zia Nina at her home.

We could check out at 7:00 a.m., and we had to be back no later than 6:00 p.m. All of us were required to carry the identification cards with us at all times; they functioned a bit like passports. We had to show them to the officials at the gate when leaving the camp in the mornings, and again upon our return at the end of the day. So the authorities could keep track of our comings and goings, the cards were stamped each time we passed through the gates. We were among the more fortunate ones: some refugees were never allowed to leave the camp, either because they couldn't be properly vetted or because authorities had suspicions about them.

My mother was terrified that somehow the military in Yugoslavia would track us down and force us back over the border. So it took her more than a month to overcome her fear of letting any of us leave the camp. Sitting idly in the camp day after day made me feel like a prisoner. I yearned for the day when we could finally get outside San Sabba's brick walls. Today, when I see images in the newspaper and on television of all the refugees living in tents, a shiver runs down my spine, and I flash back to my days in San Sabba. In a way, we were more fortunate. After all, we had a roof over our heads, and we weren't exposed to the elements like those living in tent cities today. Still, we were without a country and without a home. The number of displaced immigrants in 1956 wasn't of the same scale as it is today, but I know what those refugees are going through—the hunger, the pain, the sadness, the insecurity, the helplessness, the anguish

My mother, brother, me, and my father in
Zia Nina's apartment in Trieste—our Sunday
visit from the camp

they feel. All they want is a secure place of their
own with food and warmth for their families. I
don't know their individual stories, whether they
are being chased from their homelands or whether
they have chosen to leave in search of a better life,
but I do know that, if given the chance, most of
them would make something out of their struggles.
They would work hard for their families and make
a better life for themselves.

Finally, that April, my mother agreed to let us go
to Zia Nina's house for Sunday dinner, and the authorities at the camp had no problem with our leaving, because we followed proper protocol. We were
allowed to leave as often as we wanted to. However,

no one was allowed to visit us at the camp; non-refugees were not permitted there.

Just walking into Nina's house was a treat. It smelled like home, with the aromas of fresh-cooked foods emanating from the kitchen. There was the sound of quiet conversation among the family members, and music coming from the small radio in the kitchen. It all felt so different from the constant noise and ambience at San Sabba, where we were packed in like sardines and the smell of body odor and cigarette smoke filled the air. Nina always had something special on the stove for us, such as her Sunday gnocchi with **guazzetto**, a type of stew-like sauce. This was one of my favorite meals.

The meat for the **guazzetto** would sometimes be squab, sometimes chicken, and sometimes rabbit. It did not matter; it was always so delicious, and the joy of sitting with family in a peaceful setting with good home cooking and the warmth and security of a real home gave us a much-needed respite.

Zia Nina's elderly tenant La Professoressa often joined us for meals, and being around her brought me comfort, too. Sometimes she would invite Franco and me into her room for English lessons, helping to prepare us for the day when we would hopefully immigrate to the United States.

From time to time, Nina would tell us about things she'd heard from Pola, including word from Nonna Rosa. Unfortunately, some of the news was sad. My grandmother missed us and was upset that we had been forced to leave. Grandpa Giovanni was hopeful that we would soon be on our way to America.

While we were in the camp, Aunt Lidia was able to stay in touch with us from Pola through new refugees who came to Trieste. They would sometimes bring letters and messages. Grandma and Grandpa were anxious about our status and future plans, but communication was scarce. Though the mail did reach us, I recall that when my mother wrote letters she always feared that whatever she put in print about our search for freedom might hurt our family left behind; officials in Yugoslavia were almost certainly reading the letters before they delivered them.

We knew that Nonna Rosa was always thinking about us because of the little packages of food—pieces of prosciutto, sausage, and pancetta—that she would send from Busoler every so often. She would search for people going to Trieste and ask them if they could carry a package for her. I even remember her sending a block of butter for us to eat in the camp. There were still shortages of many goods, including cigarettes and coffee. People from Yugoslavia would journey over the border to buy goods on the thriving black market in Trieste and take it back home. For Nonna Rosa, it was fairly easy to learn who was making the trip, and give them a package. Nonna Rosa would always send the packages to Zia Nina's home, and she would include something for Nina, too. My grandmother knew that Nina worked hard to feed us when we came over for dinner, and she was anxious to show her gratitude. Getting a package from Grandma always made me miss her a little more.

We heard that authorities back home had gone to our house in Pola looking for us, and that they had stopped by Nonna Rosa's farm to ask questions. Someone from the Communist Party had even knocked on Zia Nina's door in Trieste, inquiring if we were there. But no one said a word.

Officials at the camp regularly put up signs in the courtyard whenever a country was opening its borders to refugees or needed workers. Australia had taken a number of people, and many other refugees had accepted offers to immigrate to Canada, New Zealand, and Belgium. Month after month, we watched the signs and hoped that the United States would announce that it was opening its border. We were told that we could be facing a long wait, certainly months, and perhaps years.

We were in San Sabba for about two months when my father was offered a job working in a shipyard in La Spezia, a port city in the Liguria region of Italy. His experience in the mercantile marines and his work in the navy yard made him a good candidate. My mother would be sent to northern Italy, to the city of Como, in the foothills of the Alps, where she would be given a job as a teacher. "We are not dividing the family," my father told camp officials. "We escaped. We will live together." So we stayed where we were.

My father was next offered work in the coal mines of Belgium. He didn't want to go, and my mother was wholly against it, in part because working in a coal mine was dangerous. Just a few months earlier, a mining disaster at the Bois du Cazier coal mine, near Charleroi, claimed the lives of 262 miners, most of them Italian laborers. My mother knew that my father was both educated and skillful, and she was confident that he could find something better suited to his skills. Besides, she did not want to go to Belgium, and was convinced that if we waited a better opportunity would come along: in America, she hoped.

"We will live somewhere else in the world!" she told my father.

Local businesspeople came to San Sabba, looking for day workers and part-time help. My father was hired to be a chauffeur for the Ferro family, well-to-do coffee merchants. He was tasked with driving Signora Ferro to and from the theater in Trieste. For a while, my mother even worked as a housekeeper in the Ferro home. Like many other adults, they were aggressively seeking to earn whatever money they could. My father was paid a small stipend, and my mother was compensated with food that she could bring back to the camp for the family.

One day, a woman from Trieste named Paola Leonori came by the camp asking about my mother.

Her husband owned a clothing store in the city, and they had three young sons. Signora Leonori had heard that there was an Italian teacher in San Sabba (my mother, of course), and she wanted to see if she could hire this teacher to work with her developmentally disabled son, Guido, who was six years old. The boy had suffered from an infection when he was an infant, and it had affected his development; as a result, he couldn't attend school with his siblings. She asked that my mother be allowed to come to her house five days a week to teach the boy how to read, write, and count.

My mother agreed to do it, and Signora Leonori paid her a small fee. But the woman wanted to do more for my mother. She arranged for me to attend a special school next door to the modern apartment building where she lived. The Scuola Canossiana, at 66 Via Domenico Rossetti, was a grammar school run by the Canossian Sisters, also known as the Daughters of Charity; this was where Signora Leonori sent her sons Giuseppe and Gabriele. It operated out of a charming stone building that was painted a cheerful shade of apricot and surrounded by a six-foot stone wall. The building was hard to see from the street, much of it hidden behind a mix of shrubs and tall cypress trees. The large building also served as a home to the Canossian nuns who ran the school.

My mother was able to arrange for me to leave the camp with her in the mornings to attend classes. On some days, Signora Leonori would pick us up right outside the gates; on other days, we would catch the public bus at a stop just a few minutes' walk away, on Via Flavia. The ride took about twenty-five minutes, along Via dell'Istria, to our stop at Viale Gabriele d'Annunzio; we'd walk the rest of the way from there. My mother would drop me at the entrance to the school and then walk next door to begin her lessons with little Guido.

My class photo from La Scuola Canossiana, 1957; I am next to the last on the right in the top row.

I was relieved to learn that students were required to wear uniforms—for the girls, a black smock dress with a white collar. I didn't have a big wardrobe, and having the uniform guaranteed that I would be dressed the same as everyone else.

All of us were self-conscious about our appearance when we left the camp and walked through Trieste. We couldn't afford clothing, much less the quality and styles worn by the city's permanent residents. We tried to emulate the locals' style, mixing and matching as best we could with what we had, but we still felt different. The city was small enough that we could recognize other immigrants. I got the sense that the people of Trieste could quickly identify us as outsiders.

The first few weeks in my new school were overwhelming. Even though we spoke Italian at home in Pola, we spoke a dialect that was quite different from what was spoken in school. Ours was very Venetian in its origins. The Republic of Venice had ruled that part of Istria for three or four hundred years, so that was the strongest influence on our dialect. The Italian dialect spoken today in Venice is very similar to what I spoke as a child at home. In Trieste there was also the Triestino dialect, but in school everybody spoke the pure Italian language, so I was self-conscious and hesitant to speak up in class.

My favorite teacher was a nun named Lidia de Grandis. Originally from Venice, she was a petite

Sister Lidia de Grandis took me under her
wing at La Scuola Canossiana in Trieste.

woman with tinted glasses and grayish-black hair.
Unlike other orders, the Canossian Daughters of
Charity did not wear the black cloth habit that covered their hair and draped down their backs unless they were attending a special event. Instead,
they wore smaller brown hats that resembled puffy
baseball caps with a band of white fabric across the
front, and on their outings a thin black veil was
draped over the cap. All the nuns wore their hair
rolled up beneath their caps, although strands of
Sister Lidia's hair were always falling out of hers.

Sister Lidia sensed how apprehensive I was—I
was so anxious I was literally shaking inside. But
her kind attention put me at ease. In her gentle
way, she helped me feel that I belonged in that
school just as much as every other girl there.

Over the months, she dedicated an enormous

amount of time to helping me catch up with my studies. She stayed after class to work with me on improving my Italian grammar, and she taught me Italian poetry, a subject I knew little about, even though my mother was an Italian teacher. She also opened the door to religion for me, something I had been forbidden to explore back home in Yugoslavia.

Nonna Rosa had tried to teach me the basics of Catholicism. She took me to church on Easter and at Christmastime, and sometimes, after a morning at the **mercato,** she'd sneak me into the little church by my mother's elementary school, so that we could say a few prayers together. It was always so dark and somber inside; it felt more like a hiding place than a house of worship. The only people I ever saw in there were old ladies like my grandmother, likely because the city's new leaders were more lenient with the elderly.

I knew that I had been baptized in secret, and that there were rituals that we practiced at certain times of the year. But being able to read the Bible openly with Sister Lidia allowed me to discover a side of myself that had not been possible before. Over the months, I found a spirituality long hidden inside me, and I began to develop a deep spiritual connection to Sister Lidia.

My history and geography classes also proved eye-opening, offering a refreshing alternative to the communist dogma of my childhood. I felt as if a window was opening, and at eleven years old, I was now able to see a world that I had never known.

The Scuola Canossiana slowly became a cheerful place for me. It had a beautiful garden and an open area where the children could play when they weren't in class. I enjoyed spending time with the other girls in the school and yearned to be out there with them, but I was helping the nuns in the kitchen in the early mornings and during lunchtime every day. The students were expected to pay for their meals, and since I wasn't able to do that, I would earn mine by lending a hand in the kitchen, preparing the **merenda,** the morning snack, and helping with food preparation at lunchtime.

The nuns would give me a stool to sit on and have me peel potatoes and apples, shell beans—whatever food prep needed to get done that day. I was surprised to see that the nuns wore their habits in the kitchen, too. They donned long aprons to protect their religious garments, and "manicotti" to protect their habits' sleeves. These were long tubular pieces of fabric, like white cuffs, that covered the area between the wrist and the elbows and were held in place with elastic at each end. They also wore **cuffie**—little plastic hats that covered their caps.

This was my first exposure to a commercial kitchen, one that was considerably larger than a home kitchen, and much more advanced, with big stoves and ovens and nice big clean pots. Nonna Rosa had nice pots, but she cooked on an open fire, and the pots were black on the outside from years of heavy use. The nuns did all their cooking inside, on a modern, closed gas stove with an iron top, and were scrupulous with their cleanup.

I was struck by how organized everything was in the kitchen, and how methodically the three or four nuns that I worked with went about their tasks. They knew exactly what needed to be done to feed a school-full of hungry children and staff. We always started each meal with a light **primo** dish and followed up with a hearty main course and dessert. The meals were very balanced, and included soups and pastas, cheese, and lots of vegetables. We had an abundance of apples and would often do strudels and apple cakes. There were crostatas and baked sweets with some fruits in there, too.

All the time that I'd spent in Nonna Rosa's kitchen doing food preparation helped prepare me for my new role in the school kitchen. I was a pro at vegetable and fruit preparation, and I didn't need much in the way of direction or oversight from the nuns; they liked having me in the kitchen, and I enjoyed being part of a productive and efficient team. I'd often look out the kitchen window at the playground and watch the girls on the swings. There were moments when I wished I were out there, playing with them, but I also felt a sense of self-accomplishment and enjoyed being part of a team. I quickly came to feel at home there. And I noticed that the girls on the playground would sometimes look at me with just a bit of envy as I walked freely up the back steps from the playground and into the kitchen, a place that was strictly off limits to all of the other students.

The nuns had a dining room of their own, and I would help to bring food there and assist with the cleanup as well. Sometimes they'd let me eat with them, too. They really took me under their wings and were always teaching me something new. I loved listening to them, and I loved my continued learning in the kitchen.

My time in the school kitchen marked a culinary transition point for me as I shifted from simple home-cooking techniques to cooking beyond the house, and cooking in volume. As the saying goes, "All roads lead to Rome," and the cornerstone of my life has always been food: growing it, sometimes not having enough of it, preparing it, and relishing the many tastes and smells. Whether it was on the farm with Nonna Rosa, in our home in Pola with my mother, with Zia Nina in her kitchen in Trieste, or in school with the nuns, I was always working with food. I had so much to contend with—being a refugee, not having a home, missing Grandma— but the familiar aromas, such as rosemary and bay leaves, helped soothe me and transported me back to my earlier childhood with Nonna Rosa in her courtyard, a time when I felt safe and free to be a kid.

I hadn't fully realized that I was never going back

to my life in Pola—that Grandma and her courtyard were only memories, treasures from my past
that I'd carry with me for the rest of my life. I was
too busy trying to get a handle on what lay directly
ahead of me—was I going to eat, was there going to
be enough food for the family, was I going to play
today—coupled with the trauma that my parents
were feeling. Food was like an umbilical cord, a
connection to Grandma. It was something stronger
than I was. Food was beginning to heal me, to keep
me in balance. I found I could use food to do that
for other people, too: I could provide them with a
sense of comfort and love. When I became a mother,
I tried to give my children the same security and
comfort my grandmother gave me through food.

People always ask me why I love food, why I love
preparing it for others. It is unfinished business
for me. I had not been given the opportunity to
say goodbye—not to my grandparents, not to the
farm animals I had loved and cared for, not to my
friends, and not to the lifestyle I left behind. Somehow, food could bring me back there, if only in
my mind.

In Trieste, I didn't forge lasting friendships. Most
of the children were very accepting, although there
were always a few who made it a point to say that
I was not a girl like the rest, that I was a refugee,
that I lived in the camp, that I had to work while
they played. It was in those moments that Sister
Lidia would pull me aside and talk to me about

being a good human being; she explained how God had given me this challenge of being an immigrant and how He chooses special people for His hardest tasks. She would make me feel unique and important and instilled in me a spiritual foundation that helped me become strong and resilient, to grow from a timid immigrant girl into a strong woman. Though her teachings were spiritual, they were not much different from Nonna Rosa's, molding me into a human able to accept challenges, appreciate the gifts of the earth and the family, and be strong in the face of adversity.

When I was not working in the kitchen, much of my time was spent with the nuns to prepare for my First Communion and then Confirmation. Because we were not allowed to practice religion openly in Yugoslavia, I'd never been able to achieve either of those important milestones.

In the late afternoons, I would go back to the camp. I could not invite any friends, but that was okay with me. I knew I would move on again and did not want to create any new bonds and then have to leave them behind.

Franco also attended school. Camp officials arranged for him to go to the nearby San Sabba technical school. My brother, like many boys, was fascinated with electronics and loved working with wires. He liked to know how things worked, and often took things apart, then put them back together. He reminded me of my grandpa.

My brother was just eleven years old when he wired my grandmother's **casetta nera** so that she finally had light when she was cooking after dark. Before then, she used a **lumino,** a handheld light with a felt wick and glass base that held kerosene. For someone who had toiled with a portable light for years, Franco's work was truly a big deal.

We tried to stay out of the camp as much as we could. During the week, my brother and I were in school, Mom was at Signora Leonori's doing her lessons with Guido, and my father continued his periodic work as a chauffeur.

Sundays were always reserved for a visit to Zia Nina. Sometimes my brother and I would also be invited to go fishing with Zio Rapetti. Even though he was from the landlocked region of Piemonte, he loved fishing and being on the water. He'd take Franco and me out for a few hours in the late afternoons, much as we'd done with Uncle Emilio in Pola. He kept a small skiff tied up in the port of Barcola, about two miles from his house.

Zio Nicola Rapetti, who would take us fishing on Sundays during our stay in the camp at San Sabba

There was an art to fishing on that little boat. We each had a line tied around a bow-tie-shaped piece of cork. You held on to one end and used your free hand to manage the fishing line. We'd unwind a length of the line, careful not to tangle it, and throw it into the sea. We'd hold the line between our fingers and wait for a fish to bite. When we felt a tug on the line as the fish went after the bait, we'd quickly start retrieving the line, pulling the fish closer and closer to the boat, until we were able to reach over and pull it in.

I had done this kind of fishing before, with Uncle Emilio back in Pola, so I had a sense of how it was done. In the Gulf of Trieste, the big fish, such as **branzino** or **orata,** were hard to find, but there were plenty of small white fish called **guato** or **gheozzo.** They were the size of sardines and were deliciously sweet when fried. My time on the water with Zio Rapetti brought back powerful memories of my evenings with Uncle Emilio. I didn't have the freedom and the space I had had fishing in Busoler, but I found solace in being out on the water.

My brother and I were always happy when we caught something, because we felt we had earned our supper. We would eat whatever little fish we pulled in for dinner, so, at a time when we were imposing on our aunt and uncle, this allowed us to feel we were contributing something.

When it was time for my First Communion and Confirmation, Zio Rapetti was my sponsor. He also sponsored Franco. My brother and I celebrated our First Communions and Confirmations at the same time. The ceremonies were held at Sant'Antonio Nuovo, the big neoclassical church on the Canale Grande, and a bishop came to lead the special service.

My brother and I were all dressed up for the occasion. Franco wore a gray suit and had a sash on his arm to signify that he was getting confirmed. I felt like a little bride in my beautiful lacy white dress and matching white shoes. The outfit was not that expensive, but I looked great—and so did my brother. I wore a headdress that was reminiscent of what the nuns wore, and a white veil. I vividly remember climbing the well-worn stone steps into the church with my parents and brother, and entering through the heavy wooden doors. Afterward, we all went back to Zia Nina's for a nice meal that included gnocchi and some fowl.

I had never felt as close to my religion and spirituality as I did that day. For months, I'd been infatuated with the nuns who had been helping me see that life could be both satisfying and positive, even when I was faced with tremendous adversity and hardship. The First Communion and Confirmation brought me closer to them than I'd ever been before.

That spirituality has stayed with me. I can't say I am so religious that I go to mass every Sunday, but I carry my spirituality with me wherever I go.

11

Taking Flight

In the spring of 1958, officials at San Sabba received word that the United States had finally opened its borders for immigration. The country was receiving a limited number of refugees, and we were one of the first families accepted for consideration. My mother was thirty-six years old at the time, my father forty-six, and Franco and I were thirteen and eleven respectively. We had been at San Sabba for more than two years.

Officials told us that we needed to travel to the U.S. Consulate in Genoa, where officials would interview us and we would undergo a medical examination. We would be one of several families from San Sabba making the journey, and officials from the consulate would be arranging our travel and covering our expenses.

Genoa is a port city and the capital of Italy's Liguria region, which is in the northwest of the country, and some 406 kilometers or 252 miles from Trieste,

Franco and I in Genoa for our medical visit
and interview for our U.S. visa, 1958

My father in Genoa for his medical visit
and interview for his U.S. visa, 1958

with a coastline that stretches along the Mediterranean Sea. The city is best known as the birthplace
of Christopher Columbus. During his lifetime, the
Genovese were great seafarers who made their for-
tunes importing spices, jewels, and clothing. To get
there meant a train ride of over nine hours, west
across northern Italy.

My mother had a cousin in Genoa, Lidia Bosazzi.
Lidia was the daughter of Grandpa Giovanni's sister Maria, and she and her husband had settled in
Italy after World War II, during the mass exodus
from Istria. In Genoa, Lidia was a language teacher,
and her husband worked as a surveyor. As children,
Lidia and my mother and my mother's younger
sister—also named Lidia—had been inseparable,
Lidia Bosazzi having grown up in the house next
door to Nonna Rosa's in the courtyard in Busoler.

On the day of our departure, camp authorities
handed us the necessary paperwork and travel
documents we needed for the journey. The consulate had arranged for a bus to bring us to the train
station in Trieste, where we would board our train
for Genoa. My mother had planned for us to stay
with Cousin Lidia and her family while we were in
Genoa.

Returning to the grand old train depot brought
me back to the night of our arrival in Trieste, when
I had been full of excitement at the prospect of
spending several weeks in a free city with our fam-

ily. That night, I was still naïvely unaware that it was to be a one-way trip that would change the course of my life forever.

The U.S. Consulate in Genoa was in a stately stone building that spanned an entire city block on Via Dante, not far from the Piazza de Ferrari and the Teatro Carlo Felice. Cousin Lidia knew where it was, so she volunteered to accompany us there and serve as our unofficial representative.

My stomach was in knots as we climbed the stone steps of the consulate. Like all the old buildings in Italy, this one had an enormous entry door. Once inside, we were instructed to have a seat and wait for our names to be called.

I recall that first day as being endless: we moved in and out of different offices, doors opened and shut, people came in and went out. There were endless interrogations of my mother and father, and, every now and then, a smile of kindness and word of encouragement were addressed toward my brother and me. I could see how nervous and tense my parents were. My brother and I just sat there and looked around at the walls and shelves for anything that would give us a clue of what our next home would be like.

The process continued for several days, as we walked up and down, from one office to another and one floor to another inside the consulate. There were visits to different doctors. I remember the

X-ray machine in one room; tuberculosis seemed to be a concern for the American authorities, but we were cleared of that.

The consulate offices were grand and staffed mostly by Americans. The female employees all seemed so proper, standing perfectly erect in their knee-length skirts and blouses. I was fascinated by their hairstyles; many of the women were blond and wore their shoulder-length hair in big curls that bounced when they walked.

A wall of glass separated the waiting area from the offices. Though we couldn't see through the glass, I caught a glimpse of the interior area whenever the big glass doors slid open and an official emerged to summon the next candidates inside.

When our name was finally called, we all jumped up from our seats. The process began with a lengthy interview, followed by a thorough medical examination. We had seen one family turned away after a doctor found that one of the children had lice. "Go and clean yourselves, and when you are clean, come back and try again," we overheard one of the consulate employees admonish. I dreaded something like that happening to us.

During the interview, I listened intently as my mother and father answered any and all questions posed to them. Franco and I were both dressed in our best clothes and sat quietly in our chairs. Whenever the interviewer looked my way, I made sure to smile at her. My mother's educational qualifications seemed to impress the woman, and she appeared equally pleased that my father had a transferrable skill.

I did not find the medical examination as invasive or debasing as the one I had undergone upon our arrival at San Sabba. Still, I felt tired and drained when we finally left the consulate that afternoon and returned to my cousin Lidia's flat.

My mother seemed to think that the interview at the consulate had gone well. Based on comments made by our interviewer, she believed that we had a very good chance of being selected for immigration to the United States, although it would be a month before we knew for sure.

I didn't find out until many years later how tormented my mother had been over her decision to move the family from Yugoslavia. The night after our interview at the consulate, we stayed in Genoa with Lidia Bosazzi, and my mother made a visit to the Chiesa di Nostra Signora della Consolazione, on Via XX Settembre. She would regularly stop at churches in the various cities we visited to pray for our future.

It was almost dark when she arrived at the church that night, knelt before the Madonna of Consolation, and began to pray. "God, just give me the grace to give my children an education like my mother and father gave me," she said.

Years later, my mother disclosed that she had seen a vision at that moment. A lady wearing a veil came to her from the altar; she imagined it was the Madonna. In retelling the story, my mother admits that nobody was actually in the church with her that night, and that this vision was only in her mind. But it gave her strength, and she continues to pray every night before she goes to sleep.

From Genoa, we were sent back to San Sabba to wait for word from the U.S. Consulate. When a month had passed, we finally learned that we had been approved for a visa.

Our final days in Trieste were bittersweet. I had grown exceptionally attached to Sister Lidia, and I was reluctant to leave her behind. I was so taken by the goodness of all the Canossian nuns at the school that I gave serious thought to becoming a nun myself. When it was time to go, I told my mother that I intended to stay in Trieste with Sister Lidia and become a nun. She laughed and told me it was not possible. The nuns had given me some sense of stability during a time of great uncertainty, but in my heart I knew that I could not stay in Trieste. I needed to be with my family.

As a parting gift, Sister Lidia gave me the large metal cross she wore every day. Another nun had given it to her, and now she was giving it to me. The cross, which is about three inches in height and two inches wide, was hanging on a black satin rope when she pulled it over her head and placed it around my neck. The rope was still warm as I felt it on my skin. Tears of happiness filled my eyes, and I felt such a sense of protection and security. Suddenly, I realized that I was not leaving alone; I had this cross and Sister Lidia's spirit to accompany me on my journey. I carried the cross with me to America, and kept it around my neck for more than a year. I still have it today, safely stored with other important life memorabilia. She also gave me a picture that I continue to treasure, and a small Bible; to this day, I revisit some of her favorite passages in that Bible.

➤◄

It was a glorious April morning. The sun was shining, and the smell of freshly brewed coffee filled our tiny room on the second floor of the musty old barracks. My mother was preparing what would be our last breakfast at the San Sabba refugee camp, a two-cup mocha pot for Mother and Father, and hot milk and a few of the cookies Signora Leonori had sent home with my mother for Franco and me. Zia Nina had cooked a glorious dinner for us the evening before. La Professoressa and the mother-and-daughter tenants were all invited. I do not remember our ever being so happy during our stay in Trieste. They all offered words of wisdom and tenderness. They would miss us, but they were sure we would have a great future.

There wasn't much for us to pack, just a few articles of clothing. My mother had decided we would take only a few of the garments and leave the rest for the people of San Sabba. I was surprised to see that her tiny suitcase held the set of linens from her dowry chest that she had brought with her from Pola. With the exception of these linens, we had no special mementos, and no family photographs.

Zia Nina had sewn beautiful dresses for my mother and me to wear on our big day. My mother's was grayish beige and had a matching jacket, and mine was a pretty pastel color. My mother was so appreciative; this was the first new dress she had owned in more than two years.

Officials at the U.S. Consulate in Genoa had provided us with an overview of what to expect upon our arrival in the United States. The Catholic Relief Services was taking care of getting us to New York, and would take care of us once we were in New York, and a representative from the organization would be at the airport to meet our plane. Someone from the agency would be helping us settle in. We would be provided help with housing, and there would be assistance securing a job and enrolling my brother and me in school.

A bus was waiting on Via Giovanni Palatucci to transport us to the railway station in Trieste, along with a few other families who had been lucky enough to secure visas for the journey. It would begin with a train ride to Rome. Since this trip was nearly three hundred miles, we spent the night on the train. Franco and I were too energized to sleep and passed the time running up and down the aisle, visiting the dining car, and, when it was light enough, looking out the window at the passing scenery. For us, this was the first time we got to actually see parts of Italy. We would get excited each time the next city was announced: Venezia, Bologna, Firenze, Roma. At each station, some time was allowed for new passengers to board the train. My brother and I, much against my mother's protests, would jump off the train onto each platform and make believe we were visiting the city, then hastily climb back on the train so we would not be left behind.

Once in Rome, someone came to collect us at the Roma Termini railway station. I was blown away by the sheer size of this contemporary building, which had a ceiling that soared three stories high, and a wall of floor-to-ceiling windows, some looking out onto the Baths of Diocletian, the old Roman baths, directly across the street. Now and then when I visit Rome, I pass through Roma Termini. Much has changed since our initial visit there: it has been renovated, and the adjoining building has become a food mecca. But to this day, the station remains a transfer point for refugees coming to Italy, looking for a place to make a new life there, or as a springboard to move on into other countries.

My parents were now unified and seemed happy, although my father appeared pensive and apprehensive, and my mother was emotional. No matter, my brother and I were very excited. Franco was always the quieter one, inquisitive but reserved. That day, however, he could barely contain his elation, skipping and jumping and wearing a broad smile.

There were a lot of other immigrants on our bus to Ciampino Airport, then Rome's main airport. Planes had been chartered to bring us all to the United States, starting with an old KLM jet-propeller-driven plane for the first leg of our journey, to Amsterdam, where we would transfer to a DC-7 for the transatlantic flight. There were a number of passengers on the flight with us, all refugees, not only from Italy, but from Czechoslovakia, Hungary, Russia—from all the communist countries.

As we were waiting to board the flight, two representatives from the Red Cross, a man and a woman, both of whom wore large armbands bearing the Red Cross symbol, approached my mother. The man was carrying two small bags, and the woman held a young baby in her arms. The child was bundled in a blanket with a nametag that read "Gianfranco" fastened to its coverlet.

"You were a teacher?" I heard the woman ask my mother.

When she responded in the affirmative, the woman asked if she would be willing to take care of the infant during the flight. "You know how to care for children; we have confidence that the baby will be in good hands with you."

My mother looked confused. "To whom will I

give him?" she asked, concerned that they wanted her to care for the child indefinitely.

The woman reassured my mother that there would be someone meeting her in New York to take custody of the baby, that she needed only to care for him during the transatlantic flight, and that in America she would be relieved of the responsibility. He was six months old, and was going to America to be adopted, she explained as she placed the child in my mother's arms. She next directed the man to give my mother the bags he was holding. "In one bag, you will find food for him. In the other, you will find clothes and diapers," she said. This was the first time my mother had ever seen a disposable diaper. My brother and I were happy, because Mom now had someone to take care of and would be distracted from crying and worrying about our trip. That would give us more time to explore the insides of the plane.

Indeed, having the baby to look after turned out to be a blessing for my mother. She had been crying for much of the day, and her distress seemed to be getting worse now that we were at the airport. I know she was happy that we were finally leaving the refugee camp, and that our dream of going to America was about to be fulfilled, but she was also plagued with worry. Had she made the right decision in uprooting her family? Would we really be happier in a new land? What if she and my father couldn't find work? How would they care for us? We did not know a single person in the United States, and neither of my parents spoke English. In Trieste, we had Zia Nina, and we all spoke Italian.

Franco and I had seats next to my mother on the plane, but we were so busy exploring that we hardly sat in them, so she was able to lay the baby down for a nap. The stewardesses didn't seem to mind our marching up and down the aisles, and even treated us to juice and snacks. My mother was so occupied with Baby Gianfranco, feeding him, changing his diaper, and rocking him to sleep, that she had no time to focus on anything else, and she finally stopped crying.

My father's seat was across the aisle from us. He slept for much of the flight, but every so often he'd open his eyes and give us a nod and a smile.

One leg of our journey had us landing in Reykjavik, Iceland, to refuel. No one was allowed to deplane, so Franco and I stared out the window as the ground crew tended to our flight. Looking out the window, I saw nothing but snow and ice.

As tired as I was, I didn't sleep at all during the transatlantic portion of the flight; the excitement of our journey and the effects of the three caffeinated sodas I had consumed in flight had me wide awake and eager to get a glimpse of our new homeland. Cheers erupted throughout the cabin when the captain came on the PA system to announce that we were about to land at New York's Idlewild

Airport (now John F. Kennedy International Airport). Franco and I were glued to the window, hoping to get a glimpse of the tall buildings we had seen on television.

My mother seemed surprised when she realized that we had landed. We waited while she bundled the baby into his blanket, then followed her off the plane and into the international arrivals terminal. "Such immense ceilings!" she shrieked. "Beautiful, beautiful!"

Two representatives from the Red Cross were waiting for us at the gate, again a man and a woman. They thanked my mother for the care she had provided to little Gianfranco, and allowed her a moment to say goodbye. She had grown attached to him during the flight and was a bit mournful to let him go. Then she grew upset when the woman tried to give her money, twenty-five dollars in cash, in gratitude for what she had done for Gianfranco.

My mother refused to accept it. **"Non posso accettare questo denaro,"** she told the woman. She explained that she had not paid for our flight, or for any of our travel—someone else had covered all of our expenses—and she could not in good conscience accept this payment.

But the woman insisted and would not let my mother leave without the cash.

"Madonna!" she exclaimed, turning to my father. "Here in America, they give you free money." In her mind, she was now a millionaire. One American dollar was worth more than one thousand dinars back home in Pola, and here she had twenty-five!

The immigration authorities at the airport separated us into groups by nationality. We were instructed to go with the Italians. There was again this mass movement of people. Officials were telling us what to do in a language we could not understand. My mother and father were constantly grabbing our hands, trying not to lose us. We followed the crowd to the baggage claim area to collect our luggage. Though we were tired, we were also enlivened. Once we had our bags, our group leader led us outside to the curb, where five big yellow buses awaited us. I held on to my mother as we climbed aboard the one for our group, with Franco and my father following behind us. We found four seats together and excitedly waited to see what would happen next. The bus's diesel engine rumbled to life, signifying we were on our way. I watched out the window as we merged onto a busy highway, the widest road I'd ever seen. Everything seemed bigger: the cars, the trucks, the roads. We had been driving about fifteen minutes when, suddenly, the skyline of Manhattan appeared in the front window of the bus. The buildings looked just like they had in the postcards—like needles, tall and pointy—and they slowly grew closer and closer, taller and taller. I remember passing a huge cemetery, rows and rows of headstones flashing by. I was frightened: I'd never seen a cemetery that size before. As the bus kept on driving, we kept passing more and more gravestones. I wondered if they would ever end. Concerned, I nudged Franco to look out the window. "Are we going to die here?" I asked. "A lot of people have died here." Turns out, this cemetery, the Calvary Cemetery— a Roman Catholic cemetery sandwiched between two highways, the Long Island Expressway and the Queens end of the Brooklyn-Queens Expressway— has the greatest number of gravesites of any cemetery in the United States, with about three million burials across its 362 acres.

Now and then, when my mother and I reminisce about our transatlantic flight to America, our thoughts go to Gianfranco: **Where did he end up? Who adopted him? Is he well? Did he make a good life for himself?** Although he was with our family for just twelve hours, we will always remember him. Ours was a hard road, but being left an orphan is much more difficult. At least Franco and I had our parents. Years later, as I began my own family, I could not help thinking back to the courage and strength my mother and father had summoned in facing the unknown with two children.

They had no family waiting for them in America, they did not speak the language, they did not have jobs, nor did they have a home to which they could bring their children. How much anguish must a parent feel in situations like these? Yet they must remain strong so their children can feel secure. I must say that in my young life, no matter how much adversity and hard times we faced, as long as the family was together I felt secure. I knew we would make it.

My father has since passed, and at the time of this writing, my mother is ninety-seven years old. Whenever she recalls the hard times, she seems not to have an ounce of regret or anger. Her family story ended up well, very well, and that is all that matters to her; her past pain and anguish are forgotten now. All she wants is to be surrounded by her family: her two children, her five grandchildren, and her nine great-grandchildren, all of whom she calls her "jewels."

As time passed after our move to America, the comforts of a good life became ever more evident. Periodically, I would think back to the places and the people who had been a part of our journey to freedom and a new life, and to all the kind individuals who supported us and gave us aid and encouragement. One of those very special people was Signora Paola Leonori. I often think of her special-needs son, Guido, and wonder how she found space in her heart to care about me and help me with my school tuition. I can still see vividly her gentle face and mannerisms, and how she would stop to visit me at school when she came to spend time with her other two sons. She would often bring me chocolates and candies, and always sent my mother home with a little treat, some cookies or biscuits, for the family to enjoy at the camp.

During one of my trips back to Trieste, many years later, I felt compelled to return to the apartment house on Via Rossetti, where she had lived, hoping to find her. But she had moved, and no one knew where she had gone. Then, in 2015, I was in Friuli, Italy, staying at our Orsone B&B near Cividale del Friuli, where the family now owns and operates a winery under my son Joe's direction. I was having coffee and chatting with some guests from Trieste when, during the conversation, the subject of the Leonori family came up. Much to my surprise, one of the guests knew one of Signora Leonori's sons and told me that he continued to run the family's clothing store. I immediately reached out to him, and we made arrangements for me to go and see Signora Leonori.

She had moved to Opicina, a small town on a hill overlooking the Gulf of Trieste. Her merchant son met me there and escorted me inside the home she shared with her son Giudo, now a man in his sixties. For me, it was a very exciting and moving moment, seeing her after all those years, and my eyes filled with tears as she enveloped me in a warm hug. Her gaze was as kind as it had been that first day in the schoolyard, when she had accompanied me to the Scuola Canossiana to begin my education there. We spent some hours together that day,

A photo with Signora Paola Leonori,
2015, Opicina, Trieste

reminiscing about those years and bringing each
other up to date on what had happened after my
family left Trieste. During our time together, she
spoke of my mother with great tenderness, and listened intently as I shared with her how that family
of four she had helped so long ago had found a
life and a home in America. Signora Leonori's years
had centered mostly on her son Guido. She was as
committed to him now as she had been back when
we had known her on Via Rossetti.

Two years after our first visit, I went to see her again. It was the spring of 2017, and she was ninety-four years old. As always, she was happy to see me. But there was sadness in her eyes. She told me that Guido was no longer with us: he had passed away since our last meeting, and she was taking his death hard.

There is no doubt in my mind that her resilience and her will to live well into her nineties were motivated by her lifelong mission to take care of her son. I just hope and pray to God that this remarkable strength will continue to support her and keep her alive.

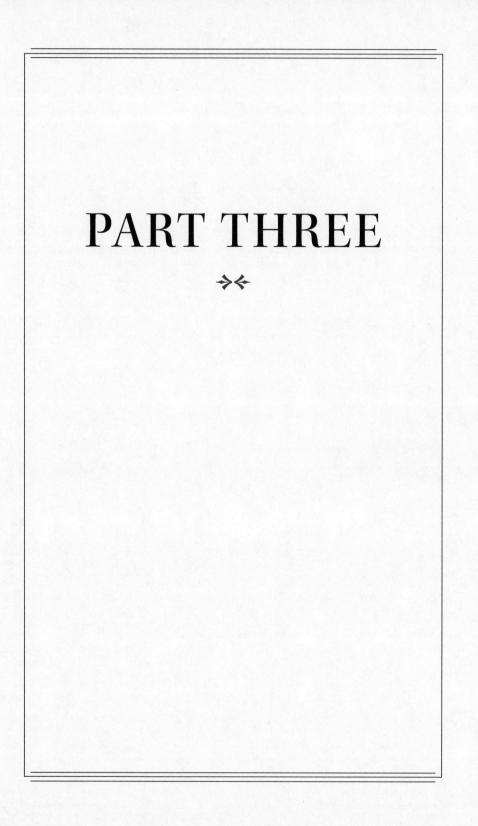

PART THREE

12

Hotel Wolcott

Our big yellow bus pulled up to the curb of the stately Hotel Wolcott at 4 West Thirty-first Street in midtown Manhattan, and the driver swung open the door, setting us free to discover our brand-new world. I stared out the window at the pink-brick-and-limestone Beaux Arts–style building, not far from the Empire State Building. The stone part of the exterior, with its elaborate keystones and ornamental scrollwork, was a bit reminiscent of some of the buildings we'd left behind in Trieste. Looking up, I wondered how many stories tall it was, and began counting the windows on the building façade until I reached the top. At twelve stories high, this was easily the tallest building I had ever seen. Grabbing my tiny valise from beneath my seat, I followed Franco and my parents down the bus's short, steep steps and jumped down onto the crowded sidewalk. The street was chock-full of cars, trucks, and yellow cabs. Horns honked, and the people on the sidewalk all seemed to be rushing to get somewhere. All the other passengers on the bus were gazing up, speechless for a moment as they took in the city scene and eyed the gleaming skyscrapers all around us. I was so distracted by all the buildings that I nearly tripped on the step leading up to the heavy steel-and-glass doors of the hotel.

A bellman in a brimless oval hat welcomed us inside. The busy lobby was beyond palatial, with massive marble pillars, mirrored panels, and a colossal chandelier suspended from the ceiling just in front of the reception desk, where we were all told to line up for check-in. The rich, patterned carpet felt luxuriously soft underfoot and added warmth to the expansive space.

Because there were dozens of us, check-in was a long, drawn-out procedure, and Franco and I, already weary from our long journey, were eager to wander off and explore. But my parents kept a tight grip on us, worried we might get lost. After what seemed like forever, we received keys to two adjoining rooms on the fourth floor. The bellman directed us to a bank of elevators, we waited for one to arrive, and then we squeezed in excitedly for the ride.

My brother and I had never been in such a big, modern elevator. In Italy, few buildings had elevators, and those that existed were usually the old-fashioned style, with open "scissor"-type doors that you slid shut once inside. Those old elevators made me feel as if I were locked into some kind of metal birdcage that carried people from floor to floor. In this one, a delicate chime alerted us that the door was closing, and as we began to ascend, I felt as if the floor were pushing up beneath my feet. People were getting off on every floor. When it was our turn, I begged my mother to let us stay on a little longer, but she wanted to get settled in. Representatives from Catholic Charities had instructed everybody to meet in the ballroom on the ground floor at noon, so we didn't have much time to freshen up. Catholic Relief Services had helped us throughout our time in Italy and, along with support from members of the Red Cross, had helped us realize our dream of coming to America. But now that we were in the United States, Catholic Charities would be the lead agency in charge of our welfare.

Franco and I ran down the carpeted hallway, calling out the numbers on the doors until we arrived at ours. We had been given rooms connected by an internal door. I was surprised to find that these rooms had wall-to-wall carpeting, which was almost unheard of in Italy and Yugoslavia, where wood floors with an occasional area rug were the norm. Each hotel room had two twin beds with wooden headboards and a nightstand with two lamps between them. The beds were immaculately made, with beige chenille duvets and decorative pillows. Matching beige-and-brown curtains covered the two expansive windows. Both rooms looked out onto an inner courtyard. There was even a little kitchen, complete with a table and chairs.

The bathroom had a full-sized tub and was stocked with fresh-smelling towels. My brother and I were so excited we hopped up on the beds and started jumping up and down, face-diving into the big overstuffed pillows.

Representatives from the Red Cross were among those waiting for us in the majestic ballroom, a jaw-dropping space with twenty-four-foot ceilings, arched doorways, and a giant stage. Some of the city's grandest social events had been held here, including New York Mayor Fiorello La Guardia's inaugural ball in 1938. Mayor La Guardia had a link to the city we'd just left: his mother was a Jewish woman from Trieste. Light refreshments and beverages were being served at a makeshift bar in a corner of the lobby. I opted for a Coca-Cola, something I had tried for the first time during our transatlantic flight.

We weren't there long when two Americans, a young man and a young woman, approached us. They had been tasked with escorting a group of us to the Catholic Charities headquarters. The offices were only a few blocks away, so we set off on foot. I could hardly believe all the people hurrying along the sidewalk. The streets were so long and wide, and I had never seen so many cars spread across three lanes and traveling in the same direction. The

cars were huge, so much bigger than the ones people drove in Italy. So much was happening, I hardly
knew where to look first.

Our chaperones led us into a tall building on the
corner of Thirty-fourth Street and Fifth Avenue.
Franco and I were excited when we saw the bank
of elevators in the lobby. This meant another ride.
Once upstairs, we were shown to a small inner office. A young woman in a stylish dress introduced
herself in Italian. She was a social worker with the
agency, and she would be helping us with our resettlement.

"How do you feel now that you are in America?"
she asked my parents.

"Ci sentiamo molto bene," my mother replied,
telling her that we felt great.

Before the woman had a chance to say anything
more, my mother began inquiring about jobs for
her and my father. We had arrived in the United
States without any money; the only cash we had
was the twenty-five dollars the woman from the
Red Cross had given my mother for taking care of
Gianfranco during our flight. With no income, she
worried that we would not be able to pay the agency
back for the flight, the two hotel rooms, and all of
our meals.

"There is plenty of time," the woman assured
her. My parents didn't immediately respond, but
I could tell that my mother was still uneasy about
finding work.

The woman explained that we were to come see her every day at 3:00 p.m. She then handed my mother sixteen dollars. "Go out and walk a little bit around the hotel," she told us. "While you are out, look at the stores, and you will find a place to buy some food. But don't wander far. Stick to one side of the street. And don't let the children starve," she added, smiling.

Italian women are often responsible for handling family finances, especially when it comes to putting food on the table for the family, so it made sense that the social worker had given the money to my mother, not my father. My mother stared at the money she had been given. She had no idea how much it was worth; all she saw were the numbers printed on the green-and-white bills.

We followed our American escorts back to the hotel, then headed west along Thirty-first Street in search of a shop selling food. As we neared Sixth Avenue, my mother spotted a little store with a sign posted in the window. **"Qui si parla Italiano"**— here we speak Italian.

Two concrete steps led down to the entrance; we followed my mother into the deli. The deli worker, in a white apron, immediately sized us up as newly immigrated Italians.

"Cosa volete comprare?" he asked, wanting to know what we wanted to buy.

"I want a loaf of Italian bread," my mother responded in Italian.

Franco and I perused the shelves. All the labels on the products were in English. Many had pictures of what was inside, so at least we could figure out what we were looking at. As we neared the register, we spotted a basket of fruit, containing apples and oranges and an elongated yellow fruit, bananas, which we had never eaten before. We begged my mother to let us try one. So far, all she had selected was the loaf of bread and a carton of milk. She seemed hesitant to purchase anything more, unsure that the money she had received from the social worker would be enough to cover it. We kept at her until she finally agreed. Our first purchase in an American store was a loaf of bread, a quart of milk, and three bananas.

The shopkeeper told her the total for the items was eighty-six cents. **"Ottantasei centesimi."**

"Qui, prenda." Take the money, she told him and handed him all sixteen dollars.

We watched as he pulled a bill from the pile and held it up to show my mother. The number "1" was printed in all four corners. He then returned the rest of the bills to her; he even gave her some coins from the register.

Back at the hotel, we feasted on bread and bananas. My brother and I each got our own, and my parents shared the third. The banana was kind of starchy—not juicy, like I expected a fruit to be. But it had a good smell, and a unique flavor. It wasn't love at first bite, mostly because of the texture, but over time I grew to love them. My brother and I shared the carton of milk, and my parents drank water from the tap in the bathroom. That was our only meal that day, but it was enough. We were used to small portions from our time at San Sabba, where dinner was often just a scoop of risotto or some pasta.

Sleep came easily to me that first night. My mother insisted we all have a shower, so I took my time in the bathroom, enjoying the deliciously hot water. A wonderful, fresh-smelling towel awaited me when I emerged. I had already selected my bed, the one closest to the window, and Franco hadn't put up much of a fight.

The bleached white sheets were crisply pressed, and the blanket had that wonderful freshly laundered smell. I had spent the last two years sleeping on a mattress so thin the metal slats of the bed frame poked at my spine. That first night in New York, it was as though I had gone to heaven, and God had provided me with a puffy cloud to sleep on.

The following morning, we finished off the Italian bread and drank the last of the milk. We didn't have to meet the social worker until 3:00 p.m., so my mother let Franco and me have a little fun. As soon as she dismissed us, we tore off toward the elevator. We spent nearly half the day riding up and down. We'd press buttons for the various floors, hop off when the doors opened, then wait for the next one to come and collect us.

I don't think my mother expected us to be gone so long, because when we returned to our floor she was standing in the doorway of her room, wearing a worried expression. It was almost time for us to head back across Fifth Avenue for our meeting with the social worker. I was beginning to feel a little hungry.

The woman was happy to see us and wanted to hear how we had fared. "How was the day?"

My mother told her about the little deli we had found.

"So—what did you eat?"

My mother hesitated. I could tell she did not want to tell this woman how little she had purchased. "Oh, so many things," she replied. "We had enough."

"How much did you spend?"

My mother opened her purse and pulled out what was left from the sixteen dollars. "I don't know," she said, handing the money to the social worker.

"Cosa stai facendo?!" the woman exclaimed. She was clearly upset with my mother. "What are you doing? You are in America. America is a welcoming country. There is no need to go hungry here. You are not in the camp anymore, you are in America."

"I have no money, no job," my mother cried. "Please, find me a job. I am ready to work, to do anything you want. I am willing, and I am healthy."

"You will have work, you will find a lot of work in America, just have patience."

My parents were surprised when the woman handed my mother some more money on top of the unspent money from the previous day. "Here is thirty-two dollars; it is double, for you to use for the next two days," she said.

With the weekend coming, we wouldn't be seeing the Catholic Charities woman again until Monday. So my parents were being given enough to get us through the weekend. In addition to the thirty-two dollars, she handed back the $15.14 that remained after our trip to the deli. When we left the office that day, my mother had $47.14—plus the twenty-five dollars she'd been given for taking care of the baby on the plane.

My parents had more than enough money for our immediate needs. Still, my mother's anxiety remained high. She was worried that we were being loaned the money by Catholic Charities and that we were essentially running a tab with the group. Her fear was that we would have to pay the group back at some point in the future, and she had no idea how that was possible while she didn't have a job.

"You need to give these children nourishing food and meat!" the woman admonished. "Don't come back if you don't feed them meat," she said with a smile.

She handed my parents walking directions, written in Italian, to the Horn & Hardart Automat

Cafeteria on the corner of Thirty-second Street and Sixth Avenue, which was only a short walk away.

To Franco's and my unbridled delight, we soon found ourselves standing directly in front of the Empire State Building that night. We had been able to see the top of the building all lit up from our hotel, but now we were actually on the sidewalk, staring up at what was then the tallest building in the world. As you would expect of children, my brother and I started shrieking, grabbing our parents as we jumped up and down in amazement. Even my father seemed excited. This was the first time he had smiled since arriving in America. For the next few minutes, we stood on the sidewalk, searching the sky for the building's needlelike top. We were too close to it to see the very top floors, and we didn't dare go inside, though I really wanted to. At this moment, all I could think was how lucky I was to be standing at the base of this famous landmark, the one I had seen on TV and on postcards.

The exterior of the Horn & Hardart was also impressive. It was covered in shiny glass and chrome and marked by a huge vertical red neon sign. People were constantly streaming in and out of its revolving doors. At the time, some fifty Horn & Hardart restaurants in New York were serving some 350,000 customers a day. It was, in a way, an early version of a fast-food restaurant—though the meals were simpler and perhaps more nutritious.

From the moment we arrived at the automat, we were in awe, beginning with the revolving door at the entrance. My brother and I couldn't get enough of it, and continued to go around and around until, finally, my mother pulled us inside. We had no idea how to buy food in a place like this, and there was no obvious person to explain it all. Besides, neither of my parents spoke English, and Franco and I had only a rudimentary understanding of the language from the private lessons we had received from La Professoressa during our Sunday visits to Zia Nina's. So we found a table and quietly observed. We watched the people pick up a tray, then get in line. "Let me go and get a tray," my mother said, striding up to the area where the trays were stacked. My father, brother, and I followed her, and we all got on the line. We watched as the people in front of us stuck their hands inside some kind of window, pulled out a plate of food, and placed it on their trays. Inside one window was a big plate of meat. Another contained roast chicken. Each item was tagged with a number, presumably the price. My mother had been directed to buy us some meat, so she chose chicken, because it was the least expensive. Next were the side dishes. Franco and I lobbied hard for the mashed potatoes. My mother filled the rest of the tray with bread, because, at just two cents a slice, it was the cheapest item available. Near the end of the line were the desserts. My brother and I immediately fixated on little cups of a brightly colored dessert. It came in three colors—green, red, and yellow. I wanted the red, and Franco wanted the yellow. My mother objected for two reasons: first, that she didn't know what it was, and, second, that it was sure to add cost to the meal. But after a few shouted pleas from my brother and me, she gave in.

We pulled the colored desserts out of the little windows. My mother couldn't help noticing how the desserts seemed to shake, even wiggle, on the plates. We'd never seen anything like them, and wondered what they would taste like.

We settled in at one of the high-backed booths to enjoy our meal. My mother prepared plates for each of us, giving my brother and me the lion's share of the chicken. Her greatest concern was that we have enough to eat; she and my father finished whatever was left over. The consistency of the dessert was strange; we were told that this was Jell-O. Mine was cherry-flavored and tasted like liquid sugar.

From the table, Franco and I watched with fascination at the people who had opted to bypass the line to purchase cold food from what looked like a mausoleum of food, an entire wall of glass doors that opened if you put a nickel into a slot next to the item. We begged our parents to let us have a nickel so that we could give it a try. My mother acquiesced yet again, handing each of us a nickel.

We ran to the wall, picked out two more desserts, and put our nickels into the slots. The little doors opened, and we reached in and took our new purchases. I remember looking inside and wondering where the hand was that was pushing out the dishes of food. We thought somebody had to be inside the great machine. But there wasn't anyone there.

My mother seemed happy after we'd eaten our big meal. I was surprised that she'd given in to our requests to buy the Jell-O as well as the second dessert. She seemed less anxious than she had been during our visit to the deli. Whatever the reason, Franco and I were delighted with Horn & Hardart and hoped that we might be able to return.

After our meal, we took a walk up to Thirty-fourth Street and saw crowds around Macy's, the biggest store we had ever seen. Inside, it was like a giant playground, and my brother and I had a ball, playing hide-and-seek among the racks of clothing on display and riding the wooden escalators. My mother and father stood by the door as we raced around the main floor. This way, they could catch us if we tried to leave the store without them. We tired ourselves out after a while, and headed back to the hotel for the night.

Over time, we ventured farther and farther from the Hotel Wolcott. We added a new city block to our repertoire every few days. My mother seemed to be enjoying herself, but my father was desperate to leave. He had lived well in Pola, but here we had no money, and he wasn't sure he would be able to find work to support his family.

It was an extremely difficult adjustment for my father, who had always been a proud and strong man, able to care for his family and provide a comfortable lifestyle in Pola. Moving to America forced him to start from scratch and rebuild our lives. We were dependent on Catholic Charities, and all the money we had was in my mother's purse. You have to be open and ready to enter a new and different culture. He was afraid he was not going to be able to make that adjustment. He was forty-six years old, and the idea of having to learn a new language and start life anew was daunting, even overwhelming, to him. For my brother and me, our time at the Wolcott was like one long vacation. It was a far cry from the way we had been living in the camp, all crammed into one tiny rectangular space, standing in line for a scoop of rice or a forkful of spaghetti and tomato sauce and a bowl of vegetable soup. We loved the hotel, and it was fantastic being in the middle of New York. The automat became our preferred dining spot when my mother allowed us to eat out.

Our meetings with the social worker shifted from once a day to once a week. We always met with the same Italian-speaking woman. First she would ask us, "How was the day?" My mother would have to explain what we did to pass the time, and what we had to eat. She would report that we were all okay and had plenty of food. The woman seemed pleased. She also learned that my mother was being very frugal with the money she was being given and saving as much as she could. Every week, my mother would pull out the money and show the woman how much she had left over from what she had been given.

My mother would always say to the social worker that she didn't need more money, that she had enough. Privately, she continued to fear that we would have to pay all the money back someday, and she didn't want to owe any more than was absolutely necessary. Time and again, the social worker admonished my mother, insisting that there was no need to worry. Still, my mother continued to keep track of every penny that she was given, totaling it up on a daily basis.

To save money, we ate many of our meals in the hotel, usually the same meal of milk, bananas, and Italian bread that we had had our very first night. When we went out, it was always to the automat.

We had been at the hotel for about fifteen days when Catholic Charities told my parents that they had found us a little house in North Bergen, New Jersey. We were the first family of all the refugees at the hotel to leave—perhaps because the organization knew that my mother was so uncomfortable.

Our social worker told my parents that she'd send two of her colleagues over to the hotel to pick us up and take us to New Jersey to see the house. All of us were really excited, especially Franco and I. We had no way of knowing it at the time, but our new home would be directly across the Hudson River from the hotel where we'd been staying. We would be able to see the Empire State Building from our kitchen window!

13

A Kitchen with a View

It was move-in day. The social workers from Catholic Charities were waiting in the lobby to bring us to our new home. Franco and I fought over who was going to push the elevator button for the last time. As much as we had enjoyed our stay at the Hotel Wolcott, we were ready to have a home of our own.

The sun was shining as we stepped out onto the busy midtown sidewalk that morning. May was here, and with it the temperate weather. The social workers' car was a big, roomy sedan, and Franco and I climbed excitedly into the backseat. There was enough room for all four of us, with me sitting on my mother's lap.

We'd all marveled over the bridges we'd seen on our way from the airport into New York, and now, as we headed to New Jersey, we wondered if we'd see even more bridges. My mother was especially curious—in part because of her years of indoc-

By the wall gate that led to the dirt path to our first house
in America, North Bergen, New Jersey, 1958

trination in Yugoslavia. The authorities there had
sought to dismiss Americans as unskilled and unin-
telligent. But when we saw the dramatic structures
connecting Long Island to Manhattan, we immediately realized that the Americans were every bit as
highly skilled and capable as the people back home,
and more. Now, as we headed toward the West
Side, we wondered if there were more engineering
marvels ahead of us. As it turned out, the people
from Catholic Charities opted to take the Lincoln
Tunnel for the one-and-a-half-mile crossing under
the Hudson River to New Jersey.

Our new house was right by the Palisades, the
massive cliffs on the Jersey side of the Hudson

River. We passed through North Bergen along the way. Franco and I peered out the car's windows as the social workers pointed out a few of the stores along Hudson Boulevard, now John F. Kennedy Boulevard, the main shopping street. We saw a supermarket, a butcher shop, and a few other businesses. The road down to our new house was just off Hudson Boulevard. Only part of it was paved; the remainder of it was gravel.

Tucked away at the end of a sloping, rocky driveway was a small wood-shingled ranch house that had been converted into a two-family home. A Canadian man and his two daughters occupied the right side of the house; we were given the other half. Our side had a little porch that squeaked and creaked whenever we walked on it, but it boasted a magnificent view of the Manhattan skyline. Though the house was a bit weathered, its scenic location, perched at the edge of the cliff and fronted by big rocks and boulders, made it ideal. Once again, I was by the water, and Franco and I had some room to run.

A door off the porch led directly into the kitchen. We were all surprised to see that the kitchen had a dirt floor. We hadn't had a dirt floor back home in Istria, although I knew that some of the older houses did. Still, we never expected to find one here in America.

Beyond the kitchen were two small bedrooms with wood-plank floors, and a tiny bathroom with a tub and shower. The Salvation Army had furnished the home for us. The bedrooms had army-style cots, and the kitchen was big enough to accommodate the table with four chairs and a couch. The cupboards were equipped with a few pots and pans, some dishes and utensils.

The charity had also left us a big box of gently used clothes. The only items in the house that weren't secondhand were the linens and towels. All of this concerned my mother anew—she was still worried about the cost and how she and my father would make reparations, still not understanding that we were being gifted these things.

Franco and I did a quick inspection of the place, let our parents know that we had chosen the bedroom closest to the kitchen for ourselves, then raced outside to play on the big rocks in front of the house. We were finally free. We could jump and run and had space to roam. Overlooking the water, the Hudson River, immediately brought me great comfort.

Before leaving us that day, the social workers went through the house with my parents. In the kitchen there was a small refrigerator and a stove for cooking. They explained that the big box on the kitchen table contained food for us to eat that evening— enough to make a cold meal, nothing that would require preparation. Someone would be by in the morning to show us around North Bergen. Until then, we were on our own.

We excitedly ripped open the box of food as soon as they left, eager to see what was inside. There were only a few things we recognized: a loaf of Wonder Bread, a package of sugar, the packaged American cheese we had come to know from our time in San Sabba, and a carton of milk. The rest of the items were a mystery. We all sat down around the kitchen table and took turns sticking our fingers into the various packages, having small tastes, then trying to guess what they were. The most baffling was the thick white substance in the round aluminum can. The red, white, and blue label featured a slice of cherry pie and the word "Crisco."

My mother suspected it was floor wax, because it looked similar to a product she had used back home to polish and shine our parquet floors. Her "finger" taste test confirmed it for her: the white substance had no taste; therefore, it was likely not food. It wasn't until some days later, when a Frenchwoman who lived in the neighborhood stopped by with a bag of groceries, that we learned it was cooking fat.

We made some sandwiches and finished off the meal with a few cookies. After dinner, we all went outside and sat together on the big rocks, marveling at the shimmering lights of Manhattan across the way. Seeing the Empire State Building all lit up, directly across the Hudson, was just amazing. Our view was spectacular. Over the next few months, Franco and I spent hours out there, perched on the cliffs, watching the boats navigating the river, the

planes crossing the sky, and, of course, the twin-
kling lights of the New York City skyline. Sometimes I would close my eyes and imagine I was back
in Istria, beneath the towering pines looking out
over the Adriatic. I wondered how Nonna Rosa was
doing, and if she missed me as much as I missed her.

My parents had to chase us into bed that first
night. The excitement of being in a new home energized us, and we wanted to stay awake and savor
our newfound freedom.

The windows in our new bedroom didn't have any
drapes, so the room felt bare. Still, it was good to
finally have a space of our own. Franco and I spent
a few minutes talking about the day. Neither of us
could figure out if our parents were happy. They
had held hands during our initial walk-through of
the house with the social workers, but offered little
comment. We assumed they must have been happy
that we finally had a family house. But we also
sensed sadness—perhaps because the home they
had left behind in Pola was so much nicer than
this one.

Looking back, I am sure they were both wondering if they had made the right choice in uprooting
the family and emigrating. At some level, Franco
and I both understood my parents' quiet inner
conflict, and were determined to show support for
what had to be an agonizing decision. Somehow,
we were confident that they'd acted correctly and
that we would be fine. To be sure, our first house

wasn't new or even all that comfortable. The furniture was worn, and the dirt floor in the kitchen took some getting used to. But when night fell, we could close the front door and be a unified family. We were no longer **in balia delle onde,** at the mercy of the waves. We had finally dropped anchor.

The following morning, I was startled awake by the high-pitched shrieks of my mother, and I ran to the kitchen to see what was going on.

"Formiche!" she yowled, pointing to the box of sugar on the kitchen counter. Dozens of tiny black ants were crawling amid the white crystals, and she was busy trying to salvage what she could of the package. It was not that she had never seen ants, but the rough nature of the house and the dirt floor in the kitchen ensured that we received visits from all kinds of insects.

It would be several days before we were finally introduced to the Canadian family next door. The girls were a few years older than Franco and me, and they spoke French, so communicating proved difficult. My mother was able to converse a bit with their father in French. Franco and I blended Italian words with the few French ones we knew. It wasn't ideal, but we could make ourselves understood.

By the end of May, Franco and I were registered in school. Franco was enrolled in junior high, and I attended Sacred Heart Elementary School. Sacred Heart was a parochial school, and, as at the Scuola Canossiana in Trieste, the students were required to wear uniforms. I was given a blue-and-green plaid skirt, which I paired with a white blouse and knee socks.

I started in the sixth grade, and I still recall the anguish I experienced during my first few days there. I truly was a foreigner coming into a school for the first time, and I wondered if the students there would ever accept me as an American. There were some other immigrants at the school, even some who spoke Italian. At one point, the teacher sent me outside of the classroom, where I sat on the steps with a study guide so that one of the "smart kids" in class could begin to teach me English. I felt devastated, so ashamed that I couldn't stop crying. When I went home, my mother comforted me and tried to explain that the teacher's intent was not to keep me out of the classroom but to give me more individual attention—assigning a good student to teach just me. The incident prompted me to re-double my efforts to learn English; it would be my route to acceptance by my peers in the school and to demonstrate that I, too, was one of the smart students.

Moments like these served as a powerful driver for me; they motivated me to exert myself daily to improve my skills and pushed me in a very strong way to want to be an American.

Though Franco and I started by speaking only a few words of English, within two months we were communicating with friends in the schoolyard and helping our parents to navigate the supermarket, the bank, and whatever else they needed us to do.

My father found a job right away, and in a very unexpected fashion. Our social worker had talked to a few of the Italians in our neighborhood and quietly spread word that my father was looking for work. A few days later, one of our neighbors stopped by the house and invited my father to join him on a visit to the barbershop in town that all the Italians patronized—they liked to congregate there, and it had become a place for them to socialize. During the visit, my father met a man who was working as a mechanic at the local Chevrolet dealership. The man told him they needed somebody to install radios in the cars, and my father went for an interview and was immediately hired. Installing radios was child's play for him after the work he'd done on his heavy-duty trucks back home. Better still, my father liked working there, because many of the employees were Italian.

Not long after, my mother found work, this time with the help of an Italian immigrant named Paola del Conte. Paola was from the island of Cherso, now Cres, in the Adriatic Sea, just off Istria. She had been in the United States for about two years, and lived a few blocks from us. Paola had four children and worked as a seamstress at the Evan-Picone factory in North Bergen, where more than four hundred Italians were employed. She was able to pull some strings and get my mother a job at the factory. My mother was not a seamstress, nor did she know how to use an industrial sewing machine, but every girl in Istria was taught how to sew by hand. And the forewoman, a Sicilian woman named Carmela Alecchi, found jobs that my mother could do, such as cutting fabric for the belts, distributing dress patterns to the seamstresses, and doing general cleaning of the facility. The salary was seventy-five cents an hour.

She was ecstatic the day she received her first paycheck. Her friend Paola del Conte warned her not to keep money in the house and brought my mother to the bank during her lunch hour to help her open a savings account. We were so fortunate to have people like Paola and my mother's forewoman, Carmela. Carmela appreciated my mother's hard work and dedication to the job, and she arranged for her to earn overtime pay. To get it, my mom had to come in one hour earlier in the mornings and stay one hour later in the evenings to clean, raising her pay to forty-six dollars a week, after all the overtime. This meant beginning her day at the factory at 7:00 a.m. and working straight through until 5:00 p.m. The work was menial in nature, and certainly not what my mother had been trained to do, but she enjoyed being with other women who spoke Italian, and valued Carmela's kindness.

Life was challenging, to say the least. Not speaking the language and not being familiar with day-to-day life in the States forced us to relearn everything, from how to shop in a supermarket or pay for light and gas bills, to finding our way around on public transportation. The social worker would come periodically to help us out until we gradually became self-sufficient.

As my brother and I learned English, it was our job to accompany our parents and be their interpreters for all the official paperwork—neither of my parents could speak the language. Franco and I communicated on their behalf, using the words and phrases we had picked up at school, both in the classroom and while playing with friends in the park and on the playground. These extra duties had some unexpected benefits: my brother and I matured more rapidly than our classmates. We also became acutely aware of each financial transaction that was made—contracts with landlords, agreements with utility companies and employers, and even small purchases at the supermarket. In a way, all those interactions prepared me for a future in business. I learned to pay attention to every detail, and to be very wary about signing any documents.

I felt a deep sense of responsibility to protect my parents and correctly interpret their needs and wishes as they negotiated a lease or applied for a job. It was not an easy responsibility for me, at the age of eleven, to lift my parents emotionally and encourage them during those first few years in the United States. They were still questioning their decision to emigrate. My mother, who was in her mid-thirties when she came to America, was much more open to and receptive of the new culture, life, and language here than my father was. She gradually learned English and adapted easily to the American way of life. For my father, nine years her elder, adapting was much harder, and he remained melancholically nostalgic for his native land for the rest of his life. At forty-six, a man should be settled down and relaxing; instead he was beginning a whole new life with all new worries. He died in 1980 at seventy years of age, still speaking very little English.

Though he loved his work, he couldn't communicate, and he had difficulties with jobs. I would have to go to the interviews with my father, and I would tell them how skillful and talented he was. Unfortunately, I had to do it time and again, because my father just couldn't find a good fit in the United States.

In the evenings, we would sit around the dinner table and share stories that highlighted the ways in which life in America was different from back home in Istria. There were so many nuances. Just trying to buy food in the supermarket proved a monumental challenge. Since we could not read the packaging, we relied on the pictures. Sometimes our guesses were wrong. We had limited resources, so, no matter what we had picked, we had to eat it.

On Friday my parents did their banking, and on Saturday we did our shopping at the supermarket, which was about a fifteen-minute walk from our house and required that we cross the big park to Kennedy Boulevard. Our visits were always an adventure. Our first time there, we watched to see what the people were doing, just as we had done at Horn & Hardart. Franco and I wandered off to find a shopping cart, and the four of us set off down the aisles. On future visits, my mother was usually busy looking at the pictures on the cartons, trying to figure out what everything was. Once we got to the fresh produce department, we fended pretty well.

We always bought the second cuts of meats, the chicken necks and lots of beef bones and smoked pork hocks to make soup. We made a lot of soups, with beans and pasta or rice. We also ate a lot of kielbasa and other sausages. My mother would always start off the meal with a salad, and our second course was all in one pot—vegetables, potatoes, dried beans. We used a lot of beans, because they weren't expensive, and with potatoes, carrots, and some meat for flavoring, you can make a lot of things.

We were excited the first time we spotted Spam on the shelves. Spam, American cheese, and Wonder Bread were our favorites. Franco and I would quietly slip items into the cart when my mother was distracted trying to decode the packaging. She didn't notice Franco and me tossing chocolates and cookies into the cart, at least not until we got to the checkout line. We would wait for her to instruct us to put the items back. But she rarely said a word; she just got on line for the register.

She would wait patiently as the woman in front of us placed her items on the conveyer belt. When it was our turn, she did the same. The ticky-ticky-tack of the cash register seemed to stir anxiety in her. I could tell from her expression that she was worried that she wouldn't have enough to cover the bill. The first time we shopped, she had cashed her paycheck that day and had forty-six dollars in her wallet. Her shoulders relaxed, and I thought I heard a tiny sigh escape her lips when the cashier said, "Eighteen dollars."

That same trip, Franco and I were desperate to try the chocolates we had stashed in the cart, so we put on a dramatic show, grunting and struggling with the grocery bags as we started to cross the park for home. We proposed a little rest on one of the benches, and, once we were seated, suggested that a chocolate or two might help energize us. It was almost noontime, and everyone was hungry, so my parents decided to make a picnic of it, fixing us a delicious meal from the items in our shopping bags. Our impromptu al fresco lunch remains a favorite memory for me of our time in North Bergen.

Not all of our purchases turned out to be what we had imagined. One of our first weekends in New Jersey, my mother got a visit from a neighbor, a Frenchwoman, with a bag of gently used clothes for the family. My mother knew very little English, but she motioned her inside and offered her a coffee, and the two sat down on the couch in the kitchen. The cushions had started to sag and were in need of some new stuffing, but it was free, and it gave us a comfortable place to relax in the evenings. My mother prepared a pot of coffee and went to the cupboard to retrieve the box of cookies she had just purchased at the supermarket. Pulling a few from the box, she arranged them on a plate and offered them to her guest.

"Take some cookies," she told her, confused by the woman's puzzled expression.

"**Non, merci,**" the neighbor replied.

My mother's repeated suggestions that she try a cookie were also met with a polite refusal.

"Why not? They are good," my mother told her in French, and she started to eat a cookie from the plate.

"You will not get angry with me if I tell you something?"

My mother shook her head no. "Of course not."

"These are not good cookies."

"Yes, they are good," my mother insisted. "To me, they taste very good."

The woman picked up the box and pointed to a picture of a dog eating a cookie. "This is a cookie for the dog, not for the human being," she explained.

My mother gasped. She was so embarrassed she didn't know what to say. But she vowed to be more careful with her selections in the supermarket. Little by little, she began to figure things out, and she learned something from every mistake.

After that, we stuck to foods we knew. Money was tight, and we feared wasting money on something we didn't like, or need. As we got more comfortable, we got a little more daring in our tastes. We would discuss the grocery list before setting off for the store, and seek permission from my mother to try a few new items as well. Crackers were a whole new taste for us. Cereal was, too. We were familiar with butter and jam on our toast, but now we were discovering cream cheese, cottage cheese, and peanut butter.

Leftover bread and coffee with a lot of milk and sugar had been a typical breakfast for us. If we had some leftover polenta, that was another breakfast treat. We'd cut it into pieces and eat it with heated sugared milk. But now we were starting to experiment with coffee cakes, and found that crumb cake and raisin rings made for a luxurious breakfast.

Convenience foods were also really interesting to us. They were very expensive, so my mother wouldn't buy frozen meals like the popular TV dinners I was desperate to try, but instant puddings and pancakes found their way into our kitchen. We didn't go out to eat very often; if we did, pancakes, hamburgers, and meatballs were things we liked to order.

The social workers at Catholic Charities had instructed us to come to their New York office in

Me in North Bergen, New Jersey,
on the road leading to our first home
in America, c. 1958

three months' time to report on how we were far-
ing. My mother dressed me in a brand-new sweater
and skirt and Franco in a crisply ironed shirt and
shorts, hoping to make a good impression and telegraph that we were doing fine. An Italian woman
from the neighborhood explained how to get to
Manhattan using public transportation: The bus
stop was just a few blocks from our house. If we
waited there, the bus we needed would pick us up
and take us to the Port Authority Bus Terminal
on Eighth Avenue. From there, it would be just a
short walk to the office building at Fifth Avenue
and Thirty-fourth Street.

We chose a Saturday to make the trip into the city,

since my parents were both off that day. The office was open, and the social worker was expecting us. She was impressed when she saw us, all dressed up in brand-new clothes.

My mother had kept close track of all the money the agency had given us during our stay at the Hotel Wolcott, and she had saved a good portion of it by watching her pennies when we were out and purchasing our meals. When she told the social worker that she was ready to return a portion of the $320 we had been given, the woman got upset. She told my mother that she did not expect or want any money back; she was happy that we were managing so well. "Go home," she told us. "Come back in one year and tell me how you are doing."

14

Bobby Socks, Saddle Shoes, and Poodle Skirts

We were living in New Jersey for about three months when my parents decided we were ready to take our first excursion as a family. We were going to Astoria, Queens, to meet a relative of my father's named Louis Matticchio. Louis's mother was my father's first cousin. She had relocated from Istria before the end of World War II, and she and her family had settled in La Spezia, on the Ligurian coast. Many of the Istrian **optanti** had settled in that area, among them Lidia Bosazzi, the daughter of Grandpa Giovanni's sister Maria, with whom we had stayed in Genoa. Lidia had taken us to La Spezia to see Louis's mother while we were in town. She had been very excited to meet us, and she gave my parents the address for her son in the United States.

Louis had worked as a waiter on a cruise ship.

When it docked in America, he jumped ship and stayed. While in New York, he met and married an Italian American woman, Marie, and together they had a young daughter, Diana. My parents promised to visit Louis once we were settled in the United States. We didn't know anyone here, so locating this young man was important to my mother and father. It didn't matter how distant a cousin he was; we were family, and that meant everything to us.

We had no way of getting in touch with Louis and his family to arrange a meeting—we didn't have a telephone, and even if we did, we didn't have a number for him—so our visit would be a surprise. We chose the second Sunday in July to make the trek, and my mother sought help from her friend Paola del Conte in mapping out our route from North Bergen to Astoria. We would need to take a bus to New York's Port Authority, then make our way to the subway station in Times Square, where we would catch the R train on the old BMT to the Broadway Station in Astoria. Paola gave us the directions, written in English, to carry with us in case we got lost.

We set off extra early that Sunday morning and arrived at Port Authority just after 7:00 a.m. A friendly pedestrian directed us to the subway station on Forty-second Street, where we purchased four tokens, went through the turnstile, and found the track for our train. My mother wanted to be in the front car, near the conductor, so she could ask for help in locating our stop. When the train pulled into the station, she walked alongside it, peering into the windows, until she located the driver. As soon as we boarded, she showed him the piece of paper with Paola's directions.

He instructed her to take a seat, but she didn't understand him and tried to explain our destination, speaking a mix of Italian and broken English.

"Mama," I interrupted, "he wants you to sit down and wait for his instructions."

As soon as the train pulled into the first stop along our route, she popped up from her seat to show him the piece of paper.

"Have a seat," he instructed. He would let her know when we had reached our stop.

But her anxiety got the better of her, and she continued to jump up and rush to him with each new stop. After being shooed back to her seat for a third time, she recognized that he was annoyed with her, so she didn't dare stand up when the train slowed as we neared the next station. The doors opened, and my mother remained in her seat.

"Get off," the conductor said, turning to look at her.

But she did not stand up.

Franco and I were busy watching all the people getting on and off the train and didn't hear the man when he addressed our mother.

"Get off!" he repeated, this time a bit more forcefully.

"**Dov'è questo** 'get off'?" she said to my father. "Why is he talking to me about flowers?" she wanted to know. "Where are these flowers?" The Italian word for carnations is **garofani,** and this is what she thought he was saying.

"Get off!" he barked a third time, then rose from his seat, came out of the cab, grabbed my mother's shoulder, and led her toward the doors, literally pushing her off the train.

My mother still jokes about this exchange, telling us she has never forgotten what the words "get off" mean.

Louis's apartment building was just around the corner from the Broadway Station. We heard a lot of people speaking Italian on our way to his address. He lived on the top floor of a four-story walk-up. I was nearly out of breath by the time we reached the third-floor landing. It was 8:00 a.m. on a Sunday when we rang his doorbell. When nobody answered, we rang it again. Finally, we heard footsteps inside the apartment and the voice of a young girl. "Mama, Mama," she yelled. "Somebody is here at the door." The next voice we heard belonged to a woman. She was looking at us through the peephole, but she didn't open the door. "I am going to get my husband," she said.

"Who are you?" he asked, talking to us through the door.

"Your mother gave us your address," my mother replied in Italian.

After a short back-and-forth on how we knew his mother, and him, he let us in.

The first thing I noticed was that the family had a television set in their living room. After speaking with us for a little while, they turned it on and left us kids to watch it.

We were there through lunchtime, so Marie fixed us a meal of spinach and hamburger. She served the burger on a plate and not on a bun, as we had come to know them from our visits to Horn & Hardart. I found this alternate presentation curious, but I enjoyed the taste.

I have no doubt we overstayed our welcome that day, lingering in their living room until nearly dusk. Later, when we got to know them better, Marie admitted that after a while she had begun to wonder if we would ever leave. Still, we continued our relationship; they soon made a trip to North Bergen to visit us.

Louis was as excited as we were to have a relative—albeit a very distant one—in the United States, and when a one-bedroom apartment became available two doors down from him, he immediately contacted my parents and suggested that we move in. By then, we were independent of social services. We had our papers, and my parents had their green cards. Franco and I could attend the local public schools, and Louis offered to help my father find work nearby. My mother liked her job at the factory, and was okay with the idea of commuting to

North Bergen. Louis even offered to help us move. Our new apartment had one bedroom, a living room, and a kitchen, so my brother and I shared opposite corners of the living room to sleep.

I was happy to leave North Bergen and the Sacred Heart School. I was glad to leave behind the memories of entering a school without knowing the language in the middle of a school year, when everybody already had their friends. Now I had the chance to begin a new school year at the same time as my classmates, and I spoke some English, which I hoped would make this transition somewhat easier.

For me, Astoria was the beginning of the reality of what America really was. The town was bustling, and full of the flavors of different ethnicities. Yes, there were Italians, but there were also Germans, and Greeks, and so on. In Istria, we were on the border, so I was already accustomed to living among people of different ethnicities.

My mother and father were happier in Astoria. You walked up Broadway and there was the el train, the Astoria Line. Italian and Greek delis and vegetable markets lined the avenue. At about Thirty-sixth Street, there was the five-and-dime store, and across the street and farther on down Broadway was the Most Precious Blood Roman Catholic Church, where we would go on Sundays. One could speak Italian in all the stores and find most of the ethnic Italian foods. If there were not Italian products, there were Greek products—that was close enough.

My mother, Franco, me, and my father, in Astoria,
in our Sunday best, c. 1963

Our apartment was on the top floor of the building, directly below the flat roof. It was summertime when we moved in, and it was really hot. Of
course, we didn't have air-conditioning, and we did
the best we could to stay cool by an open window.
The RR subway train, on an elevated platform, ran
right past our bedroom window, so the black dust
created by the train would come blowing in every
time it went by. The floors were linoleum in the
bedroom as well as the kitchen, and since I walked
barefooted, the black dust of the train collected on
the bottoms of my feet. We tried to keep the bedroom windows shut as much as possible, despite
the heat, to help keep the soot out.

We couldn't afford new furniture, so we made

due with secondhand items and things we found on the side of the road. Somebody had left a couch at the curb to be collected as garbage, so we carried it home, cleaned it up, and found a spot for it in our living room.

Astoria was a totally different setting from North Bergen. Our new neighborhood was heavily developed, and there was so much going on. For a young girl, this was incredible. I was growing up. I was developing, and I was searching for new opportunities. And I found them here. Astoria was also pretty much self-contained. Even though we were just a short subway ride away from Manhattan, we didn't go into the city much, only for big events like the Macy's Thanksgiving Day Parade. We had everything we needed right in our little neighborhood. Still, I missed North Bergen's parks, trees, and views across the Hudson River. I couldn't just run outside and sit on the grass and gaze across the water in the evening. In Astoria, I could sit out on the stoop and watch the people, cars, and trucks go by.

On weekends, we'd take short trips as a family, often visiting Astoria Park in Queens or venturing a bit farther away, to Coney Island in Brooklyn. Astoria Park, which is located along New York's East River, stretches for nearly sixty acres and is one of the most expansive green spaces in the borough of Queens. My brother would play soccer there with his friends, and I would wander off and find a quiet spot to sit under a tree and look out at the water. It took us more than an hour to get to Coney Island by train, a trip that always seemed endless. But I was happy to emerge from the subway station to views of the Atlantic Ocean and the vast stretches of white, sandy beaches, which were so different from the rocky beaches I'd grown up with. The water was a different color, too—green, not the lovely pale blue that I was used to.

Indeed, just about everything about Coney Island was new and different from what I'd been accustomed to. We could stroll the beaches or the boardwalk, ride on the giant Ferris wheel, or eat cotton candy and frankfurters. The water was so cold, and there was an undertow at the beach that we had not experienced before. It took my brother and me a while to get used to the rip currents and avoid getting pulled farther from the beach than we (or our parents) wanted. Fortunately, we knew there were lifeguards on the beach if we got into trouble.

Some Italian friends brought us to Orchard Beach, once known as "the Riviera of New York City," and the only public beach in the Bronx. There was no undertow to worry about there, because Orchard Beach was on the gentle waters of Long Island Sound. It had views of City Island, a bathing beach, a promenade, and a food pavilion.

In the fall of 1958, I entered the seventh grade at Junior High School 204, now IS 204 Oliver W.

Holmes School, on Twenty-eighth Street in Long Island City. This was on the border of Astoria and Long Island City, and students from all the elementary schools in the area fed into it. The building was huge, a massive and rather nondescript four-story tan-colored brick structure occupying a full city block. I was overwhelmed by the size of the building and the number of kids inside. It was many times larger than the parochial school I'd attended in Trieste, and there was no dress code here, no uniform. My schoolmates all wore the latest American fashions, and I immediately felt a bit of an outsider just because of the way I dressed.

Because I desperately wanted to be accepted by my classmates, I did things to prove myself worthy. I joined various clubs and organizations. I wasn't a great athlete, but I loved music, so I joined the chorus. I also became a member of the chess club, which was coed. I remember the excitement of going to a competition on Forty-second Street in Manhattan that pitted the team from my school against one from Stuyvesant, home to some of the brightest kids in the city. We won two or three games in the competition but weren't able to clinch first place. I took some lifelong lessons away from my days of playing chess. The game is very analytical, and you must change your analysis with every single move. I realized that the same lesson applies to life, too—if your course changes a little bit, your strategy must change along with it.

Chess remains one of my favorite games, and my brother, Franco, and I continue to play at some of the family gatherings. Whenever we get together during the holidays, Franco and I square off just the way we used to in the piazzas of Pola. It seems that I've passed down my competitive nature to my grandchildren, who all enjoy the game. I still view chess as challenging, and love it when I can battle it out with my brother in a game that might last two or three hours while our kids and grandkids root us on.

In the ninth grade, I was elected president of the Arista Club in school, too, which was very exciting. Arista was the New York City Board of Education's version of the National Honor Society.

One of my favorite subjects was home economics. This was something I was good at, and it didn't require that I be proficient in English to master the lessons. Though my English was good, it was always my weakest subject. It takes more than three years to become proficient, to learn the vocabulary and grammar, and to think in a new language. By then, English was my third language, and even though I was picking it up quickly, it still took intense concentration for me to process the daily assignments in my more academically challenging lessons. That's one reason why I always looked forward to the home-economics period.

I especially liked it when the topic was cooking,

because I got some new insights into the American kitchen. From my perspective at least, the lessons were quite basic—but fun. In one lesson, the teacher would take a slice of white bread, always Wonder Bread, cut off the crust, spread it with mayo, and line it with olives and pimientos or peanut butter and jelly. She would then roll it, wrap it tightly in plastic wrap, and refrigerate it overnight. The next day, she would cut it into rolls, as you do with sushi, and then serve it as an hors d'oeuvre. I'd never seen anything like that in my young life, and found it truly curious. The level of home cooking was not nearly as sophisticated as it is now. I confess that I didn't share that recipe with my parents. Somehow, I didn't think it would go over well.

My mother's long commute meant that I was now spending even more time in the kitchen. My father would arrive home from work before her, and he was hungry. Sometimes she worked overtime, and didn't arrive home until well after 6:00 p.m.

I was turning twelve years old, and now in charge of starting dinner when I got home from school at 3:00 p.m. My mother would prepare the ingredients and leave things half cooked, and leave me a note on how to follow through and finish the meal:

Drain the beans from the soaking water, then put the beans to cook in 4 quarts of water. Cook the beans for 30 minutes, then add 3 peeled

potatoes, 2 bay leaves, 2 garlic cloves, and the ham hocks. Cook all for an additional hour. Add a tablespoon of olive oil, taste, and add salt.

I would prepare some salad to be served with the main course. When my mother came home, she added the pasta, and in twenty minutes our **pasta e fagioli** dinner with ham hock and salad was ready.

In Astoria, we continued to buy only chicken necks and wings. They were the cheapest parts of the bird, but they also made the best-tasting soup. The necks and wings, along with some carrots, gave us the basic proteins and vegetables. Mom would have the pot with the chicken and vegetables all ready to go in the refrigerator. I would add three to four quarts of water and put it to boil when I came home from school. By the time my mother came home, the soup was ready. We would strain it, and put the carrots and chicken on a plate seasoned with salt. Then I'd add some pasta or rice to the strained broth, along with, if needed, a touch of salt and pepper, and some grated Grana cheese on the side, and we'd have a meal. Of course, there had to be a first course (usually a salad) and a dessert, too. I still love chicken necks and wings and use them to make soup today. My mother and I still nibble on them with a sprinkle of salt while they're still warm from the pot. Bean-based soups were a regular for dinner as well, with some smoked pork hocks or kielbasa sausage cooked in, and an escarole salad tossed with some of the cooked beans from the soup as a side dish. It filled the table and our stomachs.

My mother was concerned about my time, and fearful that I wouldn't have enough time to do my homework if I had to prepare the family meal. But I told her not to worry—I was more than willing to lend a hand, I knew how to cook, and, in fact, I enjoyed doing it. I told her that I'd make the dinner between 4:00 and 6:00 p.m., read in between and do my homework on the kitchen table while the soup was cooking, and then have dinner with the family. I'd go back to my homework after dinner if she could handle the cleanup. She acquiesced, and I shifted into my new role. I would have my schoolbooks on one side of the kitchen table and the dinner preparations on the other side, and would move from one side of the table to the other while preparing dinner, doing my reading and homework while the food was cooking. Of course, there was no one home except for my brother to help me with my homework (and sometimes he was late). If I needed assistance, I'd ask one of my teachers for a bit of time, either before or after school.

I'd already spent far more time in the kitchen than most other children my age and was starting to develop my own style of cooking. Being in the kitchen with Nonna Rosa and with my own mother had taught me the basics. And I'd continued to hone my skills with Zia Nina (a professional chef) and with the nuns at the Scuola Canossiana in Trieste.

As time passed, my mother let me take control of the menu for dinner. After school, I'd walk into our apartment, put my books down on the kitchen table, and pull out the pots I'd need for the night's meal. We usually discussed the next day's menu together, but there was always some space for me to be creative. I would pull out select spices from the cabinets, and pinch herbs from the plants that we kept in the kitchen window. I already knew numerous recipes and sometimes even knew several different versions of the same dish. I'd vary the preparation and experiment until I had something that I could be proud of.

I was too young to worry about how my parents and brother would react. Indeed, I didn't think all that hard about what I was preparing. I enjoyed cooking and didn't really see it as work. The smells from the stove were a daily reminder of being with Nonna Rosa in Busoler, of our gathering around the kitchen table in Pola, and of cooking with Zia Nina and the nuns. Working in that commercial kitchen at school had given me other skills, too, including timing recipes and scaling meals up to serve more people. I'd learned to get the second dish started and then shift to preparing a salad while things were cooking. Even then, I instinctively knew how to time things so that everything would be ready at the same time.

I was always reading books about different cuisines: French, Italian, Chinese, Greek. I was just interested in everything to do with this field. Sometimes I would scour the park to find wild herbs, such as dandelion, to use in my recipes. Boiled dandelion tossed with a boiled egg or two made a great **contorno**; I still love it today. Dandelion with some sweet onions and shredded carrots makes a great risotto; if I had picked some, over dinner I would tell my mother, "Tomorrow we will have risotto with herbs."

"What kind of herbs?" she'd ask.

"Something I picked on the hill in the park." I used to forage for wild dandelion with Nonna Rosa, and there were plenty of dandelions in the New York parks. There still are today, but with all the contaminants, it is hard now to find pristine wild dandelions.

I would clean them and try to cook with them. I was always experimenting. Every Sunday, I'd surprise my family with a meal seasoned with herbs I hadn't tried before, and complete it with a cake I'd bake from a new recipe. Sometimes I'd lie awake in my bed at night dreaming up new combinations of foods to experiment with. My parents were usually pleased with the outcome, and would compliment me on my creative use of flavors.

I even incorporated something new that was uniquely American, profoundly simple, and fun— a Duncan Hines cake. When we went shopping, I'd always go to the aisle for the ready-made cake mixes and grab a few of them for the family dinners. They were inexpensive, so my mother didn't seem to mind. Almost every night, my parents would come home to the delightful smell of a freshly baked cake wafting through the apartment. My mother marveled at how I figured out how to put these cakes together. But they truly were easy enough for a twelve-year-old to make. I just had to follow the instructions on the box, usually adding some eggs and butter. I had bought myself a hand-whisking machine, with two rollers turned by a small handle, and the batter I made with it was as smooth as silk. A cake was a small treat that my hardworking family deserved.

I was mesmerized by these premeasured, prepackaged cake mixes available at the supermarket, how easy and delicious they were. One of my favorites was the vanilla cake with chocolate icing. It was so easy to add some butter and an egg or two and whip it all into a batter.

Sometimes I would leave the door to our apartment open so everyone in the building could smell that I was baking. It was food that made the first connections between our neighbors and us. I would sit on the steps outside of our apartment and share some of those baked goodies with my little cousin Diana and any other kids who would show up.

Just as in Nonna Rosa's courtyard, food was always shared. On the weekends, we'd fix lunch in our apartment and invite Louis and Marie and their children to join us. They'd bring a little something from their cupboard to contribute, and when they invited us, we'd show up with something as well. Our kitchen was small, and there wasn't enough room for all of us around the table, so each of us kids would take a plate and find a spot somewhere in the apartment to eat, the way we had done in Busoler.

I was now at an age where I was conscious of how I looked. I wanted to dress like my classmates in white bobby socks, saddle shoes, and a poodle skirt with a big belt. Rock and roll, particularly Elvis Presley and Frankie Avalon, was all the rage. I was trying to be American as quickly as possible, and that meant looking the part and fitting in.

I was determined to make things work here. We all were. My parents had chosen America as our destination, and here we were. Perhaps our biggest hurdle was behind us, but things certainly weren't easy, and we still had to find our way. For my brother and me, that meant fitting in at school. For my parents, it meant finding and keeping jobs and creating a stable life for us as a family.

It was a time of hardship and discovery, of establishing ourselves and making friends, of learning what it meant to be an American.

15

Shoofly Pie and Succotash

O ne year after our arrival, in July 1959, we returned to the Catholic Charities office, as
promised, to give our social worker an update. My
mother was determined that we all look our best
for the meeting, and so we all wore our best clothes
and paid special attention to how we looked. Everything had to be perfect. I even wore a hat my
mother had purchased for me from a vendor on the
street for fifty cents, and I looked sharp.

"We are so happy," my mother reported. "We
have everything we want. We moved from New
Jersey to Astoria, my husband and I are both working, the children are doing well in school.

"We don't know how to thank you. We want to
repay you for everything you have done for us."

"How do you want to pay us?" the social worker
inquired.

My mother pulled out a bankbook from her
purse, which showed how much she'd been able

to save during the past year, and handed it to the woman. "People here taught me how to open a bank account and manage our money," she said. "I am frugal and planned carefully how much we can spend and how much we need to save. I have one thousand dollars, and you can have all of it." Even though my mother had been told she would not have to repay the agency, she and my father were proud people and felt a moral obligation to return what had been given to them.

The social worker smiled. "Go home," she directed. "We don't want a penny from you. Catholic Charities has covered all of your expenses. You and your family are the future of America. Continue as you are doing. Come back on your five-year anniversary and tell us how you are doing."

On the surface at least, as my mother said, we were very happy as a family; things were going as well as could be expected. But there was turmoil beneath the surface, and we were still far from settled. My father had gone from owning his own trucking company and having an upscale and spacious home in the heart of Pola to a menial job delivering newspapers and a fourth-floor walk-up next to an elevated subway line. The apartment was furnished with items we had found on the street that to us seemed still usable, or obtained with an S&H Green Stamp book. My mother went from being a respected teacher who wore beautiful clothes and hats to doing simple factory work. I was doing well academically but still striving to "fit in" and find my place in school.

Franco was perhaps the only one who was comfortable, making friends in school and planning for the future. He attended Thomas A. Edison Career and Technical Education High School, which was on the service road of the Grand Central Parkway in Jamaica, Queens. He got himself a part-time job after school at a television-repair shop not far from the school, and started working there two or three hours a day, in the afternoons. Gradually, his hours increased and he started working evenings as well as on weekends and vacations. The job seemed like a great fit for him, since he'd always been interested in electricity. There was nothing he loved more as a youngster than putting two wires together and watching them spark. Bringing electricity and light to Grandma's **casetta nera** when he was only eleven was just a start. He was always playing with things, and everyone had a hunch that he'd soon be inventing things.

When we were in the camp in Trieste, my mother asked him what he wanted for his thirteenth birthday.

"If you have five lire, give me five lire," he told her. Five lire was a token amount of money, worth slightly less than an American penny.

"What will you buy?" she asked him.

My brother just smiled. He went to a store nearby and returned with an electronic component, a diode, which looked to me like some kind of crystal.

Franco took the diode, a piece of wood, and some wires, and fashioned a simple radio receiver for himself. "Ma, I have a radio," he told my mother.

"A radio?" she asked.

"Put it to your ear," he said. My mother did, and heard a faint noise. "I made a radio!" Franco said proudly.

Once we were in Astoria, we were able to buy an actual radio, and even a small television set. Franco and I spent hours listening to English-language programs, which not only were fun, but helped us with our English. My brother's interest in electronics and tinkering with things seemed to offer a diversion for him, along with providing some extra money for the household. He didn't seem to care as much as I did about fitting in or wearing fashionable clothes.

❧·❧

Sometimes, the trade-offs that we'd made seemed extraordinarily difficult. We'd left family, friends, and all our belongings behind. We were literally starting from scratch, and that was incredibly tough for my father, who had always been a proud man and respected in the community. But we knew, too, that we had freedoms here in the United States that we would not have had in the communist society that we'd left behind. We could pursue our dreams, knowing that no one could suddenly claim ownership of things—like my father's truck—that we'd struggled to buy.

There were the smaller, more intimate things, too. I missed Nonna Rosa's courtyard, the fig and cherry trees that I used to climb in, and the fields that I ran through. I missed the shoreline and the crystal-clear pale blue waters that I'd gone swimming in with my friends as a young child. I hoped that someday I'd be able to experience some of those things again. But for now my immediate world in Queens was one of concrete, steel, and soot.

In a way, it was easy to remember, and long for, the lives we had left behind. The daily hardships were easy to forget while the daily pleasures of friends and family were magnified. I worried about whether my father could pull himself out of the past and move forward. I hoped that he would find his own path, but worried about his difficulty mastering English.

In many ways, my mother was happy with our new life in America. She and my father both had jobs (finding work here had been her biggest worry), we had our cousin nearby, and she was pleased with the progress Franco and I were making. In one year, my brother and I had learned English and were using it comfortably in school. There was always more than enough food on the table, and my mother was putting money aside in a savings account while still managing to send packages of food—rice, sugar, and coffee—back home to her parents in Busoler. And we were able to treat ourselves to special activities and outings on the weekends.

My mother was slowly picking up the language here, too. She and a friend at work, Paola Franceschini, arranged to practice speaking English together, and she'd been using her daily commute to study. Paola sat next to my mother at the factory, and the two women would talk while they were cutting the belts and sewing. Neither one could sew particularly well, so they tried to help each other with their tasks. Neither woman knew more than the most basic English, but they desperately wanted to learn. My mother suggested they each purchase the same book, something written in simple English, to read during their commutes, so they could discuss what they had read, speaking only in English, when they returned to work the following morning. My mother found this a great way to pass the day, sewing and conversing in English with her Italian friend. They would read simple children's books and stories of animals. The subject material didn't matter; it was all about the vocabulary. She had even begun attending night school.

I would sometimes hear her crying in her room at night. She did her best to hide her sorrow from us, but I knew that she dearly missed her parents and the lifestyle she'd once enjoyed. One of the first things my mother had done after moving into the house in North Bergen was to prepare a care package to send back to Busoler containing a variety of foodstuffs. She quietly approached a neighbor to ask if she could borrow some money to ship the package. The neighbor loaned her some money and also explained how to mail the items. My mother continued to send things back periodically—more food, and even shoes and dresses. Her parents and other family were always appreciative. Still, she tried not to tell us too much about what they said, because she didn't want us to worry, or miss them even more than we did.

My mother's moods would often oscillate between active and joyful and quiet and sad, depending on what was going on, and the latest letter from home. When she broke down, my father would emerge as the stronger of the two and help cheer her up— always using their native language. In the long run, though, she was the one who adjusted to life here better and pushed us all to succeed. My father was almost always more sentimental and pensive. He was sad in America. He felt that having to leave his homeland was a huge injustice, and he longed for the day when the communists were no longer in power, and he could return to the life he had left behind.

My greatest challenge was fitting in with my American peers. I didn't enter the social scene at the junior high school right away. Our family had befriended some of the Italian immigrants in the neighborhood, and on the weekends I would stick with them, rather than going to the homes of my American classmates. My best friend was a girl named Wanda Radetti. My mother had introduced us. Wanda worked at a five-and-dime store, Star Economy, on Broadway between Thirty-sixth and Thirty-seventh Street.

Everything in the five-and-dime cost under a dollar, and I loved to shop there. What I remember best is the lacy undergarments, the bras, underwear, and slips. I bought my first bra there for ninety-nine cents. We didn't have these styles in Pola, just plain cotton. They were all such a treat. Shopping for them was unusual, too. Everything was stacked in big piles on tables in the middle of the store, and we had to sort through the things one at a time, looking for the size and style that we wanted. In Pola and Trieste, the stores were far smaller and there were only a few items in stock. Here there were hundreds of choices.

Wanda was a couple of years older than me, a slender sixteen-year-old with reddish-blond hair and freckles. She was from Fiume, now Rijeka, one of the major seaports of Istria, which became part of Yugoslavia after World War II. It was about sixty miles from Pola. She and her family had stayed in a refugee camp in Liguria, near Genoa, before immigrating to the United States. She also had a brother, Giorgio, so our stories were similar. Her father was a chef, and the organization that was bringing the family to America had found him a job at a restaurant in Chicago. But he died two weeks before they were scheduled to board a flight to the United States, leaving Wanda's mother with no place to go. A friend of the family agreed to take them in, and they made Astoria their home. Wanda's mother worked for Loft's Candies in its chocolate factory in Long Island City. After a few years, Wanda's brother joined the U.S. Army, which alleviated his mother's concern about how to support the family. It was also his way to become ever more American.

The more we talked, the more that I realized that Wanda and I had a lot in common, in addition to being immigrant girls and speaking Italian. We both loved nature and being near the sea. Although we did not attend the same school, we socialized together on the weekends.

Wanda introduced me to her friend Graziella, whose family had come to the States from the Istrian town of Albona (Labin, in Croatian), which was halfway between Pola and Fiume. Graziella's father had been a sailor, and he had come to the United States first before sending for his family. Now he worked in a restaurant, and her mother was a housewife. She also had a sister and a brother. They owned a two-family house in Astoria; Graziella and her family lived on the top floor, and they rented the bottom level to tenants. We rarely went inside the house. The floors were always immaculate, and all of the furniture was covered in thick, clear plastic to keep it clean and pristine. It wasn't all that unusual, in the Italian American community, to see furniture covered in plastic like this. Still, it was something we'd never done back at home, and it felt weird to sit on or touch.

The home's cellar was where we all congregated. Graziella's father made wine and cured sausages there. Her brother would invite his friends—young, single immigrants from the Albona area—and we all listened to music while some shared stories about the home country and coming to America.

I was glad to have Wanda and Graziella as my friends, and I enjoyed my time with them. Fifty-five-plus years later, we are still the best of friends. But because they attended a different school, we didn't get to see each other very much. I was still having trouble making connections with American kids my age, and I felt lost and alone. My low moments had me reminiscing, feeling nostalgic for happier times, and pining for my old home. I was missing Grandma and the courtyard, and I wondered how all the animals were doing. I missed the farm fields and the beaches with those crystal-clear waters.

When we got letters from our relatives, Mom would start crying, and I wished we could somehow do everything over again. I just didn't feel settled yet in America. I kept asking myself, **Why did this separation need to happen?** Emotionally, I still had strong ties to everything and everyone we'd left behind.

As I began to learn and understand more about the political system back home, I started to wonder if my grandparents and relatives were being treated well. They weren't allowed to write about things like that in their letters; it was common knowledge that all outgoing mail was read and censored, so they needed to be nonpolitical. I would write to them asking how my friends were doing, and I'd hear back that they were growing up, and doing fine. But when I wrote directly to my old friends in Yugoslavia, they never wrote back. I suppose they didn't want to continue our friendship after we fled—whether for political reasons or because they felt personally abandoned I didn't know.

The loss of my old friends made me feel empty inside. Once again, as when I was both Giuliana and Lidia, I felt like two different people—one, the young girl running in the courtyard in Busoler like a butterfly, flying in the fields without any worries (Grandma took care of all the worrying), the other the far more serious young woman I was becoming in Astoria. I was growing up, becoming a teenager, and trying to find a connection with new friends and customs in America. I oscillated between the two very separate worlds.

Since we left Pola, our life had been so transitory. We had moved five times, living for weeks in some places, months in others, and a few years in others. By the time we landed in Astoria, I was completely focused on what was directly ahead of me—adjusting to a new setting, a new school, a new culture, and a new language. I still hadn't fully grasped that we were not going back to Busoler— that this was our future now, and Busoler, the court- yard, and Nonna Rosa were strictly part of my past. I longed for the freedom I had felt as a child.

I always wondered: was Busoler the real world or only a childhood fantasy, made more important to me because I was surrounded by so much love and such a beautiful setting?

In Astoria, I longed for the sense of safety and security I had felt in that courtyard. Perhaps what I was really missing was the innocence of childhood, a time when I did not yet understand or appreciate the struggles of the adults around me. In Astoria, I couldn't find a way to simply relax, and I didn't feel centered. I suppose my mother could see that in me, and so she decided that it might be time for me to get away from busy Astoria for a while and find open spaces and nature, where I could be free again to smell the grass and run after the chickens and through fields of grain and corn.

After locating our cousin Louis in Astoria, we had sought to find Nonna Rosa's older sister, Anna. We managed to locate one of her children, and through her we arranged a visit. The family was still living in central Pennsylvania, in a small city called Sunbury, which was on the Susquehanna River about seventy miles north of Hershey. We learned that Anna had four daughters, Stella, Olga, Mary, and Betty, and two sons, Mario and Johnny. She had been paralyzed by a stroke, and was now living with Olga, who had recently been widowed. Olga kept in contact with us after our visit and even came to see us in Astoria.

She understood that I was missing home, especially my time with Nonna Rosa, and she invited me to come live with her in Northumberland County. I stayed there for about a year. This was my first exposure to small-town America, and I loved the rolling hills, the mountains, the river views, and the vast open spaces. I also had Nonna Rosa's sister and the cousins. Even though none of the cousins spoke Italian or Croatian, having family here in America soothed me. Being with Anna brought me great comfort—in some little ways, it helped me feel connected to my grandmother. Her tender, gentle look reminded me of Nonna Rosa, and even her soft, wrinkled skin reminded me of Grandma. I would often just sit and caress her paralyzed hand. Unfortunately, she died soon after I arrived, so having me as a houseguest provided Olga with much-needed company and a welcome distraction from her family situation.

Olga and I spent many happy hours together. We went regularly to mass and to church festivities. Olga was a good baker, and she and I baked cookies and cakes to bring to the church fairs.

The family had a little cottage on the river, and we spent weekends there with my extended family. It felt good to be together, another reminder of the close-knit family I'd known when I was younger. Olga also took me to the Amish countryside. To be sure, the life of the Amish was different from the cultural norms that I'd experienced, but they worked with the earth and loved the land, and in that we shared a common bond. I loved the food, the shoofly pie and succotash. Now, when I make periodic trips to Philadelphia, I visit the Reading Terminal Market there and patronize the stands with the Amish pies. Their aromas take me back to those quiet days in the Pennsylvania countryside.

My time in Sunbury made me a stronger person. I spent one year at Shikellamy High School, where I completed the ninth grade. Reinvigorated, I now longed to return to Astoria. Somehow, I no longer saw Queens in the same way. I missed my mother, father, and brother, and often wondered if my mother missed my work in the kitchen. Who was helping her with all the things that I'd once done—the bills, the banking, and other family chores? I was ready to go home. And home was now Astoria.

16

America the Beautiful

I had matured considerably during that school year in Sunbury, and I realized that my future was my own to build. My memories were mine forever to keep and cherish, and I had been given an extraordinary gift and opportunity for a new life; to show my mother and father my gratitude for the sacrifices they had made for us, I needed to make the most of it. Small-town America had welcomed me and made me American; this truly was my country now.

That summer, I got my first job as a salesperson at Walken's Bakery, diagonally across the street from my parents' apartment at Thirtieth Street and Broadway. I had often gone to the bakery to check out their delicious cakes, and my father loved their kaiser rolls as well as their apple strudel. I had gotten to know Josie, the store manager, and now and then I would see Mr. Walken emerge from his office in the corner of the store to check on the goods and his customers. He was a gentle man and a great baker. I discussed the possibility of a part-time weekend job with Josie, and she encouraged me to go to the office and talk to Mr. Walken. "A bakery always needs weekend help," Josie assured me.

I got my courage up, knocked on the office door, and waited for Paul Walken's response. When I opened the door, I saw him sitting at a desk squeezed into the corner of the little office. I told him that I was looking for part-time work. I knew that I had to be at least sixteen years old in order to apply—and that was still one year away. But I had blossomed early as a girl, and looked older than I really was. Mr. Walken decided to give me a chance and never asked for any papers to prove my age. He and his wife, Rosalie, were also immigrants. Paul had come to the States from Germany in 1928; Rosalie was born in Glasgow, Scotland, and made the transatlantic journey from Hamburg, Germany, in 1937. Both of them seemed eager to help other immigrants succeed, as they had succeeded so many years earlier.

I went to work behind the counter as an assistant salesperson. My duties were to fold all the boxes for the salesgirls, stack them neatly behind the counter, and replenish the supply whenever needed. I was also responsible for going downstairs to get more paper bags to refill the stock behind the counters for all the breads and rolls, and to sweep regularly behind the counter and around the store. The bakery employed many people, including Mr. Walken's three sons, Ken, Christopher, and Glenn. Christopher, the owner's middle son, delivered cakes. The two of us wound up becoming friends, in part because we worked weekends together.

The family had a summer home on the North Shore of Long Island. Sometimes the Walkens would invite me out to help Rosalie with the cooking and cleaning, but I was also included in the fun parts with the boys and their friends, mostly swimming and waterskiing. When I was a little older, Mrs. Walken took a few of us to see Christopher's first performance as an actor. It was an Off Broadway show, **Best Foot Forward**. Liza Minnelli also debuted in it. This was my first time ever going to such a performance. Over the years, Christopher and I have stayed in touch, and I admire his work as an actor. He is not only an extraordinary artist, but also a good cook, and we have cooked together at my house.

I felt at home in the bakery; the constant hustle-and-bustle reminded me of the school kitchen in Trieste. The weekends were especially busy, with customers stopping in to buy special breads, cakes, and pies for family dinners and celebrations.

On Sundays, the bakers would come before 3:00 a.m. and leave early to get home to their families. They would quietly exit through the back door, leaving plain cakes—with no icing or decoration on them—for others to dress if needed. I gradually took on that task, adding icing, flowers, and other designs, and carefully adding names, along with birthday and anniversary sentiments. I had honed my cake-decorating skills with the instant Duncan Hines cakes I had made from the box for our family desserts. Now I was in a professional baker's kitchen with access to all the professional decorating tools.

I was a hard worker, and I appreciated having the opportunity. I also appreciated having a little pocket money. Often I'd bring home bread or a dessert for the family—usually something that was less than perfect, or a cake that had an inscription with a misspelled name. With my new job, I was able to bring home the bread (literally!), save the family some money, and contribute a portion of my weekly salary to the household. My mother took my first two paychecks; after that, she let me keep most of what I earned, though part of it had to go into a savings account at the bank.

A big motivator for getting a job was being able to buy myself special things. All the girls at school were wearing nylon stockings, and at two dollars a pair, my mother refused to purchase them for me after I got a run in one the very first time I wore them. Now I could buy a few more pieces of clothing, a hat, and even stockings! My new clothes allowed me to feel more comfortable when I was at school or out with friends.

My mother was pleasantly surprised when I

dressed up for the Easter church service at Astoria's Most Precious Blood Roman Catholic Church that year with a new hat, stockings, dress, and matching pocketbook and shoes, all in a coordinated beige tone. We had begun attending services there regularly on Sunday mornings, and I was looking to emulate the styles of the girls my age.

And I was finally able to buy myself the frozen TV dinner that I had long wanted and that my mother had refused to buy because of the cost. After heating the frozen food in the oven, I put the aluminum-foil container on my TV tray table and set myself up in front of our TV to watch a show. "I am American!" I exclaimed.

I also treated myself to my first opera in America, at New York's Metropolitan Opera House, a performance of **Aida** with Leontyne Price and Franco Corelli. I love opera, and all types of classical music. I had grown up hearing it in the background as I played outside the arena in Pola as a child, and it blared from Nonna Rosa's radio on Sunday mornings in Busoler.

My graduation from William Cullen Bryant High School, 1965, in Astoria

The night of the show, I got all dressed up and I went by myself to the performance. My seat was all the way up in the rear of the hall—that was all I could afford. It didn't matter. The music just came straight to me, right to my seat.

⇒ ⇐

Franco completed his studies at Thomas A. Edison High School and was accepted to the Brooklyn Polytechnic Institute on a full academic scholarship. Scholarships were the only way for us to continue our education; it was the only way (and still is today) for a lot of immigrants to attend university. I was determined to follow my brother to college, and I worked hard during my years at the William Cullen Bryant High School in Long Island City. I was studying the sciences and thought I would become a doctor. At the time, there was a floating hospital ship called the SS **Hope**, making stops all over the world and providing critical medical services to a wide range of people, oftentimes around Africa. I imagined myself joining the ship and traveling the globe to provide medical care to children and families in crisis in foreign lands. Perhaps I was seeking a way to heal the hole in my heart from having left all of my relatives and childhood friends at such a tender age.

When I was fifteen, I began volunteering at the New York Infirmary, founded in 1857 by America's first woman doctor, Elizabeth Blackwell. The hospital was on Third Avenue between Fifteenth and Sixteenth Streets, in what is now the Stuyvesant

Franco and I, awaiting guests to celebrate my sixteenth birthday, in our apartment in Astoria

Square Historic District of Manhattan. The infirmary had a unit for orphans, and I went there after work at the bakery on Saturdays and Sundays to care for the orphans. It was heartbreaking to see them in their little metal cribs. The minute I came through the door, they would all put their hands out, wanting to be held, to be touched. The experience affected me greatly. I cleaned them and changed their diapers, but mostly I would just hug them. I'd go from crib to crib, spending an equal amount of time with each child. Sometimes it was difficult to put them back in their cribs, because they just wouldn't let go.

It was amazing to see how quickly they grew. At seven or eight months, they were standing up.

My work with the orphans solidified my desire to become a doctor. I loved the sciences, especially biology and chemistry. I found physics a bit challenging, but studied hard, because I was motivated to excel.

When my sixteenth birthday was approaching, I begged my mother to let me have a little party. She agreed to a small gathering in our apartment. We didn't have much room, so the guest list was short: Wanda, Graziella, and a few of the young men we had befriended at the gatherings in Graziella's cellar. Graziella took it upon herself to invite an Istrian immigrant named Felice Bastianich, who had an accordion that he played at weekend parties at her house, where everyone would sing along. Felice would be playing the instrument, too, at my party.

Felice was seven years older than I was. He had come to America on his own, and I had met him a few times when visiting Graziella. He was a joyous young man, gentle and kind. He was good-looking as well, with wavy dark hair and expressive green eyes. Sometimes I would catch him looking at me, but I was too young to do or say anything. Felice had an impressive job. He had started at Romeo Salta, an Italian restaurant on West Fifty-sixth Street in Manhattan, as a waiter, but had already become an accomplished captain. Romeo Salta was one of the first restaurants to introduce fine Italian cuisine to Manhattan, and it had a stellar reputation.

Felice charmed me at my sweet sixteen. He was a

gentle guy, and even though I was young, and my mother set rigid limits on how often I could go on dates, he was relentless, bringing my mother flowers and stopping her whenever he saw her on the street—at the beginning, it seemed he was courting my mother. My parents were not too happy about my relationship with Felice. I was young and doing very well in school, and they felt the relationship would interfere with my education. Both Felice and I were always respectful of my parents, but falling in love was out of our control, and something my mother had to deal with.

Our courtship was a lot about going to try the best restaurants in New York—Italian, French, and others. We both had a love for food and could talk for hours about a dish or a recipe.

❧ ☙

I continued to work at Walken's Bakery throughout my high school years. Eventually, I convinced my mother to apply there as well. Since moving to Astoria, she had continued her long commute to North Bergen without so much as a complaint. But after five long years, she agreed to interview for a job as a salesperson. Mr. Walken did not hesitate in hiring her, and she loved working there. The other employees at the bakery struggled to pronounce her name, "Erminia"; in English, it would be "Hermione," so everyone called her "Herminie," a name

Erminia with Josie as a salesgirl at
Walken's Bakery, 1968

Erminia bicycling to work

that stuck. Soon she became known all over Astoria as simply "Herminie."

The year my mother began working at Walken's Bakery marked our five-year anniversary in the United States. It was again time for us to return to the Catholic Charities office in Manhattan to provide our social worker with a final progress report. This time, my mother arrived bearing gifts— cookies for everyone. By now, Franco and I had mastered the English language, and my mother, too, was speaking English.

She proudly reported that Franco was now earning his undergraduate degree at Brooklyn Polytechnic on a full academic scholarship, and that I was excelling in my studies at Bryant High School.

Before leaving the offices that afternoon, my mother tried one final time to repay the agency for all the money they had spent on our resettlement. She explained that, through careful budgeting, she had managed to save more than five thousand dollars since arriving in New York.

"We will not take a penny from you," the social worker told her yet again. We had made them proud through our hard work and dedication to succeed in our new land; we had proved ourselves model Americans and should continue to contribute to the future of this country.

For me, our seven-year anniversary in the United States marked a number of important milestones.

That June, I put on a cap and gown and accepted my high school diploma during a graduation ceremony in the auditorium of Bryant High School. On the afternoon of my graduation, I joined a group of friends at the Neptune Diner on Astoria Boulevard, where we all ate hamburgers to celebrate the important moment.

That fall, I boarded the subway in Astoria, bursting with excitement when the doors opened at Sixty-eighth Street, the Hunter College stop along the Lexington Avenue Line. My strong academic performance had earned me two Regents Scholarships, which would go toward my tuition. I couldn't stop smiling as I walked to campus to begin my freshman year at the college.

Hunter College was part of the City University of New York, CUNY, and the school had a stellar reputation. Being accepted there filled me with a sense of pride and accomplishment, and I was proud to be a member of the second coeducational class at the college's Manhattan campus.

Hunter College was a women's college when it first opened its doors in 1870. In the mid-1940s, it began admitting men, but only to its Bronx campus. In 1961, it became part of CUNY, and in 1964, male students were allowed to attend the Manhattan campus. I was a member of the 1965 freshman class. I was going to study the sciences, with a focus on biology. The Regents Scholarships I had been awarded covered my tuition, and I began waitressing at various restaurants in Manhattan to pay for train fare, books, and to contribute to household expenses. I preferred restaurant work to office work, because it enabled me to expand my knowledge of food preparation. Thirsty to acquire new cooking techniques and recipes, I would work at an establishment until I had learned all I could there, sometimes staying only a month or two, then find work at another restaurant to enhance my skills.

My mother worried that I couldn't keep a job. Throwing her hands in the air, she asked me, "What are you doing wrong, that they keep firing you?"

"Mom, I am not being fired," I assured her. "Don't worry."

I marked my seven-year anniversary in America by applying for citizenship to the United States. The day I turned eighteen, February 21, 1965, which is when I was allowed to file for citizenship, I filled out the paperwork. As soon as I was able, I took the tests—the naturalization test, the civics exam, and an English-language test. I went for an interview, and I attended all of the required meetings.

My parents and brother were not in the same hurry that I was, and they waited several more years before applying. For me, putting down permanent roots was extremely important, and I wanted to do it as soon as I was eligible. I had no trepidation at all. As a young child I had been tossed from one government to another, one country to another, until the United States took me in. I was extremely grateful, and I was going to stay here for good. I didn't have an ounce of doubt. I wasn't going to turn the opportunity down. I was going to anchor myself in America.

My naturalization photo, 1965

On June 22, 1965, I attended the swearing-in ceremony at the U.S. District Court in Brooklyn. I was allowed to invite two people to witness my swearing the Oath of Allegiance to the United States of America. Since my mother and father were both working that day, I invited my cousin Louis and his wife, Marie.

I got very dressed up, elegantly dressed up, out of respect for the occasion. As the first one in the family to receive this honor, I fully appreciated the magnitude of what I was about to become a part of.

The event began at 10:00 a.m. in the ceremonial courtroom. As I looked at the smiling, anxious faces around me, I was struck by the diversity of backgrounds of those in the room. There were Chinese, West Indians, Hispanics, and many, many more; we exemplified America. After we sat down, U.S. District Clerk of Court Sidney R. Feuer made a series of emotional remarks about being accepted and what it meant to be an American.

I feel very proud to be an American and to be in America. The United States is the nation that accepted my family and me. It gave me security and stability. It is my children's country, and the country of my grandchildren.

At the same time, I continue to celebrate my Italian and Istrian heritage. I celebrate both. I think everyone should look into his or her own family heritage and explore that added richness of diversity.

PART FOUR

PART FOUR

17

Finding Home

At eighteen, I felt like I had it all. I was an American citizen, a college freshman, and I was engaged to the love of my young life, Felice Bastianich, called Felix by his American friends. It was a moment of intense happiness for me.

I was already making plans for my wedding and dreaming about going out to buy a tasteful white wedding dress. But my mother was upset that I had accepted Felice's proposal, and she did little to hide her disappointment. The night we announced our engagement, she pulled me aside and told me, "I don't want you to do this right now. I want you to finish college. There is always time to get married."

My father was much calmer. "If this is what she wants to do, let her do it," he told my mother. In a way, he put the responsibility—and therefore the consequences of the decision—on me.

Franco didn't offer an opinion either way. He was

My father escorting me to church
on my wedding day, May 29, 1966

Felice's and my wedding

never very intrusive, and we had always been sup-
portive of each other. Like many boys, Franco had
probably been slower to mature than I was. Still, he
was very focused on his future, knew his path forward, and was determined to become an engineer
someday. I, too, had a vision for my future. Deep
down, I felt like an adult and was confident that I
could act like one, too.

I was a little bit rebellious—a typical teenager, I
suppose. I heard my mother's words and the worry
in her voice. At some level, I sensed that she might
be right; she'd always had my best interests at heart,
and I had no reason to doubt her now. Still, I was
determined to put aside her objections and forge
ahead with the marriage.

Felice was 100 percent behind the idea that I
should get a college degree. He said he would support and encourage me to finish school after our
wedding.

My mother remained skeptical and pressed me
to reconsider. Her concern was that, once we were
married, I would be expected to assume the role
of wife—which meant putting my husband's needs
before my own, as she had done when she married
my father. This was both customary and expected
of women in the Italian culture; the man was the
leader, and the wife was expected to follow. No
matter how much I reassured her that I would not
let my marriage interfere with my college plans, she
never fully embraced my assurances and continued

to lobby against my teenage marriage right up until we set a date for the wedding, May 29, 1966.

Spring is probably my favorite season, a time when the earth and nature come back alive. Felice and I chose the Sunday of Memorial Day Weekend for our wedding date, because the holiday would allow people to travel and not have to rush home immediately after the party. Also, that's when roses and peonies are in full bloom. I envisioned my wedding as a spring blossom. My bouquets were white roses and orange blossoms, which had a beautiful aroma. The twelve bridesmaids had simple, flowing pink chiffon dresses with a cascade of pink roses and carnations. By then I had developed many friendships in the Istrian-Italian community, and my soon-to-be husband had two sisters who had come to America as well. Aunt Angelina Cavalli, Felice's father's sister, who had sponsored him, had an extensive family. From not having anyone in America, I now had a growing and extending family, and that also made me happy.

We decided the ceremony would be held at the Most Precious Blood Roman Catholic Church in Astoria, followed by a reception at Villa Bianca, a stately English Tudor-style house in Flushing, Queens, that had been converted into a catering hall. Most of the Istrian weddings in Queens took place at the Astoria Manor or the Oyster Bay, a Greek catering hall on Thirty-first Street, but Felice and I picked the Villa Bianca in Flushing because it had more of a country feel. Villa Bianca was also known for its lavish smorgasbord luncheons and beautifully executed weddings and affairs.

We felt proud of our knowledge of good food and took great care in selecting our menu. Following the cocktail hour there would be **prosciutto e melone** and tortellini in **brodo di capone,** capon broth, and the main course was American prime rib, with bowls of salad on each table. The symbolic wedding cake of strawberry-and-pineapple filling was made by Walken's Bakery. We hired our friend Dante to perform at the reception, with his musical group consisting of two accordionists, a guitarist, and a drummer.

Dante's band usually played at the White Oak, a club on 108th Street in Corona, where we would often go and dance. Felice would sometimes end up on the stage to play the accordion. Dante was an Emiliano, and Emilia-Romagna is known for its **balere,** from the word **ballare** (to dance). **Balere** are large gatherings, usually on an open dance floor with local accordion music—waltzes, tangos, and Italian folk dances such as the **mazurche** and **liscio.** We extended the reception for one and a half hours, until 1:30 a.m., and danced away.

Our guest list topped three hundred people, most of them immigrants we had befriended during our years in America. Some relatives and friends were able to fly in from Istria and Italy to attend. Unfortunately, my grandmother was unable to come. She did not travel at all, except to go to the fairs in the small towns of Istria: she was elderly and alone, and had the animals to tend to. Besides, I knew I was going to be seeing her soon; Felice and I planned to go to Istria later that summer for what would become the second of two honeymoons we were planning.

Felice had purchased a house in Astoria before we were even married, and he moved in and lived alone there until our wedding day, when I joined him. The newly constructed house, on the corner of Forty-fifth Street and Twenty-fifth Avenue, contained three apartments, two of which would generate some money to help pay the mortgage. From a purely economic perspective, the house made sense: it was in Astoria, and a bit removed from the busy, noisy commercial district. The house was on a corner plot, forty by a hundred feet, twice the width of a New York brownstone, with enough room for a small vegetable garden on the side yard. We could plant some tomatoes, basil, and radicchio.

I bought a simple white silk gown with sheer lace sleeves, and small pearls and crystal beads in a floral appliqué. Selecting the dress was a twelve-month process. In those years, especially among immigrants like me, the bouffant-lace dress was in style. But I had fallen for a very simple A-line shantung gown with a long, plain train, and a beige veil. Part of the veil was as long as my train, and part of it puffed out at my shoulders. I had long hair, which

I wore pulled up into a shapely bun atop my head, and the veil was pinned in front of my gathered hair by a cluster of satin orange-blossom flowers. I still have the dress and veil boxed and stored in my attic. I had suggested it to my daughter, Tanya, when she was getting married, but she made her own choice. I still have two granddaughters—Olivia and Julia—growing up, so who knows!

I vividly recall all the excitement and emotion of that first big event and celebration in America. For me, it was also further affirmation that, forever-more, this would be my home. America was where I would start my family and have my children. They would be born Americans, and that would make me the mother of Americans. I have never let them forget that they are of Italian roots and made sure that the first language they spoke was Italian, but they were born in America.

➤◄

After spending our wedding night in our new house in Astoria, we drove about seven hours north and west across New York State to reach Niagara Falls, a popular honeymoon destination at that time. In addition to the majestic and breathtaking water-falls that straddle the border between the United States and Canada, there were numerous hotels and restaurants and panoramic views of the area. You could see the Toronto skyline from there. Now

I go back regularly to Buffalo, Syracuse, and Toronto. **Lidia's Kitchen**, my show airing on Public Television, has a large following there, and I travel gladly to do fund-raising for the local Public Television stations as well as book signings.

Our trip to Niagara Falls was lovely, but the highlight of our nuptials would be our second honeymoon, a summer trip to Istria. Felice's parents lived in Brovinje, near Albona, and I had Nonna Rosa in Busoler. More than ten years had passed since I'd last seen my grandmother.

Holding our new U.S. passports in hand, we left for our three-week trip to Istria with a mixture of excitement and trepidation. It was our first time going back to what was now Yugoslavia, and we both harbored very real fears about returning to a country that we had once escaped under difficult circumstances. We didn't expect any problems, since we had all the correct documents. But at some deep level, we were both wary of what might happen—Felice more than I, because he was eighteen when he escaped from Istria. The decision to leave had been his own, whereas I was just a child and had not actively participated in my parents' decision to leave the country.

We carefully planned our trip to take advantage of lower airfares and rental car fees, by flying into Stuttgart, where we rented a Volkswagen. We drove to Villach, Austria, and continued through Ljubljana, Slovenia, before arriving in Istria.

We first went to see Felice's mother and father in the small village of Brovinje, on the Labinštinja Peninsula, overlooking the Gulf of Kvarner, in the northern Adriatic Sea. Brovinje is a community of no more than about thirty houses, all made of stone with traditional **coppi** (curved terra-cotta tile) roofs. The village hasn't grown much over the years; as of the 2011 census, Brovinje had a population of eighty-one. The setting is on a rocky hill overlooking the beautiful Quarnero, now Kvarner, and the small port of Valmazzinghi, now Koromačno, where an intrusive cement factory stands. Though it sprinkles dust on the local vegetation and coastline, it provides employment to the residents of all the local small towns, so it is a welcomed eyesore.

I was nervous about meeting Felice's parents, Milka and Giuseppe. And though I knew he wanted to spend some time visiting with them, I was deeply conflicted about the visit, because I was dying to go see Grandma. I struggled to keep my emotions in check and not pull him away from his mother and father. Felice's paternal grandparents, Nonna Caterina and Nonno Mia, were still alive and in their nineties. They lived in the house adjacent to Milka and Giuseppe's, in front of which they had a water cistern to collect rainwater and a big umbrellalike mulberry tree, around which were heavy sections of tree trunks that had been shaped into stools for sitting.

I still hold distinct memories of his grandparents'

home, including the huge stone hearth, blackened from decades of soot, which was just inside the front door, on the right side as you walked in. The walls of the home were made of stone, like most in the area, and the floors were tile. A tiny curtain over the hearth hid a shelf where Nonno Mia kept a pitcher and some glasses. There was a small table to the left, with two chairs. Above the table was a nook in the wall, hidden behind another curtain. There he kept some small treasures—foods, coffee, and the strong menthol mints that he enjoyed and offered to his guests. Only a few steps beyond this one room were wooden steps that went up to the bedroom. There was no bathroom in the house; everyone used a nearby outhouse.

Caterina and Mia loved their coffee, which was still scarce and expensive. On later trips, I would bring coffee from Trieste, and after every meal, to sweeten the situation, as they sat on those stumps in the shade of the mulberry tree, I brought them hot espresso that I made in the **napoletana,** or Neapolitan, style. Grandpa always had his little bottle of grappa. He would pull it out of his jacket pocket and would say, **"Bisogna un caffè corretto,"** Let's correct this coffee. The addition of a splash of his grappa did the trick. I still enjoy my **caffè corretto** that way. None of them are alive now, and the house is closed. Felice's sister Jolanda is the only sibling left; she returns to Istria now and then for a summer vacation.

The drive down to Pola took only about an hour. During the ride, my early-childhood memories all came flooding back. I looked anxiously out the car windows as I began to recognize my surroundings, and my heart started to race. I began pointing out landmarks to Felice as we got closer to Pola's Šijana—the Cathedral of the Assumption of the Blessed Virgin Mary, where my mother was married, the fields where I used to run, and the road we used to walk with the cart when we went to market in the morning.

There had been some construction during the decade since I left, and I noted the occasional new building. Everything seemed smaller, the roads seemed narrower, and Busoler was so much closer to Pola than I remembered. To a child, everything seemed so vast and distant; the walk to town had seemed so long, as had the walk to school from our apartment in Pola. The road through Busoler had been paved. Along each side, where there had been open fields, houses now stood, and in their courtyards were people I did not recognize.

Felice pulled the car onto the side of the street and parked. I hopped out and ran into the courtyard, where I spotted Nonna Rosa standing on the concrete steps by the animal pens. She was in her usual black dress and black headscarf tied like a babushka.

"Nonna! Nonna!" I exclaimed.

She stopped what she was doing and looked

around. **"Ti son proprio ti Giuliana?"** she cried out. "Is that really you, Giuliana?" Nonna Rosa still called me by the name I had used for the first five years of my life, as did many of my Istrian relatives, including my parents. Even Franco still calls me Giuliana.

I ran up to my grandmother, grabbed and hugged her, and raised her off the ground; she was much smaller and lighter than I remembered, but her smiling eyes, now wet with tears, and her warm smile were the same. It was so comforting to have her tight in my arms. Her dress and headscarf carried scents that immediately took me back to my childhood, when I was little Giuliana, helping Grandma in the courtyard. It was the smell of cooked food mixed with the smoke from the **casetta nera,** the little black house with the open hearth where she cooked for the pigs and smoked the prosciuttos, sausages, and bacon. For Nonna Rosa, not much had changed in those ten-plus years.

There was nothing easy about her life; she'd worked hard for as long as I could remember, and this petite woman showed no sign of slowing down. Seeing the courtyard and Nonna Rosa again, smelling the scents of my past, and recalling the wonderful times we'd spent together gave me a euphoric sense of happiness, joy, delight, and love. It was something that I couldn't adequately describe to Felice. But I believe he understood my emotional outpouring in some way. I was finally back home, in the comfort and security of that courtyard, and with Grandma. I was back in the blissful time of childhood, where the important things were family, security, food, and love.

Nonna Rosa took my face in her hands and kissed me; she smelled of smoke and had the color of the red earth on her hands and feet. When we finally stopped crying, I introduced her to my husband. I had sent wedding photos, so she knew what he looked like, but not much more. She took his face between her hands, kissed him, and welcomed him into our courtyard. Felice was relaxed, outgoing, and determined to charm my grandmother. Perhaps it had been wise to visit his parents first, for he seemed content and willing to spend time here in Busoler and in Pola.

Unfortunately, I was unable to see Grandpa Giovanni again. He had suffered a heart attack and died on January 1, 1966, just six months before my return home to Istria. That was one of the few times I had gotten to speak to Nonna Rosa on the phone. My mother had to set up an appointment for the call; authorities then notified my grandmother at what time she needed to be at the post office to receive it.

Grandpa was buried in the family tomb in the Cimitero Civico di Monte Ghiro, in Pola. I was happy to hear that my mother had been keeping her parents apprised of our activities via letter, and was heartened when Nonna Rosa told me of my grandfather's pride at receiving a photo of Franco on the podium with New York's Mayor Robert F. Wagner Jr. the day he was awarded his scholarship to the Brooklyn Polytechnic Institute. Grandpa had gone from house to house, showing the photograph to all their neighbors.

Grandma's routine seemed unchanged from when I'd left so long ago. The courtyard looked much smaller than I remembered it—as did my grandparents' home and the trees outside. Otherwise, everything was as I remembered. The fig tree in the courtyard was still providing shade—and fruit—the animals were in their pens at the top of the stairs, and there was still no indoor plumbing in the house.

I felt comfortable coming there. But I also realized that Busoler was different, and so was I. A decade had passed, and life had moved on. Grandma Rosa had aged, and I had grown older, too.

Felice and I spent a week in Busoler and Pola, and together we visited many of the places that I had loved as a young girl: the farm fields, the beaches where I'd gone with my friends, the forest where I'd picked wild asparagus, and the old Roman arena where I had played house with my friends and attended concerts with my parents. Once word reached Pola that I was in town, my aunt Lidia rushed to Busoler, bringing her daughter, Sonia, who was now about eleven years old. Aunt Lidia and her family were still living in our old apartment. I was anxious to see the city, the market,

Giardini, and my house at Via Castropola 7, which had been changed to Ulica Matia Gubaz 7. I had to revisit all of the places that I had longed so much for after our escape. I needed to accept and close the door to that chapter.

Life has a path for each one of us. We need to embrace our destiny and move forward while still cherishing and safeguarding our memories, because they give us strength and a reason to keep moving on. It took some time for me to take it all in, to see things as they were, and to absorb it all.

I visited all of the aunts and uncles who remained in Pola, as well as all of the cousins who were still there. There was my cousin Sonia on my mother's side, and two of my father's brothers, Franco and Tonino, both of whom had five children. I searched out some of my childhood friends, too, including my pal Silvia from Busoler and my friend Lilliana, who had lived next door to us in Pola. I had so been looking forward to seeing them again and had somehow imagined that we would be able to pick up where we'd left off years earlier.

Unfortunately, it wasn't meant to be; they were adults now, and they'd grown up under the communist regime. More than just miles had separated us over the years. They were not as open and affectionate as I remembered them. I had the feeling that they almost considered me a traitor for leaving Istria and abandoning them.

Our visit to Busoler ended way too soon, and

we had to say tearful goodbyes to Nonna Rosa and others. But this time, I knew that I could return, and that I would return. I knew that I could come back as often as I wanted, and that I would be able to say goodbye each time I left. I would never again leave under the cover of darkness.

After visiting Grandma Rosa in Busoler, we returned to Brovinje to be with Felice's parents for another week. During that week, we drove to Trieste to visit with Zia Nina and do some shopping. Yugoslavia was still missing a lot of commodities, like towels, linens, detergent, delicate soaps, and food items such as coffee and rice for risotto. Delicacies—chocolates, candies, lemons and other citrus fruits—were even harder to find.

Zia Nina was still living at Via Cecilia de Rittmeyer 6, in her apartment on the third floor. My heart began palpitating as we crossed the border from Yugoslavia into Italy. The road into Trieste passed about half a mile from Campo San Sabba, and I could not stop thinking of the years we spent there. I was told that it had been shut down and no longer harbored immigrants. As curious as I was to see it, I could not bring myself to make the visit, although I would finally find the courage on subsequent trips to Trieste.

Nina was expecting us and buzzed us right in. The climb to the third floor seemed much faster than when I was there as a child. Just as all those years ago, Nina was standing in the doorway when we reached the third-floor landing. She was dressed all in black, but her skin was as beautiful and peachy as I recalled it, though perhaps with a few more wrinkles. Her long hair was braided in the same style it always had been, except for a few strands of gray falling around her temples.

I immediately fell into her arms. Nina was a big-busted woman, and she seemed to envelop your entire body in her embrace. At that moment, I felt as secure in her arms as I had those ten years ago. But now my heart was full of gratitude and love, not fear and worry, as it had been the morning we arrived from the train station. Much to my chagrin, Zio Rapetti and La Professoressa had since passed away. But Nina's home was not empty; she had new tenants sharing the apartment with her. As we stepped inside, the aromas coming from her kitchen reminded me of those precious Sunday meals she cooked for us when we visited from the camp. It was so comforting to sit at her kitchen table and eat her food again.

I would see Nina another time, in 1969, when Felice and I traveled to Italy and Istria with our new son, Joseph, in tow. He was just nine months old, but we were anxious to introduce him to the special people in our lives—Nina; Felice's parents, Milka and Giuseppe; and, of course, Nonna Rosa. I was thankful we made the journey, especially because, only a few months after our visit, on January 3, 1970, Zia Nina passed away.

My mother finally summoned the courage to make her own journey home to Busoler in 1968, two years after my honeymoon trip to Istria. Tito had broken away from the communist bloc. That year, Yugoslavia became the first communist country to open its borders to foreign visitors without visas, and materially reduced restrictions against its citizens' travel abroad, although it retained its communist economic and political system. Tito continued to rule the country until his death on May 4, 1980.

Both of my parents had sworn their Oath of Allegiance to the United States two years after I became a citizen. But only my mother would go to Istria on this trip. Although my father was always nostalgic to return to his homeland, he remained fearful of political reprisal and elected to wait and see how her journey turned out before deciding if it was safe for him to travel there. He was never happy that he had left his birthplace, and he always held out hope that one day he would retire to his homeland and end his life there. But he never stopped worrying that communist officials would be waiting for him at the airport, to arrest him and throw him in jail. My mother had a similar fear, but her desire to see her mother outweighed her concern. When she alerted my grandmother to her travel plans in a letter, she urged her to share the information with no one. She even planned to arrive in Busoler after dark to ensure that she would not be seen.

She was so nervous that she couldn't stop sobbing. Later, she confessed that she had continued to cry for much of the transatlantic flight, and right up to the moment she arrived in Busoler.

"What kind of Gypsy is this lady?" Nonna Rosa cried upon seeing my mother. I had bought her a dress with a colorful floral pattern to wear for the reunion, and on the day of her departure, I presented her with an orchid corsage that she pinned to her lapel. Since coming to the United States, she had begun to wear her auburn-colored hair in an upsweep, which was all the rage back then. I guess she was hardly recognizable to my grandmother, who was accustomed to my mother's more proletarian style of dress and to seeing her wavy hair fall loosely past her shoulders.

My mother told me that, once Nonna Rosa recognized her, the two fell into a long, tearful embrace.

"Don't tell anyone I am here," my mother said, "not even the neighbors. I'm afraid that they will come to take me and put me in jail."

"Don't be afraid," my grandmother replied. "The system has changed. It's a bit better now."

Despite my grandmother's assurances, my mother didn't dare venture out of the house for the first five days of her stay. Only after a chance encounter with a neighbor who reassured her she had nothing to fear did she find the courage to leave the courtyard and walk around Busoler. But that was as far as she was willing to travel during her fifteen-day stay; not once did she venture into Pola, not even to go to the market.

For my parents, returning home proved much different from my own trip; whereas I found peace and closure, they experienced disappointment and despair. For my mother, the only thing bringing her back each year was her mother, my grandma Rosa. My father accompanied her on a subsequent trip to Yugoslavia, and he, too, was disappointed by what he found. Neither of his parents was still alive. His mother had died before I was even born, and his father had passed away shortly before we fled to Trieste in 1956. He and my mother spent their days visiting the fields they had once tended. Their time in Pola proved disheartening. While there, they visited the house at Via Castropola, where my aunt Lidia now lived with her family, and they tried to find some of their old friends. Most had left Yugoslavia and were now expats, just like them. The few who remained were cool and standoffish. And there were a lot of strangers. Tito had repopulated the city with people from Bosnia, Herzegovina, Serbia. My mother said she felt more of a stranger in the house where she was born than she did in America. My father vowed not to come back as long as Tito was in power.

Felice and I returned almost every year thereafter, always in summertime. Grandma Rosa got to meet and hug and kiss both of my children, Joseph and Tanya, who spent many summers in that magical courtyard in Busoler. The children also enjoyed their time with Felice's family in Albona. They especially loved to play with the water from the cistern in Caterina and Mia's front yard. They would throw the pail tied to a string into the well, fill it with water, then hoist it up to splash themselves in the hot summer sun.

Nonna Rosa died of old age on June 24, 1975. My aunt Lidia had written my mother to say that my grandmother did not want to eat anymore. There comes a time when we all just give up, and I guess this was her time. I am so thankful that I was able to return home to see her, and I feel fortunate that I was able to introduce her to my two children; I am also grateful for the legacy of love for family and nature that she instilled in me.

18

Taking a Chance

Life is all about taking chances. My parents had risked everything to bring us to America in search of a better life. One of the most important elements of my mother's plan was for me to graduate from college. I had started down that road when I enrolled at Hunter College and began my studies. But God had other plans for me, and, looking back now, I am convinced I followed the path I was meant to travel. In one way or another, food had always been at the forefront of my life—whether growing it, harvesting it, not having enough of it, or having more than enough and selling some at the local market; or preparing it, eating it, sharing it, and enjoying it.

From the age of two, I used to mimic Grandma Rosa, sitting on the rocks in the courtyard preparing "sauce," by filling old tin cans with rocks to emulate tomatoes and pouring them into my pretend pot to stir and simmer. From there, I planted and harvested the crops alongside her, and learned the art of simple cooking in my role as sous-chef in her tiny kitchen. My visits to the open-air market with Zia Nina in Trieste became lessons in how to select the ideal vegetables, fruits, and meats for the evening menu. Observing her in the kitchen introduced me to spices I had never tasted. I also learned about the art of food presentation by watching her meticulously arrange and garnish the meals for her private clients. Lunch duty with the nuns at the Scuola Canossiana was my first experience in a commercial kitchen, and it was there that I learned about cooking for large numbers of diners.

Later, my after-school hours in the kitchens in North Bergen and Astoria provided me latitude to experiment with newly discovered ingredients and to conjure up recipes I could test on my family members in the evenings. Baking became a passion of mine—even if it was only with prepackaged mixes. I was then able to upgrade my cake preparing and decorating skills at Walken's Bakery. Even my time with Aunt Olga in the Pennsylvania countryside had me in the kitchen baking cookies and cakes for the church fairs and festivals. There always seemed to be a close relationship between me and food, so it came as little surprise that my courtship with Felice had also centered on dining. We both enjoyed sampling and critiquing the Italian American fare in pizzerias, cafés, and restaurants around Queens and Manhattan. This was a cuisine I was unfamiliar with when I first arrived in the United States. Such peculiar offerings as meatballs and spaghetti and veal Parmigiana had not been part of our repertoire back home; I was fascinated—and even a bit puzzled—by them.

One of our dates was at Mamma Leone's, on West Forty-fourth Street, an enormous and extremely popular Italian American restaurant in New York's theater district. The original Mamma Leone's was founded in 1906 by Louisa "Mamma" Leone as a twenty-seat restaurant in her New York City brownstone, reportedly at the request of the great tenor Enrico Caruso. He loved her ravioli and would often bring cast members from the Metropolitan Opera House to enjoy her **cucina,** seated on wine crates at tables in her living room. By the time Felice and I dined there, the restaurant had moved to 261 West Forty-fourth Street and had recently been sold to Restaurant Associates, which owns well-known restaurants all over the United States.

Felice and I were curious to learn the reason for this Italian American restaurant's great success. I can still see the red-checkered tablecloths, bricks of lasagna oozing with cheese, spaghetti with big meatballs, assorted antipasti of cold cuts and pickled vegetables, amid the live opera arias that were performed in the dining room.

What I learned is that the much-loved Italian cuisine in America began with the cuisine of the Italian immigrants, who started coming here in the late nineteenth century. The majority of those emigrated from the south of Italy, basically Calabria, Campania, and Sicily. They came with all of their memories, culture, and passions for food. But when they arrived in the new land, traditional ingredients such as olive oil, prosciutto, Grana Padano, good dried pasta, and ricotta were missing, so they had to substitute the ingredients they found here. The tomatoes here were beefsteak tomatoes, not San Marzano, which are sweet and have thin skin, lots of pulp, and fewer seeds. American garlic was the one ingredient that was close to the Italian version. The immigrants ate a lot of it, because it reminded them of home; to this day, Italian American cuisine still calls for lots of garlic. Another difference also stemmed from a crucial difference between America and Italy. Here beautiful cuts of meat were readily available; in Italy, meat was far more expensive, and the good cuts were hard to find. Chefs here were able to load their Sunday sauce with lots of meatballs, sausages, and **braciole**. In Italy, the Sunday sauce often had a tiny piece of fresh pork meat and usually some **cotenne**, salted rolled pig skin. And so the Italian American cuisine was born, a delicious and venerable cuisine—but not a regional cuisine of Italy.

At myriad waitressing jobs, I learned about different menu options and recipes, and I observed the cooks and chefs as they prepared thousands upon thousands of orders. I made mental notes of it all. I could not believe that pasta was precooked and then just reheated in boiling water, sauced, and served. Not to cook spaghetti **al minute** and **al dente** was sacrilege in Italy. Veal cutlet topped with mounds of oozing mozzarella was unheard of in Italy, where a **parmigiana** was a cutlet sprinkled with grated cheese and baked in the oven until crisp, and served on a thin layer of tomato sauce. In the Italian American restaurants in America, everything was heavier and loaded with sauce. Even the pizza was, and still is, a far cry from the thin-crusted, lightly dressed pizzas of Rome and northern Italy.

One of my favorite jobs was waitressing at Pete's Pizzeria, on Amsterdam Avenue between Seventy-second and Seventy-third Streets on Manhattan's Upper West Side. It was a small place, and Pete was the **pizzaiolo**. He employed a dishwasher, and one server in the dining room during each shift. I mostly worked on the dinner shift, and would come straight from my classes at Hunter College, beginning before I was married. The restaurant was quite busy, and I made good money. A young Bette Midler came in for dinner once or twice a week, and I was her server.

Pete was from Genoa. The Genovese have delicious local dishes, such as **pesto alla Genovese** and the delicious **focaccia di Recco,** a classic dish from the Ligurian town of Recco, made with crescenza or stracchino, a fresh and creamy cow's-milk cheese that has the consistency of cream cheese. But Pete was cooking none of the regional Genovese specialties; he was making the Italian American rendition of the cuisine: pizza, eggplant Parmigiana, and spaghetti and meatballs were on his menu.

Working at the pizzeria was, of course, a far different experience from working at a restaurant like Romeo Salta, which was considered one of the city's top dining establishments. Its location just off Fifth Avenue and in close proximity to Broadway theaters, TV studios, and publishing houses made it a frequent haunt of celebrities, including movie and TV executives. At the time, Romeo Salta was one of only a handful of restaurants in New York serving fine northern-Italian cuisine. That cuisine was the next step in the evolution of Italian food in America, and the new up-and-coming Italian restaurants classified themselves as northern Italian. **Ossobuco**, risotto, veal cutlet Milanese, **prosciutto e melone**, and **gnocchi al pesto** were on those menus, and the sauces had no tomatoes. A lot of the pasta dishes and flambé dishes at Romeo Salta were prepared tableside. Finishing some dishes tableside, such as **bollito misto** and **stinco di vitello**, was common in restaurants in Italy, but finishing flambé desserts and pasta dishes tableside was usually done only in the more elegant restaurants. And so the new northern-Italian restaurants opening in New York finished some dishes in the dining room; that was part of the charm. Felice, while working at Romeo

Salta, did a lot of this finishing. A showman with his accordion, he now loved having the customers' eyes on him as he worked in the dining room.

Even when we had friends over for dinner at home, he would end up making a flambé dessert at the table, and everyone loved it. I was fascinated by this kind of showmanship, and when Felice took me to Romeo Salta to celebrate a birthday, I got to see where and how he learned his tricks of the trade. It was an extraordinary experience. The elegant décor, the crisply pressed white linen tablecloths—nothing was lost on me. I observed the changes of china and silverware with each course, and the swapping out of the wineglasses, from champagne glass to white wine glass to red wine glass. I loved the servers' attention to details—the waiter artfully unfolding the napkin in my lap or grating fresh cheese on my pasta, the flaming dessert made at my table and served deliciously warm. I marveled, too, at all the little extras—the cookies, biscotti, and chocolates that came as unexpected surprises after the dessert was served. To think that maybe I was sitting in the seat that Sophia Loren had occupied when eating at Romeo Salta!

Little did I know that, thirty-plus years later, I would be cooking lunch for Ms. Loren and then dining with her in celebration of her eightieth birthday. It all started when I was invited in July 2014 to cook for the Festival del Sole, a festival in California's Napa Valley. Sophia's son Carlo Ponti, Jr., is a wonderful conductor and comes to the festival to perform. In 2013, he founded the Los Angeles Virtuosi Orchestra, an ensemble emphasizing music's educational value, of which he is artistic and music director. His mother came to participate in the festivities and listen to her son. While in Napa, she stayed at Villa Mille Rose, an authentic Tuscan-style villa on sixty acres with an olive orchard that produces gourmet extra-virgin olive oil, as well as artisan balsamic vinegar **"tradizionale."** This beautiful setting is owned by a mutual friend of Sophia's and mine, the philanthropist Maria Manetti Shrem.

The day after the wine festival, I cooked lunch for Sophia Loren, her son and his family, and Maria and her husband, Jan, and we all enjoyed ourselves tremendously. In 2016, the festival honored Margrit Mondavi, the widow of the Napa Valley winemaker Robert Mondavi, and Sophia Loren. It was a great evening, including dinner at the Far Niente Winery in Oakville. The next day was Sophia's birthday, and, to my delight, we all celebrated at Villa Mille Rose.

I first heard the name Sophia Loren when I was in Trieste in 1958. Her film **Houseboat** had just been released, and everyone was talking about her, how beautiful she was. At the time, I was just beginning to develop as a young woman, and I yearned to be like her. I was enamored with her looks, her shape, and the way she carried herself. But I became even more fascinated with this absolutely stunning movie star from Rome as I learned more about her and her struggles as a young woman. Sophia is the daughter of Romilda Villani and Riccardo Scicolone, a construction engineer. Scicolone was married to another woman and wouldn't marry Villani, and so the piano teacher/aspiring actress was forced to provide for her children, Sophia and Anna Maria, who was born three years after Sophia. The three of them lived in Pozzuoli, near Naples. Even when she was young, Sophia had to help her mother support the family. She pushed herself, and at age fifteen, she won a beauty contest, where Carlo Ponti (her future husband and producer) noticed her and took her under his wing.

Over the years, I came to admire her strength as a woman, her commitment and skills as an actress, and her capacity to be a warm and loving mother as well. She was able to handle it all, as I, too, have sought to do as an adult. What I noticed at our encounter in Napa was that she was a loving grandmother regardless of her fame. That only reinforced my long-standing admiration for her. And even as her birthdays passed and she grew older, she managed to retain the grace, poise, and moves that had cemented her place in history as one of the greatest actresses ever. Though older, she was still the same Sophia Loren that I remembered in the movies from my childhood.

❖ ❖

Felice was a good cook, and he loved cooking at home. Together, we liked to prepare sumptuous meals and invite friends and family over to dine with us.

We lived on the second floor of our three-family house, renting out the top and ground-level apartments to help pay the mortgage.

Having a husband and a home gave me a great sense of security. It was like the completion of a journey, even though it was certainly not what my mother had hoped for me, and perhaps not even what I had envisioned for myself. But life is like a running river; sometimes it just takes you with it, and I was fully on board, wherever it might lead me.

I was in the middle of my sophomore year at Hunter College when I learned that I was pregnant. I was enjoying my classes immensely, especially my time in the science labs. But I put my education on hold when our son, Joseph, was born at Astoria General Hospital on September 17, 1968; I promised myself I would return to university as soon as I was ready. My motherly instinct kicked in the moment I laid eyes on my infant son, and I immediately began planning all the things we would do together. I wanted him to experience the kind of freedom and closeness to nature that I had enjoyed during my childhood in Busoler.

When Joseph was about eighteen months old, we noticed he was limping, and he complained of aching in his hips. He was diagnosed with Perthes disease, in which circulation of blood to the head of the femur bone becomes inadequate and the bone becomes brittle and crumbles. It is a children's disease, and, thankfully, one that was treatable. He had to wear a brace to keep the femur bone open without pressure—which also meant that he wasn't allowed to walk for more than a year. My son's doctors had explained to me that, as long as he didn't walk, circulation would slowly return to the area and the bone would strengthen. Once the bone's condition had improved, he would be able to walk. But he wound up having to wear the brace for eighteen months. As a young mother, I focused all my attention on him.

At first, seeing my son in a brace was very frightening. He wasn't in any pain, but because he couldn't walk on his own, getting around was very difficult. I was still waitressing in Manhattan, so my mother would watch him until I got home in the evenings. She and my father were still living in the walk-up in Astoria, so I would have to carry him up and down four flights of stairs with the brace resting against my stomach. My father thought back to his days of working on cars, when it was common to sit down or lie prone on a "dolly" with four casters to slide under a car to perform repairs. He fashioned a dolly for my son to use for getting around the house. With a simple push, Joseph could wheel himself from room to room by himself—and it was fun! But we were all thankful when, after a year and a half, he was walking on his own.

Joseph was still very young when my husband voiced his desire to open his own restaurant. He had plenty of experience from his years at Romeo Salta; Gian Marino, another fine dining spot, on West Fifty-eighth Street; Mario's, on East Forty-sixth Street; and Gargiulo's Restaurant in Coney Island. He felt he was ready to have his own place, and he began looking for a business partner. After a search, he found a partner, and then spent the next year looking for a location. We needed something outside of Manhattan, because space was too expensive there. We wanted a high-end neighborhood in Queens.

Felice found a little place, Chez Françoise, a restaurant on Queens Boulevard and Sixty-seventh Road in Forest Hills that was up for sale. It had ten tables and held thirty-nine seats, with a small four-stool bar up front. At that time, Forest Hills was considered a chichi neighborhood, with its mix of single-family homes, low-rise apartment buildings, and attached town houses. There was also the leafy suburban enclave of Forest Hills Gardens, a planned community of English Tudor-style homes.

Italian restaurants at the time served Italian American food, food of adaptation, cooked by Italian immigrants, basically the dishes they remembered from back home, but made with the products they could find in America. Most of the Italian restaurants of that period had an Italian American menu, and we were not going to be any different. To cook regional Italian cuisine, one needs traditional Italian products, such as **aceto balsamico, prosciutto di Parma**, Grana Padano, Italian olive oil, and **Arborio** rice for the proper risotto. Most of these traditional ingredients—which are readily available in the United States today—were nowhere to be found in 1971.

We made a smart choice with the restaurant's location. The Italian restaurant down the street, La Stella, was doing well, and other restaurants were operating successfully in the area. Things seemed to be falling into place when, at the eleventh hour, Felice's partner announced that he was pulling out. That's when my food gene overtook my science gene, if you will, and I fully committed myself to making my husband's dream a reality.

"You can do it," I told him. "I will assist you."

I realized it was going to be difficult for us, but nothing had ever come easily to me, and my heart and soul were fully in this venture. We were a husband and wife, a team, and we were determined. Family was everything for me; it always had been, and always will be. Felice and I had some savings, and my mother and father loaned us what they could. It was a big decision, and

Matches from
Buonavia

Our first restaurant

one we didn't make hastily. We managed to scrape up enough money to buy the restaurant and reopen it as an Italian American restaurant.

We didn't have a lot to invest in renovations, so we left the restaurant almost as it was, just freshened it up a bit and changed the name and menu. We papered the walls with a red grass-cloth wall covering, a kind of natural hand-woven wallpaper, and on the bottom we put wainscot wood paneling; on the floor we installed marble-looking linoleum tiles. We covered the front with a green, red, and white striped awning, the colors of the Italian flag, with a new name in large letters, **Buonavia,** Italian for "a good road."

We named our restaurant after one that my

husband recalled from Fiume, now Rijeka, Istria. Before opening our doors, we studied what other restaurants were serving in the area. We examined every detail of their menus to learn what was selling, and not selling. We hired an Italian American chef, whom Felice knew from one of his prior restaurant jobs. Felice liked both his demeanor and his food. My mother got involved, too. She helped with the homemade pastas—gnocchi, pappardelle, garganelli, or, as it is called in Istria, **fuzi**—and watched Joe in the evenings while we prepared for the grand opening.

We began promoting the restaurant while we were doing the remodeling. People were curious, so we printed up flyers and started putting them in the lobbies of apartment buildings around the area, and we offered passersby a free drink or a glass of wine when they came in. We tested and retested the recipes to make sure they were just as we wanted them. Even before we formally opened the doors, people came in to look while the place was being remodeled. We took advantage of the impromptu visits, sharing our testing dishes and soliciting people's opinions. With each passing day, it seemed that more local residents started to pop in. I guess that word probably had spread of a young couple giving tastings—not only a little taste of the food, but a sip of wine to go with it.

The skies opened up and it started pouring rain the night we opened our doors to customers,

April 17, 1971. We could hardly believe the line of people huddled beneath the awning waiting to be seated. The restaurant was busy right away, and people just kept coming. Felice served as maître d' and bartender. I started first in the front, welcoming people and seating them. It was very exciting—the energy of having people fill our restaurant and enjoy our food was like shots of adrenaline for me. After ten to twelve hours of work, I was ready for more. I began jumping from the dining room to the kitchen. When the dining room was full and the orders began accumulating, I would run to the kitchen to help the chefs, and sometimes I would

At the bar at Buonavia,
c. 1975

end up serving the food to the tables. In that little restaurant, I learned all the essential stations. I even tended our four-seat bar when Felice was busy.

We worked long, grueling hours, and I had to juggle my responsibilities at the restaurant with my role as caregiver to our young son. Determined to make it all work, I approached my mother and proposed that she and my father give up the apartment in Astoria and rent the ground-floor apartment of our three-story house. After some consideration, they agreed. Having them with us meant that my mother was able to care for Joseph in the evenings, while I was at work.

It felt good to provide them with a comfortable, more permanent home. There was also a great sense of unity, with all of us together under one roof. My brother, Franco, had completed his engineering degree at Brooklyn Poly. When he graduated in 1968, he got a job with IBM as an electrical engineer in the company's offices in East Fishkill, New York, about ninety minutes north of New York City, and he moved there with some college friends who were also hired by the technology giant. After all these years, he still works for IBM, having acquired a Ph.D. and amassed many patents for his innovative work.

In 1969, he met his wife-to-be, Margaret O'Donoghue, at a social event in an Irish dance hall in Woodside, Queens. Margaret emigrated from Ireland with a degree in nursing. She was working as a midwife at St. Joseph's Hospital in Far Rockaway, where she lived in a nurse's residence with several other young Irish nurses. Margaret and my brother were married four years later, on July 7, 1973, and would go on to have three children—two sons, Paul and Eric, and a daughter, Estelle. Today they also have four beautiful grandchildren, Sofia, Adrian, Desmond, and Ruby.

Our first year after opening Buonavia was an exciting time. The business was growing, and we were learning how to be restaurateurs, managers, bartenders, sous-chefs, and most of all, hosts in the welcoming Italian style. We endeavored to make everyone feel at home when seated at our tables, and we served them fresh and delicious food. Our spirits were high; we were paying our bills and paying off the loans we had accumulated in opening the restaurant. I guess our celebratory mood got to our very core, and one of the greatest products of that mood was our daughter, Tanya, who was born on May 24, 1972.

19

Villa Secondo

In Italy, people believe that babies always bring good luck, and Tanya was our good-luck charm indeed. I worked until just one day before I gave birth at Astoria General Hospital. She was like a cherub, pink and smooth-skinned, and all she wanted to do was eat and sleep. Almost from the moment we brought her home, Joseph took on a protective big brother attitude. I stayed home for six weeks with the baby, and then I began a slow return to work.

One question I get asked most often is how a woman can find success being a chef and raising children, too. I was lucky to have the support of my family, especially my mother, who helped me raise my children, but I must say I had moments of personal guilt after Tanya was born. **How can I leave my infant child and go to work for the whole evening?** I fretted.

My husband needed me to help keep the restaurant operating smoothly, and we had a number of loans to pay off. But the mother-versus-work conflict was growing within me. My new baby needed her mom near her, and the business needed me to survive. I could not find peace and turned to one of the few people I knew and deeply trusted at the time, Dr. Stein, my children's pediatrician (I needed advice, and psychiatrists were not in vogue then, at least not with my crowd).

Dr. Stein was a very wise man, and in a few simple words he resolved my predicament. He told me that, basically, children want happy parents, and they are happy when the home is happy. He saw the passion I had as a new mother, but also the need and desire I had for cooking and the restaurant. He understood that I would not be a happy homemaker if it meant giving up my work life. "If you are going to be at home with the children and you are going to be sad all the time, that is not a plus," he explained.

Dr. Stein assured me that, within my busy schedule, I would find the time to give Joe and Tanya the love they needed. And if I was happy because of the work I was doing, that would be evident in the way I interacted with and loved my children. Pursue your passion and always include your children in your journey, he counseled. Let them know that they are contributors to your career and success.

I really took Dr. Stein's advice to heart. When I was at work, I was indeed happy and involved, and when I came home, I did so with the desire to be with my kids, to hug them, kiss them, and play with them. I tried to keep them with us as much as we could, so we schlepped them all over the place. Like so many parents today, I learned to juggle my responsibilities and carefully manage my time.

The children would often come to the restaurant, beginning with short stints when they were small. Either we would have an early dinner and then Grandma would take them home, or I would take them home, prepare dinner, and return to the restaurant after the meal. We didn't live far, so it wasn't a hardship. At the time, my mother was still working at Walken's Bakery, but after Tanya arrived, she agreed to leave her job and step into the role of full-time caretaker.

The children were always part of what we did; they knew the restaurant and were comfortable being there. It was simply where Mommy and Daddy worked. The hours we spent there together only made us closer as a family.

Once they started school, I improvised a place for them to sit in the back of the restaurant where they could do their homework, using low stacks of empty tomato boxes as "desk" and "chairs" for them. As they got older, they would come to the restaurant after school and do their homework at one of the tables. Felice and I both stressed to our children the importance of a good education. "You are going to get an education and get a real American job" was our mantra. There were moments when I regretted not completing my college education, and I was determined to ensure that both my children took their studies seriously, worked hard, and attended university. I wanted them to be able to choose a career path based on their interests and skill set, and I didn't want them to simply follow Felice's and my footsteps.

On Sundays, we would sometimes take them to dances and other social events. As little ones, they would end up sleeping on chairs. The bigger they got, the more involved they became. When we took them to weddings and Istrian dances, they'd run around, having a ball. If it was late and the children were tired, I would put two chairs together, lay them down to sleep, and then continue to dance. The kids were listening to the music and seeing their parents dancing and having a good time.

As they grew older, I spent as much time with them as I could. It was important for me to be there for them and their special moments. Joe played hockey as a boy, and I sometimes took off from work to drive him to games. Some days, I wasn't able to make it and relied on the other players' mothers to take him or bring him home. The other moms counted on me, too; I was the one they could depend on to provide the food for the whole team after an afternoon game. There were other parents who were immigrants, some who worked in factories and didn't have the luxury of a live-in relative or the flexibility in their schedule that I had, so I considered myself fortunate. Though I wasn't always available to take my children to and from school, they managed. I organized bus pick-ups, and my mother and father helped out when needed. Sometimes I think that my parents played a far more pivotal role in the upbringing of Joseph and Tanya than I did. Their unconditional love, as well as the wisdom they provided, gave my children a deeper understanding of their roots and helped them grow up to be great human beings.

I feel that today the importance of grandparents' role within the family is not fully appreciated; chil-

In the garden at our first house in Astoria, Queens, corner of Forty-fifth Street and Twenty-fifth Avenue: Joseph, Tanya, and I, 1974

dren do not usually have the opportunity to be enriched by close proximity to and strong relationships with their grandparents. I know how important those relationships were in my life, and how a lot of the basic understanding I have of life and its values is rooted in my relationship with my grandparents.

Buonavia was so successful that, when the storefront next to us on Queens Boulevard became available in 1973, we took out a lease and expanded into that space. It was at that point that I got involved full-time in the kitchen. Even though I had been working in restaurants for a long time, I was not yet a chef. Now that we had tripled in size, expanding from thirty-nine seats to 120, I found myself in the position of sous-chef. I wanted to learn how to run a kitchen, but I also wanted to learn the Italian American recipes and share the Italian regional flavors with our customers. As I was learning this cuisine, I realized how different indeed the recipes were from the recipes prepared by my grandma, mother, and aunt. I knew that at some point I wanted to cook and share those recipes, the regional recipes of Istria and various regions of Italy, with my guests. Many of the ingredients we used in Italy were not available in the United States, so we had to improvise with what was here. You need special rice, short-grain rice such as **Arborio** and **Carnaroli**, to make risotto. There was none to be had in the States until the late seventies, when it began to be imported, so we made risotto with the long-grain rice available at the supermarket. My father loved risotto and wanted it at least once or twice a week, but every time it was the same story: he would complain that it was not creamy, that it was not as good as he remembered. Then **Arborio** rice started coming from Italy, and everything was fine again.

It was during these early years at Buonavia that I learned how to manage a restaurant kitchen, butcher whole legs of veal, and fillet fish. The more I worked in the kitchen, the more regional dishes of my childhood I introduced, such as all the fresh pastas Nonna Rosa and I used to make. I also began to prepare regional sauces to go with them: pappardelle and mushrooms, garganelli with duck **guazzetto**. In the winter months, polenta with venison **guazzetto** was on the menu. **Guazzetto** involves the long simmering of tougher cuts of meat or game meats along with fresh herbs, bay leaves, rosemary, and sage, as well as dry spices such as cloves, black peppercorns, and dried mushrooms. We made delicious **guazzettos** out of squab, quail, and duck, as well as tough free-range chickens. Lamb, pork neck, and ribs also made delicious **guazzettos**.

I love making **guazzetto** with the meat still on the bone. At home, we just take the bones in our hands and eat it as if we were eating ribs; the fun and taste are in getting every morsel off that bone. However, in our current restaurants—Felidia, Becco, Lidia's

Kansas City, and Lidia's Pittsburgh—we pluck the tender meat off the bones and shred it back into the sauce, making it like saucy pulled pork. Then we dress our pastas with it.

We slowly introduced polenta to our customers at Buonavia. It was not a dish typically found in Italian American restaurants, but it was a beloved item from my childhood.

Although corn is a New World product, introduced to Europe after Columbus discovered America, corn dried and milled into polenta is the starch of choice in Istria and the Friuli–Venezia Giulia region of northeastern Italy. Corn does not need much space to grow, but gives great yields. It was the basic food during the lean periods in the northeastern part of Italy. Almost everything from the corn was used. The kernels were for corn flour (polenta) and for feed for the courtyard animals. The husk leaves were dried and used for summer mattresses and to line the animal pens. Even the cob, after the dried kernels of corn were shucked, was milled, and the rough flaky white flour was cooked into a porridge with vegetable peels to feed the pigs. Even though corn is American and grits are a common staple in the South, I had to be careful in introducing the Italian version, polenta, to my American customers.

Slowly, one dish at a time, in my corner of the Buonavia kitchen I would cook recipes from my regional memory. I was not sure how these dishes would be accepted. Most of the time, we would not put the item on the menu, but would offer it to customers in a small tasting dish alongside the things they had ordered. I would go around the tables, enthusiastically explaining the dish and its origins. We kept introducing new dishes, including venison, as we tried to go beyond what other restaurants were serving. We had friends who were hunters, and they sometimes brought us deer meat from their expeditions, which we would share with our customers as a dish of venison **guazzetto.** We also introduced our patrons to **cozze alla Triestina,** mussels in a white-wine-and-breadcrumb sauce, a regional recipe that differed from the commonly prepared mussels marinara with lots of red sauce that was being served by most of the Italian American restaurants. Not every try was successful, and people were skeptical of some of the dishes. For instance, liver **alla Veneziana** is a typical dish in which the calf's liver is cut into thin slices, then smothered with an equal amount of sliced onions, a few fresh bay leaves, a splash of vinegar, and plenty of ground black pepper. Served with a mound of steaming polenta, this was a delicacy for us. These days, liver **alla Veneziana** is widely accepted, and those who love liver will order it if they see it on the menu; we offer it regularly at our restaurants. Tripe was another story. Customers were downright defiant in refusing dishes that included tripe. But I love tripe. To this day, most Americans will not even try it, but I still make it at Felidia for those few customers, like me, for whom tripe is a fond-memory food.

I enthusiastically jumped into my role as sous-chef at Buonavia. I even returned to Queens College in Flushing (right off the Long Island Expressway, and close to home) to take new courses, including the anthropology of food and the science of food. I'd head there in the morning, right after the kids went off to school. I wanted to know everything I could about food—and I still do. My courses at Hunter College in biology and chemistry helped me understand a lot about why things happen in a pot, why egg yolks and oil whip up into creamy mayonnaise, how yeast rises, and why whipping egg yolks, sugar, and Marsala yields a delicious zabaglione. I recall being fascinated by Harold McGee's first book, **On Food and Cooking: The Science and Lore of the Kitchen,** and I kept it, and still have the latest version of it, in the kitchen as my Bible. The more I studied, the more questions I had. I wanted to understand how the food culture of a people and a country evolves, and I realized how the different foreign occupations of parts of Italy through the centuries have shaped what is on the plates of Italians today.

The occupation of Sicily by the Moors, the Arabs, and the Spaniards is evident in Sicilian cooking. The diversity of spices in Veneto and the surrounding areas goes back to La Serenissima, the Venice city-state, when seafaring traders brought back black pepper, cloves, cinnamon, nutmeg, and ginger from the Middle East and the Orient. Farther north, in the Friuli–Venezia Giulia region—ruled by the Austro-Hungarian Empire for years and bordering Eastern Europe—the cuisine uses sauerkraut and paprika, and is known for its strudels and the dessert culture of the Austro-Hungarians.

It's easy to spot examples of foreign influence on the foods found in Istria and Sicily. For example, sauerkraut, which is commonly found in Eastern Europe and can also be found in Istria. My grandmother would pickle cabbage into sauerkraut, and she'd use turnips to create **brovada,** a typical Fruilian dish. **Brovada** is made with whole purple turnips, marinated, and fermented for forty days. Stuffed peppers, which can also be found in Istria, are a common dish in Hungary, Bulgaria, and in old Yugoslavia. **Ćevapčići,** a grilled dish of minced meat, and **sarma,** a recipe close to the Greek stuffed grape leaves but using cabbage leaves, are both served throughout Eastern Europe and the Balkan countries.

Many of the traditional dishes of southern Italy were inspired by foods introduced to the region by invaders and occupiers over the centuries. The Phoenicians, Moors, Greeks, Germans, Austrians, Hungarians, Yugoslavs, Spaniards, and French all contributed to what is now Italian cuisine.

The Phoenicians, great traders and seafarers who

originated in Lebanon, introduced the Sicilians to beans such as lentils, sea salt, and cereals, most notably durum wheat. They also brought the fig, a crop that is native to the Middle East and now grows throughout Italy. During their occupation, they also planted vineyards with grape species brought from their homeland, thus introducing Marsala and other sweet dessert wines to the Sicilians.

During the area's colonization by the Greeks, in the eighth to sixth centuries B.C., seafood dishes using octopus and squid took root; seafood was a dietary staple for the ancient Greeks, as well as for the Romans. These early Greek settlers also cultivated spelt, an ancient wheat grain used in many Italian baked goods these days.

The Moors, who conquered parts of Italy in the tenth century, brought pine nuts, sugarcane, citrus, apricots, and raisins from North Africa. They also planted the first nut trees, yielding pistachios, almonds, cashews, hazelnuts, and walnuts, now all very much a part of the Sicilian cuisine. **Frutta di Martorana,** or **pasta reale**, the sugary almond paste we call marzipan, from which many Italian desserts are made, was also introduced into the cuisine by the Moors, as was coffee—a product that would later spark an intense trade war between the Moors and the Venetians. **Granita** (similar to sorbet, but coarser and richer), another contribution of the Moors, was created by bringing blocks of ice down from the mountains and flavoring the shavings with sugary syrups. Adding milk or cream to these frozen treats created gelato.

Tomatoes did not arrive in Europe until the mid-sixteenth century, when Spanish conquistadors from South America introduced the tomato plant to the Continent; the first written account of the tomato reportedly surfaced in Tuscany around that time. Before then, Italians dressed their pasta with olive oils, cheeses, vegetables, and anchovies. Had it not been for all these foreign influences, dishes such as **aragosta alla Catalana** (a salad of spiny Mediterranean lobster and fresh tomatoes that originated in Sardegna, or Sardinia) wouldn't exist today. And the famous Austrian dessert **Schmarrn,** a crêpe sprinkled with icing and sugar often served with jam, popular in Trentino–Alto Adige, would also be absent from Italian cuisine.

My desire to know ever more about food remains, and I continue to learn and experiment each and every day. I love attending the annual Oxford Symposium on Food & Cookery, which began in 1979 as a series of seminars on science and cookery and has since morphed into an international weekend conference held at St. Catherine's College in Oxford, England. Academics, chefs, food critics, writers, and others with an interest in food gather each year to exchange ideas and discuss current and historical issues surrounding food and its culture.

Some of the regional dishes that Felice and I introduced to our customers at Buonavia have become chic, such as sweetbreads and the once-unpopular liver **alla Veneziana**. I still encourage my chefs to work with all of the parts of the animal, just as Grandma Rosa did; she wasted nothing once the animal had been sacrificed to be our food. When she killed a chicken, usually on Saturday for a Sunday meal, she had me help her pluck all the plumage, and then she would dangle the whole chicken over an open fire to burn off any remaining hairs. She saved the head, the neck, the tip of the wings, and the feet after chopping off the claws, some loose skin, the cleaned stomach, and extra fat for soup. The liver, heart, and intestines were made into a frittata with some onions. The cluster of unborn eggs found in the body cavity—all of different sizes, from the size of a blueberry to the size of a mature egg—were also made into a frittata, which was usually the **merenda**, the midmorning snack.

My job was the cleaning of the intestines, not a pleasant one. Grandma would squeeze all the food out of them under running water, and then I had to cut them open with scissors and wash them well in vinegar and water. When they were clean, she would let them soak in clean water and vinegar for an hour, then cut them, and into the frittata they went. The rest of the chicken was cut into pieces on the bone and simmered for an hour or two, depending on how old and tough the chicken was, into a delicious **guazzetto**. By then, the gnocchi or **fuzi** (garganelli) would be made, and lunch for the family was ready. Steaming soup, pasta with chicken **guazzetto,** and a salad—Sunday supper was delicious. I cannot help but wonder what happens these days to the rest of the chicken, after all those chicken breasts being requested at the restaurants and sold at the butcher shops and supermarkets are consumed. Where do all the other parts of the chicken go?

Felice and I worked hard to include dishes that were meaningful to us, and as a result, much to our delight, our popularity and our customers' trust in us continued to grow. After the lunch service, we would have our staff lunch. The chefs and the assistants would sit with us, tasting and working on current recipes and giving us new ideas. The brainstorming never stopped. We did it in the restaurant kitchen and when we were home. Stuffed cabbage, **jota** (a soup of sauerkraut and beans), beef goulash, **palačinke** (a Croatian crêpe), Hungarian **rigo jansci** (chocolate cake filled with a chocolate mousse filling) all eventually found their way onto our menu.

In a way, the work never ended. Even when the restaurant was closed, there was always shopping for the best-quality ingredients, or staying late to test out new recipes. We were constantly trying to do better and to surprise our clientele. We always stayed at the restaurant until the very last customer went home, sometimes until midnight or 1:00 a.m. On some nights, I would go home earlier and Felice would stay behind to tend to our customers and close up. I needed to get up in the morning to give breakfast to the children and send them off to school. Once they were out of the house and on their way, I would go back to bed for a nap.

At the end of a long night, especially on a Friday or Saturday evening, Felice and I would look for ways to unwind and have a little fun after closing time. Often that meant going to one of the **tavernas** in Astoria, to listen to music and dance until we were ready to drop. It made no difference if we had worked until midnight at the restaurant; we still went out. A lot of adrenaline comes with working in the restaurant business, and it keeps you awake. One of our favorite haunts was Come Prima, at Forty-fifth Street and Thirty-first Avenue, which was run by a friend of ours, Carlo Sivocci, and often featured live music. They had a guitarist, an accordionist, and sometimes a local singer. We would usually get there after midnight, right around the same time that other restaurateurs were arriving, and dance until closing time. For Felice and me, it was our opportunity to relax and think about something other than Buonavia. We knew the kids were safely home with my mother. Even on the nights when we didn't go out after work, I would still come home and have to do something: laundry, ironing, planning the meals for the coming week. I needed time to wind down before going to sleep.

Keeping costs low was of particular concern to

our young business, and Felice had a lot of inge-
nuity in this area. He would go early in the morning to the Fulton Fish Market, a wholesale market,
then on South Street in lower Manhattan, where
fish vendors sold their goods, all fresh and at a low
price. We had a yellow Chevrolet station wagon,
and Felice had a stainless-steel tray made to cover
the cargo area behind the seats so he could easily
transport the fish, which were packed in ice to keep
them fresh. Unfortunately, the tray didn't always
protect the car from damage. Invariably, the ice
would start melting the moment Felice pulled away
from the market. If he made a short stop in traffic,
the load would shift forward, and the water would
slosh out of the tray—and drench the back of the
car. The water would eventually dry, leaving the car
smelling of fish. Our son, Joe, always talks about
going to the market with his father and remembers
the fishy stench. And it wasn't just the smell of fish
that had the kids complaining. We used the station
wagon to transport all of the meat and poultry from
the markets to the restaurant, so the odor of the
juice of chicken guts was frequently intermingled
with the fishy smells. In the hot summer months,
the car smelled to holy heaven. Tanya and Joe were
embarrassed to invite their friends to drive with us
in the station wagon, and avoided offering our services as carpool drivers as much as they could.

Felice often insisted that Joe accompany him to
the Fulton Fish Market in the early mornings to

buy the fish, or to the Hunter's Point Market in the Bronx for the produce. He wanted our son to understand that achieving success in the restaurant business didn't happen through some kind of magic. The key was hard, hard work and many long hours; there were no shortcuts to success. The people who made it were the ones who had all the right skills—picking the right dishes for the menu, finding the right staff, choosing the right location—and a deep-down determination to succeed.

Tanya was also invited along for Felice's fish-buying trips to the docks of Freeport, Long Island, where the fishermen sold their catches right off the boats. Tanya enjoyed these weekend excursions with her father, because it meant lunch out with him. Felice would order a big pot of steamers for himself, and a hot dog for Tanya, something I would never have allowed her to eat if I had been there with them.

To this day, one of the most important jobs in all of our restaurants is the sourcing of the best local, seasonal, nutritional, and environmentally sound vegetables, fish, meats, and cheeses.

The children were ever more involved with our work, and began to accompany us on our annual research trips all over Italy. Every summer, we closed the restaurant for three weeks to visit family and travel to different regions of the country to learn more and more about the food of Italy, about the traditional regional products, about the wines and the now iconic Italian wine producers. We dubbed these yearly pilgrimages abroad our "summer vacations." In reality, they were endless research-and-tasting trips.

Tanya and Joe experienced the fun and adventure of travel along with the occasional challenges that came with being on the road. Sometimes we'd eat two lunches or two dinners in a single day, simply because we were eager to sample the local fare and discover new tastes and recipes that we could bring home to our customers. As we did these constant restaurant stops, we would hear the kids moan from the backseat, "**Oh no!** Not another restaurant!"

We would also explore local wineries and track down interesting wines and new sources of foods for our restaurant. Some of the wineries we visited were in centuries-old medieval castles; others were in more contemporary structures that could easily have been mistaken for mansions. No matter where we went, there were surprises for the eyes and the palate as we toured winery after winery and sampled countless reds, whites, rosés, and dessert wines.

Some winery visits were memorable because of the trips down long, damp corridors filled with huge, ancient barrels. Others were impressive because of the quality of the product. The wineries also offered a shaded and cool respite from the hot Italian sun. Every so often, I caught Tanya eyeing a cute Italian boy, or wandering off to explore majestic structures and beautiful grounds.

Over time, I established contacts with the local Italian journalists and food reviewers, and they would tell me the "must-try" restaurants, wineries, and food artisans to visit in a particular area. I would call or have the journalist or restaurateur call in advance, and tell them that we would like to taste their products and possibly spend a day or two with their chef. We would introduce ourselves to the local restaurateurs and winemakers, and to the producers of various local products, including the olive growers. During our continuing visits to Italy, we visited all twenty regions of Italy multiple times. The children got to meet iconic chefs such as Gualtiero Marchesi of Milan; the Cerea brothers, Enrico and Roberto, of the Ristorante Da Vittorio in Bergamo; Ernesto Iaccarino of the Ristorante Don Alfonso 1890 in Sant'Agata sui Due Golfi (near Sorrento); Mauro Uliassi of Uliassi in Senigallia; Aimo and Nadia Moroni of Il Luogo di Aimo e Nadia in Milan; and great wine producers, including Antinori, Livio Felluga, Angelo Gaja, Bruno Cerreto, Bruno Giacosa, Donatella Cinelli Colombini, De Bartoli, and Vietti. Not only did we visit and do tastings with these great people; our whole family developed lasting friendships.

The seventies and eighties marked the introduction of many Italian wines and traditional products in America, and we wanted to have all these great products in our restaurants to share with our customers. To a great degree, we succeeded.

As luck would have it, next door to Buonavia on Queens Boulevard was a liquor store, Goldstar Wines and Liquors, owned by an Italian American gentleman by the name of Lou Iacucci. Lou was an aficionado of Italian wines. When he came to the restaurant to eat, we would always talk wine. He had a lot of direct contact with wine producers in Italy. Whenever he knew we were traveling there, he would tell us where to go. Okay, he'd say, you need to go here and taste this or that wine. I would come back and tell him, "Okay, Lou, import this for me." He went on to develop a bigger, important company, and he continued to expand. But by then I had a whole network of importers, and the producers would come to me directly. I became a kind of liaison for the wines and other products as a result of our many trips across Italy.

Those vacation-research trips had a huge impact on our children. Joseph and Tanya absorbed all of what they saw and tasted, and these experiences came to shape their adult lives and ultimately steer their professional choices. At the time, they viewed these marathon excursions as tiresome work-holidays to be suffered through; the trips were more about endurance than pleasure for them, especially the never-ending drives from here to there in the sweltering August heat, in the backseat of rental cars with no air-conditioning. The seats were all velour back then; drenched in sweat, we would be plastered to them. When going fast on the Autostrada, we could only open the windows a little bit or the inside of the car would get too windy; this made for hot and unpleasant car rides.

Sometimes Joe and Tanya would refuse to get out of the car to join us inside the restaurants for our second or third meals of the day, which inevitably led to fights. There were no single-serving plastic water bottles back then, so we traveled with large glass bottles of San Pellegrino. The kids would wait for Felice and me to disappear inside a restaurant and break out the bottles of Pellegrino. They would shake them to gas them up, then spray each other, drenching themselves and the backseat. It was a good way for them to cool off, and the seats were usually dry by the time Felice and I returned.

❧ ❦

Buonavia was in its seventh year when, one day, on our drive home from Forest Hills, we noticed a "For Rent" sign in the window of a little Italian restaurant on the corner of Horace Harding Boulevard, now Horace Harding Expressway, and 184th Street in Fresh Meadows, Queens. By then, we had sold our three-story house in Astoria and moved to leafy Bayside, Queens. Astoria was becoming increasingly crowded, and we wanted to provide our

212 762-7355
LIDIA AND FELICE

Villa Secondo

ITALIAN RESTAURANT

184-22 HORACE HARDING EXPRESSWAY
FRESH MEADOWS, N.Y. 11365

The business card for our second restaurant

children with a home where they could run and play and feel safe. Bayside, a bit farther from the city, had lots of greenery and open space. Since my parents were moving with us, we chose a split-level mother/daughter house on a lovely tree-lined street.

It was the middle of summer when we moved in, and the temperature reached a scorching ninety degrees as Felice and I schlepped back and forth between Bayside and Astoria, lugging furniture and boxes. The new house had a grass front lawn with inground sprinklers that we turned on more for the kids than to keep the grass green. Tanya still recalls fondly the hours she spent happily racing around, cooling off in her favorite bathing suit, which had a watermelon design; she told us later that coming to the new house felt like we had moved to heaven.

The only downside to the house in Bayside was that the commute to Forest Hills was a little longer and required that we take the Long Island Expressway, which was always crowded with traffic, no matter what time of day or night. Still, it was our daily drive along this new route that had led us to discover the available restaurant space in Fresh Meadows: the storefront was visible from the highway.

Felice and I were both excited at the prospect of opening a second location, and we arranged a meeting with the landlord to learn more about the terms of the lease. The size of the restaurant was something that we could handle—about twelve tables, which could seat fifty to sixty people—and it was located in an upper-middle-class neighborhood, which meant a restaurant-going clientele. Its visibility from the LIE made it even more desirable, and the movie complex up the road and the Bloomingdale's just behind it would bring people to the area. Knowing what good food we could offer, we felt confident this was the right location for us to expand into.

After some discussion, Felice and I signed a fifteen-year lease on the restaurant. We decided to keep its current name, Villa Secondo, or second villa; it seemed appropriate. We hired a young Italian American chef and sent him to work in the kitchen of Buonavia for a few months until the grand opening. Felice and I decided that he would continue to manage Buonavia, while Villa Secondo would be under my direction.

In 1978, we opened Villa Secondo with basically the same menu as Buonavia. We were busy from opening day, with a line out the door almost every night. Part of running a successful restaurant is providing a comfortable setting for your customers, taking their needs into consideration, making them feel welcome and at home. We had worked hard to develop this kind of rapport with our patrons and earn their trust in the food we were providing them, and we kept this philosophy at Villa Secondo. Many of our customers from Buonavia came to Fresh Meadows to support our efforts and sample the fare, and the feedback was very positive. During our seven years in Forest Hills, we had developed a loyal following, and I am still grateful to all the old-timers who supported us in those early years. What is amazing is that I have customers from Buonavia, and their children, who, to this day, continue to come to our New York flagship restaurant, Felidia.

At Villa Secondo, we offered more traditional Italian recipes on the menu, dishes we had learned and honed during our yearly pilgrimages to Italy. My involvement in the kitchen continued to grow, and I became more and more comfortable putting my touches on the meals we served. I saw that Americans were finally ready for **real** Italian cuisine, and I boldly served it to them, and the results were gratifying. Tanya loved coming to Villa Secondo in the afternoons, mostly because of all the stray cats that gathered behind the Chinese restaurant next door. There was always a litter of kittens for her to play with, and she never seemed to get bored with petting and naming them.

My father was retired by then, as was my mother. They loved the new added outdoor space of our Bayside home. My father turned a piece of the backyard into a vegetable garden, which kept both of my parents busy. He was very handy, and used old glass doors and windows to turn part of the garden into greenhouses, so we could have our salads and zuccherino during the winter months, too.

Our new home had a double garage, so my father turned the area along one wall into his workshop. He had golden hands and could fix anything that needed fixing in the house, as well as in our restaurants. If the slicing machine broke, he would repair it. When the rivets on the sauté pans got loose, he would replace them and make the handles stable again. He would even hammer the base of the pan back to make it even, so instead of buying new ones we could keep using them.

In our backyard garden we now had bushes of rosemary, sage, and bay leaves. My mother would make bouquets of herbs to send to the restaurants. Not only were the aromas more intense; harvesting the herbs for cooking from our garden felt like it had when I had done it with Grandma Rosa in Busoler.

I loved collaborating with our restaurant chefs and developing new presentations and combinations of dishes. The praise and accolades coming from the customers, and the dining room full of guests, gave us ever more affirmation that we were on the right path. I loved sharing my craft and excitement; in the restaurants' off hours, I began giving demonstrations of recipes. People came to those and then stayed for dinner.

Soon we had journalists coming from Manhattan to review our restaurants, singing our praises, prompting diners from the city to make the trip to Queens to give us a try. One of our new customers was an Italian American woman named Rose Gatto. Rose lived in nearby Rego Park, and she soon became a regular at Buonavia. I liked Rose, and over time we became good friends. A heavy-set woman, she reminded me a lot of Zia Nina. Rose owned her own public-relations firm and was well known in the Italian American community. Through her work, she was somehow connected to a newly launched Italian television station that was airing a cooking show in Italian called **In Cucina con Luisa.** She suggested that Felice and I appear on the show as guest chefs. The program was filmed out of a studio in New Jersey, and we would have to make our own way there.

I was a nervous wreck on the drive. I had spent hours choosing my outfit, agonizing over my hairstyle, my makeup, even my apron. I thought that for television you had to be glamorous. I was so worried about how I looked, but once the cameras started rolling and Luisa, Felice, and I started conversing, I slowly relaxed.

Luisa was a lovely woman, blond and attractive, and talking to her about what I knew best— food—helped put me at ease. I just chatted with her as if we were together in my kitchen at home. Even though the television cameras were present, I just focused on what I was doing; I transcended the cameras and focused on the food. It was not as easy for Felice. It quickly became evident that I was the more eloquent one and that he was uncomfortable in the spotlight. I loved sharing my passion and knowledge with the audience, and it showed.

Interest in Buonavia continued to grow, and we were getting more and more requests from customers to bring our cuisine to Manhattan. The idea was enticing, and Felice and I began weighing our business options and growth. For me, cooking was about sharing with my guests the authentic cuisine of the various regions of Italy. I wanted—and felt I was ready to—cook and bring these flavors to the big stage that was Manhattan.

Felice and I began to research the value of our two successful restaurants in Queens, how much could we sell them for, and what we could afford to buy in Manhattan if we did. We wanted to sell them while they still had allure and a strong, loyal clientele. We dreamed of opening a place like many we had seen in Italy—cozy, with a comfortable, homey feel, and at the same time with real character and with the elegance of fine linens and silver and beautiful china and glassware.

In 1979, we found a location we both liked on New York's East Side. It was a brownstone at 243 East Fifty-eighth Street, between Second and Third Avenues. With its cozy feel and exposed brick-wall interior, the building reminded us of places we had seen and loved in Italy. In Italy, a lot of the restaurants are part of the houses where the owners live— **casa e bottega,** as they say in Italian, a home and a store all in one dwelling.

The brownstone had that feel, although we were not planning to reside on the premises. The living area on the upper floors was already rented to Tom Penn, the son of Irving Penn, the well-known American photographer. If we did manage to raise enough money to buy the building, we would need the rental income to help us pay the mortgage.

At the time, Fifty-eighth Street was buzzing with great Italian restaurants: Tre Scalini, La Girafe, Altri Tempi, Gian Marino, Bruno's, Anche Vivolo, and La Camelia. We figured that if diners were filling these popular dining spots, some of those customers would surely visit us and try our food. The current business operating on the site was a Spanish restaurant called San Martin. Their commercial kitchen was operating from a makeshift extension the owner had added in the building's rear yard.

Felice and I could use the restaurant currently operating on the premises as a foundation for the one we envisioned. Another plus was the parking lot on Second Avenue, which meant that people coming in from Queens and Long Island would have a place to park their cars.

The more I thought about the possibility of opening a restaurant in Manhattan, the more excited I became.

I had a story to tell, and I wanted a forum from which to tell it. I wanted to serve real Italian food. Not American Italian food, but **Italian** food. Still, I knew that Felice and I would be taking a big financial gamble, and there was no guarantee that we'd be able to turn our dream into reality.

Even with the sale of both restaurants, Felice and I needed to borrow money from my parents in order to purchase the brownstone and create the new restaurant. My mother and father were always on the cautious side. "You know what you have," they told us, referring to the two successful businesses in Queens that we had built. They wanted us to be pragmatic when making a financial decision of this magnitude. But, in the end, they were encouraging. They had faith in us and would support whatever we chose to do.

Felice and I met with the building's owner, hoping to hammer out an arrangement that would work with our financial constraints. We were thrilled when he told us he was willing to wait for the deposit payment until we sold our two businesses, and a verbal agreement was struck.

That night, we went home to Bayside, where my mother had prepared a simple dinner for the family. Excited, we opened a bottle of wine and continued to make calculations on the money we had and how it was going to last to build our new restaurant.

Little did we know how over-budget the project would go—or how close we would come to not being able to afford to open our doors to customers. Launching our dream restaurant in Manhattan would prove to be perhaps the most difficult business undertaking ever for Felice and me. We had no idea what lay ahead, and maybe it was better that way.

PART FIVE

20

Building Felidia

At thirty-two, with two young children and two successful restaurants under my belt, I took on what would prove to be the most daunting and risky project of my life, the building of Felidia. Picking a name for our restaurant was the easy part. Felice and I opted for a conjunction of our two names—reflecting our decision to make this restaurant a team effort that we were both fully vested in. Though owning a restaurant had initially been Felice's dream, it had become mine as well, and now we'd staked everything we had on the future of this one turn-of-the-century Manhattan brownstone. From that point on, it was one challenge after another, each bigger than the last. Toward the end, as project costs soared and deadlines loomed, I feared we weren't going to make it—and we almost didn't.

We were now going to be competing against some of the top Italian restaurants in the nation, and we knew we were going to have to up our game. Man-

Felidia's original business card

hattan is a highly competitive market, where not just the cuisine but also a broader "vision" for the restaurant is key. Doing things on a shoestring budget and repurposing things we already had, as we had done with Buonavia and Villa Secondo, wasn't going to work in this market. We were going to have to do things differently this time around, and that meant hiring outside professionals to assist us in bringing our vision to fruition.

We'd never used a designer for either of our restaurants in Queens, so hiring a professional firm was a new step for us, as well as a significant added expense. In the past, Felice and I had created our own vision for each of our restaurants, and always with a strict budget in mind. We were accustomed to visiting different restaurants, and making mental notes of what we liked and didn't like. It could be a specific type of chair that could draw our attention, or table, or the design of an entrance, or even artwork hung on the walls. All those various design elements played into a diner's experience at a restaurant, and our goal was to create a comfortable environment where people could enjoy not just our cuisine but a memorable setting. For budgetary reasons, we hadn't changed the interiors all that much in our first two restaurants; we tried to economize by recycling what we could, and spend where it counted most to us—which often meant new pots and cooking utensils for the kitchens. But this was a whole new ball game.

We chose Antonio Morello and Donato Savoie of Studio MORSA on Centre Street in New York's Little Italy to design the interior, confident that they could create a space that would be elegant, understated, and breathtaking. The two men had the uncanny skill of bringing their separate visions together to create a restaurant that blended contemporary and traditional elements to delight both the eye and the spirit.

The brownstone we had purchased was on a lot that was twenty feet wide and a hundred feet deep. The brownstone itself was sixty feet deep, meaning that we had forty feet of vacant property at the rear of the lot. Our plan was to excavate that area, create a cellar there for storage, and then erect a two-story structure above that space. The first floor would house a kitchen, and the second floor would house an additional dining room. We envisioned connecting the new space in the back to the existing building with a skylight that would help create a "**giardino**," a little enclosed patio. With the two dining areas and the bar, the restaurant would hold a total of ninety-five to a hundred people.

Our architect found beautiful old mahogany panels at an estate sale in upstate New York. The panels, rescued from an old mansion on the Hudson River that was being torn down, had a rich patina and shine that reminded me of maple syrup. The woodwork was going to be finished off with a matching mahogany crown dental molding. A dentallike crown molding was already in place, and we continued with that theme in the rest of the woodwork in the restaurant. We knew it would be a wonderful look, and perfect for the restaurant. But, of course, the woodwork added further cost to the project.

The existing parking lot near our brownstone, at the corner of Fifty-eighth Street and Second Avenue, which we expected to be a big plus for our customers driving in from Queens and the suburbs, did not last long, unfortunately. Within a year of our opening, the parking lot was sold, and construction started on a high-end apartment building.

On many a night, Felice and I sat at home to work through our budgetary projections and cost estimates, doing our best to ensure that we could make a go of our new business.

We had fun creating our first two restaurants. We knew what we wanted, and we also knew exactly where to go to find what we needed. We purchased most items, including pots and pans, utensils, and more, at Zahner's in Queens, and restaurant supply shops on Bowery Street in Lower Manhattan. These stores recycled a lot of items from failing restaurants, so we were able to save money on appliances, utensils, and many other pieces of equipment. You could find just about anything you wanted, including furniture, overhead lights, glassware, and linens. Felice let me decide on certain things, and I let him decide on others. Fortunately, we agreed much more than we disagreed.

Over the years, we'd come to know many immigrants who were also skilled tradesmen—painters, electricians, cabinetmakers, and more. Felice was able to call on a number of them. He obtained quotes, and we selected the best, with an eye toward both the finished product and price.

We stepped forward to take on the role of general contractor on the renovation of the entire building—a task that quickly grew in size and scope. We were often talking to the contractors while backhoes and other heavy machinery worked a few feet away, excavating beneath the building to turn the unfinished area into a usable wine cellar and storage. The order of the day was hard hats and work boots, which was certainly new territory for me.

We were about one month in when we discovered that the foundation was unstable and needed costly underpinning—a major expense that we hadn't planned on. Correcting the problem would put us way over budget and potentially delay our opening,

243 East Fifty-eighth Street, the initial demolition
before the construction of Felidia, 1979

Examining the backyard of the
Felidia brownstone, where we were
adding the extra floor and kitchen.
I was thirty-two years old.

which we had targeted for December 1980, in time for the winter holiday season. But we also knew that there was no way to avoid the work, so we green-lighted the project.

At this point, Felice and I became concerned that we would not have enough money to finish Felidia—or any way to come up with the additional financing. Our only remaining tangible asset was our home, which had a partial mortgage. A home is sacred to the Italian family, and we dared not consider a second mortgage. No matter what happened with the restaurant, Felice and I were still fully able to work, and we knew we could find work no matter what happened with our project. But we were desperate to make a go of it. The initial budget for Felidia was seven hundred thousand dollars, but the new underpinnings for the building drove the cost to more than one million, the equivalent of three million today, and there were worries that the cost could go even higher.

That is not a lot of money when compared with the corporate costs for opening a high-end restaurant today, but we were doing this on our own, with no backing from a partner. My mother and father pulled money from their personal retirement account to help us as much as they could, but even that wasn't enough. We wondered, too, whether the previous owner of the building had known about the crumbling condition of the building and kept silent about it.

It was a very dark time for me. I couldn't sleep; night after night, I would just lie in bed worrying if we were going to lose everything. Many a time, I asked myself, **Do I want too much? Am I pushing the edge? Am I at the edge?** I had two young kids—Joe was twelve, and Tanya was eight at the time. We had loans all over the place, and we couldn't start paying them back until we had the restaurant open and were able to generate some revenue.

I suppose you could argue that we shouldn't have extended ourselves so far and taken on so much debt. But we were pursuing a dream, and had done all the research and homework possible. There was simply no way we could have foreseen the massive additional work that was required on the brownstone's foundation.

I didn't know much about depression at the time—no one in our circle talked openly about mental health in those days. But in retrospect, I realize that Felice did fall into a depression amid all the stress. He became quiet, withdrawn. He would not call or talk to his friends, and he could not sleep at night. He was anxious, and no longer seemed interested in the project. I didn't know how to best support him, and, frankly, I didn't have the time. We were in way over our heads, overleveraged, exhausted, and with no way out. There was no one that I could turn to for help. I had to forge ahead and figure out a way to make it happen.

With all the bills, we couldn't even afford to have

the Queen Anne–style chairs we had purchased for the restaurant in Italy stained and upholstered. So we decided that we would try to do it ourselves. My mother, Tanya, and I hopped in the car and drove to a fabric shop, where we picked out a beautiful brocade of roses like you would find on couches in Renaissance Italy. Fabric in hand, we headed home. Later, I went to see an upholsterer, who gave me some tips on how to put the fabric on the seats at home.

We brought the chairs home one at a time and put them in our Bayside garage, where my father spent hours meticulously sanding each one, with its myriad curves, careful not to miss a spot. Because we needed so many chairs, this was a huge undertaking. Still, I think he was happy to be able to contribute and help alleviate one source of stress for Felice and me.

After his trip to Istria with my mother, he had returned there on his own. For years, he'd dreamed of retiring to his hometown, so that he could renew old friendships and live out his final years in an area that he loved. But his trip back proved disastrous, and he slowly came to realize that it was pointless to even think of returning. The buildings and the land in Pola were still very much the way he remembered them, but everything else was different. The state had taken some of the land from his family's farm in Busoler. Although the house in Pola remained in the family, it had fallen into disrepair.

His plan was to fix it up so that he and my mother could retire there. But Erminia did not share my father's dream of moving back to Pola, although she did not dissuade him from going back to Istria to work on the house.

Once there, my father searched for some of his old friends, going to the bars and taverns he used to frequent, but found few that he remembered—and those who did remember him had no interest in picking up where they'd left off so many years ago. He was largely unable to even communicate with people in Pola, because he spoke only Italian and our dialect—not the official Croatian. It was truly difficult for my father; he was like a fish out of water. The neighbors did not welcome him, and he awoke one morning to find that someone had tossed rotting fish heads on his doorstep. Though he stayed there for two months, he didn't find any comfort, and his mood was low when he returned to the States.

"I feel like a stranger there. I have no friends; they all went away, they all escaped," he told us after his return.

He went so far as to tell my mother that he no longer wanted to be buried in the family cemetery in Pola: upon his death, she should just cast him into the sea.

My family's decision to leave Pola had effectively severed our relationship with many of the people outside of our family there. I suppose I wasn't all that surprised by his experience, after what I'd gone through trying to reconnect with my childhood friends. It was time for us to move forward; we had our treasured memories of the area, and that would have to suffice.

Papa seemed a bit happier to be in the United States after his visit to Pola. He now realized that his future was here, and he had to stop daydreaming about a return to the old country. He even sold our home in Pola to a family from Eastern Europe in a quick cash sale, accepting well below market value for the once-beloved dwelling. But he was never truly happy in the States. He worked hard to save money, and he loved his family, but he was always melancholy. He found solace in tinkering with cars, electronics, and just about anything that had moving parts. He spent a good deal of his time in the garage, so working on the Queen Anne chairs was a good project for him.

We were deep into the restaurant renovation, and falling further and further behind our projected schedule of a December opening, when my father suffered a massive stroke. He was not a sickly man, but he had his vices: he smoked a pack or more of Kent cigarettes a day, and he made himself a little pot of mocha coffee at least five times a day, preparing it half espresso, half sugar. Perhaps his habits got the best of him.

I was at Villa Secondo collecting my sale payment and tying up some loose ends when I received a panicked call from my mother that late-September day. She was so hysterical I could barely understand her; my father had been in the garage, pinning the tapestry on the Queen Anne chair frames, when he collapsed onto the hood of his beloved car—a Mercedes-Benz he had long dreamed of owning. He would literally pet the car as if it were a purring cat as he lovingly stroked the hood. At night, he covered it with blankets so that no one would scratch it. I immediately called an ambulance to the house and then rushed to Booth Memorial Hospital in Flushing to meet it there.

When I arrived, my father was unresponsive and his prognosis was grim. The stroke had impacted the pons, the lower region of the brain that controls breathing and motor skills, among other functions. Doctors could not offer much hope. We didn't know if he would survive. If he did, there was concern that he would likely remain in a permanent vegetative state.

For the next eight days, we held vigil by his hospital bedside. The family gathered around him, as we tried to console each other. We cried, we hugged, and we prayed. Day after day, I sat at his bedside, holding his hand. I wondered if he knew that I was there with him. One afternoon, when he and I were alone in the room, I put my index finger in his palm, squeezed his hand around it, and asked, "Papa, can you hear me? If you can hear me, just squeeze my finger."

Suddenly, I felt a light squeeze of my finger. Heartened, I began to cry. This was the last communication between the two of us, but I was grateful that we had connected, if only in a small way.

A few days later, on October 4, 1980, my father passed away. His death was unexpected and added to the stress we were already feeling. We buried my father in the family plot in St. Denis Cemetery in Hopewell Junction, New York. My brother and his wife, Margaret, had buried their first child there—Christina, who died at just two months of age during surgery attempting to correct a heart problem. Now my father would be with her, something that brought us all comfort. Following my father's wishes, Franco made sure to place the items my father had carried with him from his homeland—the stone from the Roman arena in Pola, and the card with the picture of the Sacred Heart of Jesus that his mother had given to him—under the pillow in his coffin.

My mother was depressed and lonely without my father. The two had been together since she was nineteen years old. It was a blessing that she lived with us in Bayside, and she had her hands full with the children and the opening; all the activity helped keep her mind off her husband's death. I felt a big loss, too. In such a time of need, it is important to have the support of your family. Although we had lost a big part of ours, having my family around me was my greatest consolation. I continue to surround myself with family. Together we can overcome everything, as we did during those dark days in San Sabba.

My father never got the chance to finish the Queen Anne chairs, so we all pitched in to complete the job. We did all we could to stain, paint, and upholster them as well as the bar stools. My mother and even eight-year-old Tanya helped with the application of the fabric to the seats. But my father was always with us, especially at Christmastime. He loved **baccalà mantecato,** whipped cod, a typical dish in Istria for the Vigilia, Christmas Eve. I still prepare it every year, thinking about my father.

We missed Dad greatly, but our challenges kept us going. Still, there were moments when I truly had to fight to continue. Sometimes, when you are pushed up against the wall and have no alternatives, you find the strength and make your way forward. I have always been a risk taker—calculated, but a risk taker. I mostly gamble on knowing I will work hard to make things happen. But I was exhausted and terrified that we might lose everything.

By early December, it was clear the restaurant would not be ready to open for the Christmas holiday. We were seriously behind schedule, and we were running out of money. There were months when we couldn't make a mortgage payment and pay the workers and the additional loan we had with the building's former owner, who knew how cash-strapped we were and agreed to let us pay late—with interest.

Near the end, there was absolutely no money left to pay the mortgage or the workers who were still putting in long hours to complete the project. I was cooking every day, well into the evening, as I tried various recipes for the menu. To encourage the workers to stay and continue laboring, my mother and I started cooking for them at the restaurant. I'd bring the leftovers home for the family. Mom and I undertook other jobs, tasks in the renovation that we'd hoped to assign to others, to save us money. We also cleaned up after the workers each day, so they could continue construction on the restaurant. And we spent hours cleaning and shining all the pots and pans we had bought secondhand to save money. Little Tanya would help to scrub and clean whatever she could. Though it was difficult and time-consuming work, it had to get done, and there was no one else to do it. Everything hinged on getting the restaurant open so that we'd finally have a source of revenue.

The situation was so bad that there were days when we almost didn't have enough money to eat. Joe took a job making bagels at a bagel store in Bay Terrace in the early mornings, before school, and he had a paper route, too. Chipping in all the money he could toward the household finances so that we could eat; he was our secret financier in those dark days.

Even the owners of some of the other restaurants on Fifty-eighth Street reached out to lend a hand. The chef from Bruno's, across the street, and the owners of Tre Scalini, down the block, brought food and drinks and came to encourage us as we labored late into the night. We knew that the camaraderie would likely cease once we opened our doors and were competing for some of the same clientele. And maybe to some extent it did, but we remained friends. We were all part of the Gruppo Ristoratori Italiani, an organization of Italian restaurants in America promoting good Italian food and traditional Italian products. As a group, we did many promotional and fund-raising events together, and I forged many great friendships that are still strong today. Our fellow restaurateur Angelo Vivolo, owner of Vivolo on East Seventy-fourth Street, and I established an especially close brotherly bond, and we continue to do many fund-raising events together.

21

Grand Opening

By April 1981, we were four months past our target date, exhausted, and fully leveraged. We had used up all the money generated from the sale of our two restaurants, plus the money from a bank loan and some of my parents' savings. We owed money not just to the bank but also to the electrician and some of the other contractors. And opening day was still ahead of us. It was all hugely overwhelming.

Felice and I had to make a decision: either we opened the restaurant in its current state or risked losing everything. We saw no other choice. We had to open—even though there were some little unfinished corners inside the restaurant—painting here and there, and the completion of the wine racks and the area behind the bar.

We decided that any work that couldn't actually be seen by diners in the restaurant would have to wait until we had additional funds to pay for com-

The finished front and sidewalk of Felidia,
ready to open

pletion. Our main focus was on making sure we had all the utility connections properly made, and all the major equipment, including refrigerators, the stove, and other appliances, in working order.

We chose Wednesday, April 15, 1981, to host an invitation-only launch party for friends, family, journalists, and customers of our two former Queens restaurants, Buonavia and Villa Secondo. All the hardships we'd endured would be set aside, at least for one important evening. We had to put on a smiling face for all the people waiting to experience Felidia.

Time was of the essence, and most of the invitations would be going to family and friends, so I decided to keep their design very simple and easy to reproduce. The invitation would be done on a standard-sized, eight-and-a-half-by-eleven-inch sheet of paper that would be folded in half. One half of the sheet would feature an image and become the front of the invitation. When you unfolded the paper, the actual invitation would be handwritten inside. I quickly dashed something out on a piece of paper. We wanted to telegraph that we were going to use nothing but the best ingredients and everything was going to be farm-fresh, so I found a picture of Nonna Rosa in her black dress and apron with a basket full of fresh eggs by her side, and cropped it to add emphasis to the apron and fresh eggs. I had it Xeroxed, along with my handwritten invitation:

WE CORDIALLY INVITE YOU TO CELEBRATE

THE OPENING OF

FELIDIA

243 EAST 58TH STREET NEW YORK CITY

WEDNESDAY APRIL 15, 1981

5:00 PM TO 11:00 PM

PLEASE COME FELICE AND LIDIA

R.S.V.P. 758-1479

To help get the word out, I enlisted my friend Rose Gatto, my longtime customer from Villa Secondo and owner of Gatto Communications, to assist us

The antipasto table in Felidia's dining room,
soon after opening

with the promotions. I knew she had press contacts in both the American and Italian communities, and asked her to reach out on our behalf. Rose quickly got to work, contacting journalists and extending invitations to our opening-night gala. She also sent out a press release touting Felidia's "newly created interior" and "innovative Italian menu."

"The experienced restaurateurs, FELICE and LIDIA Bastianich . . . have labored over the menu and produced the most innovative Italian menu on the block," the release boasted.

Meanwhile, Felice and I did some good old-fashioned outreach of our own. Though we had plenty of people on the guest list for our opening-night event, we needed to fill the restaurant with customers come April 16, when we would open our doors to the public. Together, we walked Fifty-eighth Street, placing messages about Felidia in the lobbies of all the buildings in our neighborhood, inviting people to stop by for a welcoming glass of prosecco on us. My mother, who was then in her early sixties, would continue to distribute our flyers even after the opening-night festivities, positioning herself on the corner of Fifty-eighth Street and Third Avenue to hand them to passersby.

The day of the party, we decorated the front of the restaurant with magnums of wine and a huge spray of flowers. The dark, rich mahogany walls gave the space a wonderful warm feeling and served as a perfect backdrop for the blossom-filled arrangements and the gorgeous assortment of antipasti we set out on a buffet table next to the bar. The table itself was a work of art, with a green marble top and brass legs in the shape of swans. Atop this table (which is now in the sunroom of my home) sat a mini-version of the table on which we placed a huge flower arrangement.

The antipasto buffet was something we had seen in Italy. I wanted to replicate it at Felidia, and we continued to feature it once the restaurant was open for business. We had marinated fish, vegetables, whatever was in season, anywhere from ten to twenty different dishes, including octopus salad, seafood salad, and grilled eggplant, all at room temperature. The meal we offered was very much like one in Italy, and included dishes such as boiled chicory, string beans, and potato salad. Diners ordered what they liked, and the captains prepared the plates and delivered them to the tables. We would dress them up with a little vinaigrette or oil, and **voilà**!

What was great was that you could order each dish for one, or to share from the center of your table. Of course, now the health department does not allow us to set food out at room temperature, and probably rightfully so. At some point, we had to place plastic wrap over all of the offerings, which didn't look quite as appetizing. And, ultimately, we had to do away with the buffet table altogether. But back then it was a big hit, and something that set us apart from the other Italian restaurants in the area.

❧ ❦

A small line was already forming when we opened the doors to Felidia for the launch party. By 6:00 p.m., the place was so packed that guests could barely move. My mother, my kids, and Franco and his wife and two of their three children were there, along with many of the relatives and friends Felice and I had here in the United States. A good number of journalists showed up that night, as did many of the faithful customers from our two restaurants in Queens. It was so heartwarming to see them all there, and I was incredibly thankful for their patronage and support. For me, it was a big relief that there was finally food on the table of this restaurant!

Felice and I decided we would do something that was memorable and appropriate for the regional Italian cuisine that we would be serving. We opted to serve a whole suckling pig, and its entrance into the dining room on the platter was met with oohs and aahs and plenty of applause.

Past the bar on the right, we set up a long buffet table upon which the suckling pig, with its crispy, shiny skin and an apple in its snout, served as the centerpiece. Next to the pig was a cutting board, in front of which were oval platters featuring different appetizers: **sarde in saor** (sweet and sour sardines), octopus-and-potato salad, mussels vinaigrette, shrimp and beans salad, marinated zucchini, eggplant **rollatini,** sweetbreads with capers, **vitello tonnato,** roasted whole salmon, prosciutto and figs, mozzarella and tomatoes, string-bean-and-potato salad, beet-and-goat-cheese salad, and on and on, with boards holding different cheeses set out with fruits, **affettati** of all kind—**mortadella, culatello, salame Genovese**—accompanied by baskets full of warm **focaccia, grissini,** and assorted Italian semolina breads.

The waitstaff was parading around the room with trays of hot hors d'oeuvres: fried calamari, **polpette, arancini, bruschetta,** and more. At the other

A special dish at the opening of Felidia

end of the dining room, by the kitchen, a table was set up with a portable stove; pan after pan of different pastas alternating with risottos would come out from the kitchen. I would toss in the cheese and dish out a tasting of it to the continuous line of guests. At about the middle of the evening, when most of the guests had arrived, Felice put himself behind the **porchetta** and began carving it limb by limb on the cutting board.

Toward the end of the evening, the serving tables were cleared and reset with platters of desserts: cheesecake, apple strudel, peach crostata, chocolate-zabaglione cake, cannoli, **sfogliatelle,** and all kinds of cookies and fruit.

Joe and Tanya took their cousins and some of the

young customers around, and I could see with the corner of my eye that they were proud, very proud, because they had been an important part in building Felidia. It was an exhaustingly glorious evening, even though the next day was our official opening.

It's funny to hear now the recollections of this grand evening from members of my family, especially from my children. Tanya, who was just eight at the time, spent most of the night sitting under the lip of the bar, a great spot from which to observe all the "fancy Manhattan people," many smoking "long filtered cigarettes," as she recalls. For her, the evening was a dizzying array of colorful flowers, an abundance of delicious, beautifully presented food, swanky New York guests, and the smell of cigarette smoke.

For me, it was all that and more. It was the realization of a long-held dream. I had found my place here in America. In some ways, it was as if all those stops along the way—Grandma's courtyard, Zia Nina's kitchen, the refugee camp, the kitchen at the Scuola Canossiana—had been meant to prepare me for this very moment. I was now the chef of my very own Italian restaurant in New York City, the greatest city in the world. I had long heard people say, "If you can make it here, you can make it anywhere." And while there was plenty of hard work and hardship ahead, in that moment I was thankful for what was.

The night was not without its mishaps. Some of

the refrigerators didn't chill down fast enough, and there were a few tense moments in the kitchen. Still, we were open, and it was a momentous occasion for Felice and me. We truly had reason to celebrate our accomplishment.

Sadly, my father did not get to witness the opening of Felidia, but he was there with me that night, in my heart and in my soul. It was because of his and my mother's courage in bringing our family here to America that I had come this far, and I remain forever grateful to them both. I am also grateful to my own children, who, as young as they were, understood the importance of this undertaking to Felice and me and worked alongside us to make it happen. I will forever lovingly remember Tanya in the garage, helping my mother and me with the upholstering of the chairs and the cleaning and scrubbing of the pots, and Joe, toiling in the early mornings before school, making bagels and delivering newspapers, so that he could contribute something to the household and help us feed the family.

And, of course, I could never have done it without the love and support of my mother—having her with us caring for the children and pitching in wherever and whenever she was needed. No matter how dire the circumstances, she always remained positive and encouraged me to look at the bright side. She had suffered the greatest loss of her life with the death of my father, and yet she persevered, working tirelessly to help make Felidia a success.

❧ ❦

The next day, Thursday, April 16, we were open for business, beginning with lunch. I had hardly slept, and there I was in the kitchen, in my new role as chef of Felidia. I had sous-chefs, and they were all great, but I was now the one literally and figuratively wearing the big white hat, the woman in charge. It all depended on my leadership of the team and getting them to understand the flavors of the different regions of Italy and teaching them the technique of cooking in the regional style of Italy. Each chef has his or her own style and profile of flavors, and now we had to join our talents and, under my leadership, cook the true flavors of the regional Italian cuisine. Not only did they have to learn these new recipes and the new style, we had to reproduce those recipes over and over, every single day. A plethora of concerns swirled about in my mind as I stood over the stove that first day: **Will the guests like my flavors, my style of cooking? Will they compare my food with the food at the popular Italian American restaurants? Will they recognize the difference? Will they like it?**

At my side was Edgar Torres, one of the **chefs de cuisine** we had brought with us to Felidia from

Buonavia. Edgar, who was Puerto Rican, was second in line, and I depended on him a lot. He had a great palate, and he really helped me. We worked in symphony and made good music together. He understood my flavors and my ideas, and he really did a lot of the hard work and preparations.

When I wanted to step out of the kitchen to say hello to the customers, I felt confident knowing that Edgar was there to hold down the fort. Back then, we didn't have orthotic clogs, like the chefs wear today, so I would "slipper" around the dining room in my Dr. Scholl's slippers, greeting diners and soliciting their feedback in those silly shoes.

I had spent a big part of my life in the kitchen, assisting important chefs, but now here I was, the captain of the ship. I was the conductor of this orchestra, and I had to make beautiful music, beautiful food. In a busy restaurant, it is not enough that you can make a delicious and beautiful plate of pasta or chicken **scarpariello**; you have to make twenty to thirty portions of each of them every evening, plus all the other dishes that come on order. And you have to synchronize their cooking, so the food for all of the diners is ready and reaches the table all at once. The pasta has to be **al dente,** the risotto creamy, and the meat at the customer's requested temperature. Each dish has its own **contorno**, side dish, and decorations, and so on, table by table, the whole evening. Then there are the dietary requests, and the new guests who join the table halfway into the meal. No matter what the challenge is, the chef has to fit the deviation into the rhythm and continue. The dining room has to flow smoothly, like oil, but it is not always so in the kitchen: sometimes chefs lose their cool and pans fly.

Timing is extremely important in the restaurant industry. You have to wait to serve the food at that table where one of the guests has gone to the restroom. It all happens in the hot, albeit well-laid-out, but small kitchen of Felidia. There is always a mishap—the pan of scaloppini that fell from the stove, the pasta that slipped out of the strainer, and the salad man who put salt on a "salt-free" salad. It feels very much like juggling balls, and some invariably get dropped.

Most important is that the guest must never feel what is going on in the kitchen—the glitches, the hiccups in timing and serving the meal, must never become part of the diner's experience. I quickly learned that as a chef, it's all about the team and the understanding and collaboration between its members. Of course, preparation, the **mise en place**, is crucial; you must be ready to go when the gate opens.

That first day, I recall, looking frequently over at the dishwashing area, checking to see if any uneaten food had come back on the plates. If it had, I interrogated the server. "Did they not like it?" I asked. "Did they tell you why? Were they upset?" I then cracked open the kitchen door and, scanning the table like a laser beam, tried to locate the discontented diner, curious to see if he or she was angry or unhappy. When there was a lull in the orders, I folded my apron over to hide some of the stains and went around the dining room to connect with and thank the customers. I loved them for coming, and I love cooking for them. The busier it was, the happier I was. My thoughts were not on the revenues we were collecting, or on the bills to be paid, but on the food that was being served and the hum in the dining room. I guess subliminally I was confident I would be able to begin to pay those long-overdue construction bills.

My new role at Felidia had me working incredibly long hours, and I cannot stress enough how fortunate I was to have my mother living with us and lending her support. I needed to be at the restaurant from 10:00 a.m. to 10:00 p.m. every day, and even longer when there were big preparations for events and parties. As soon as I arrived, I'd pick up the products Felice had delivered. We would butcher the leg of lamb, the racks of lamb, the chickens, then clean and portion the fish. Edgar and I worked on what the specials would be for the day, depending on what was coming into the restaurant via Felice or the purveyors.

I'd try to grab some rest on the couch in the upstairs office in the lull between lunch and dinner preparations. Felice always had a recliner nearby to nap.

My mother would come to the restaurant from Bayside every morning, after the kids went to school, and help clean up and receive the deliveries so that I could get a little rest. She would stay until midafternoon and be back in Bayside to meet the children when they arrived home from school in the afternoons.

Felice and I were on totally different schedules. He was often up before the sun, to shop the meat, fish, and vegetable markets of Lower Manhattan, the Bronx, and even Freeport, selecting only the best and freshest products for our kitchen. Sometimes, if he had a little time to kill, he'd stop at his sister's house in Jackson Heights to relax, or go home to shower and rest, before coming back to the restaurant for the evening shift. He knew I was already in the kitchen, taking care of things, so he didn't have to rush. On the days when he didn't go early to the market, he was in the restaurant before 11:00 a.m. and ready to work the floor for lunch. He was the one who stayed in the evenings to close, which sometimes could be as late as 2:00 a.m. He always waited until the last customer left the restaurant before heading home to sleep; we never wanted our patrons to feel pressured or rushed.

To attract customers, we employed some of the same strategies that had worked so well for us in our first two restaurants in Queens. We continued to offer our neighbors and customers a glass of prosecco or a taste of something from the kitchen, and we introduced regional dishes not on the menu at other Italian restaurants, such as **pasutice all'Istriana** (fresh pasta with seafood sauce), **krafi** (Istrian wedding ravioli, pillows stuffed with rum, raisins, and three different Italian cheeses), **frico** (Montasio cheese crisp), **polenta e cacciagione** (polenta with wild game), and **insalata di polipo** (warm octopus-and-potato salad).

At Felidia, I felt comfortable being the chef. Soon our cuisine began attracting the attention of journalists and food critics, as well as chefs and others who had learned about us by word of mouth and came to give our restaurant a try. Felidia was a novelty, with a regional Italian menu and a woman as a chef. It didn't take long—with all the attention we got—to fill the chairs.

By June, we were drawing a pretty steady crowd. But we really caught the spotlight in late July with an unexpected visit from **New York Times** food critic Mimi Sheraton. At the time, none of us was savvy enough to recognize her in the dining room, so we had no idea she had even been to Felidia until we learned of her review in the **Times** on July 31, 1981.

Her review gave us three stars, but she did have some criticism. Ms. Sheraton was known to be a tough reviewer, blunt and with strong opinions, and she took us to task in some areas, calling the food "disappointingly inconsistent," the noise in certain parts of the restaurant "deafening," and the service "badly organized." But more important was her praise of the "kitchen's most serious efforts," and those three stars.

Ms. Sheraton's review really launched us. Our phone was ringing off the hook, and we could hardly keep up with the demand. The dining room at Felidia was consistently full, a momentum that lasted well into our second and third years. It amazed me that diners would follow a reviewer with such dedication and trust.

We were lucky enough to get those three stars. But what if the reviewer had come in and we were having a bad day? His or her write-up could have wiped us out. I can't help but think how many new restaurants are out there in the same place as we'd been. Every time I see a one-star review, my heart really aches for that owner or chef. Most likely, the restaurant owners put all of their money and all of their effort into the project, and one review like that could cause irreparable harm.

In my opinion, a new restaurant should only be reviewed if it is worth going to, if it is a new discovery, or if it is offering something different, out of the ordinary. It would be better to share with the reader the positive experiences of a restaurant. The customers today are savvy and know food, and if a place is really not worthy, it will die its own natural death.

In those early days, I would tense up whenever I learned we had a reviewer in the dining room. I began asking myself, **What can I do that is extra?**

What I quickly came to realize was that the reviewer was there because of what I did, the food that I was preparing, and there was nothing extra that I needed to add, no curlicues or fancy garnishes to add to the plate. I just had to do what I do best, and do it well. I needed to make sure that my cooking time was correct, that my dish was on target, truly representing the flavors of the Italian regional cuisine, trusting that the reviewer wants to convey the passion and talent of the chef, the honesty in the products he or she uses, and the intensity of the flavors.

Still, some of the early reviews really catapulted us. The food writer Jay Jacobs, then a contributor to **Gourmet** magazine, became a fan. In 1984, he wrote an extraordinary piece on Felidia and the uniqueness of the regional Italian dishes we had on our menu. He also became a regular, sitting at the bar in the evenings, sampling my regional dishes and enjoying some of the selected Italian wines we carried, although he always began the evening with a straight-up gin martini with olives. Jay loved his martinis!

Sam Peros was our bartender, and he made a mean convex martini—a martini poured to the brim of the glass so that the drink seems to be higher in the center than on the sides. It earned him—and us—a feature article in **Cosmopolitan.** Sam playfully made his clients "bow" to his martini in order to take the first sip without spilling it. These two articles continued to whip up interest and enthusiasm. Our dining room continued to be full of customers every night, and all of our bar stools taken by patrons waiting for one of Sam's martinis.

Thank goodness, because we still had many loans to pay off.

22

Table for Two

It wasn't long before prominent New York personalities and even celebrities started coming through our doors.

By then, Felice and I were lucky enough to have brothers Dante and Nino Laurenti working with us in the front of the house. They had come to us from Brussels Restaurant, a fine northern-Italian establishment that was owned by Albert Giambelli, the brother of Francesco Giambelli of the iconic Giambelli's Ristorante on Fiftieth Street. Dante was an extraordinary cook, but for us, he was maître d' par excellence. He loved working in the dining room, finishing pasta, deboning pheasants, chicken, and fish, and the customers loved him. He also made a big show for customers who ordered our dessert crêpes or **palačinke,** which we served tableside and flambéed with some Grand Marnier. His brother Nino was a sommelier, great with wine; together, they made a terrific team.

Felidia, finally finished!

The brothers were from the Emilia-Romagna region of Italy, where Parma is located, and we really connected in our passion for food. Since the restaurant's opening, Felice had been alone in the dining room, so having the brothers join us was a huge relief. I had been able to come in and out of the kitchen to say hello to the customers at our two previous restaurants. But Felidia was multilevel, which made my appearances in the dining room much more challenging, and Felice's role in the front of the restaurant equally difficult. With Dante and Nino on board, each could work a level, and they could switch off as needed. The two men really captivated our diners with their enthusiasm, and I attribute much of our success at the time to their professionalism. Their contributions went well beyond the scope of their job titles. I have Dante to thank for teaching me how to make tortellini **in brodo**, pasta Emilliana, and all kinds of savory and sweet crostatas. I would pull him into the kitchen between the lunch and dinner hours and, along with my sous-chefs, we would talk food, while Nino and Felice shared their appreciation for wine. We became such great friends that the two brothers would come to our house and together we'd all make prosciutto or **cotecchino**—a big sausage made from the snout of the pig—and even vinegar in our garage. We'd visit them at their summer house in Ronkonkoma, Long Island, where they taught me how to go foraging for mushrooms.

The restaurant had been open for about eight months when we learned that Julia Child was coming to dinner with a guest, who turned out to be none other than James Beard. Someone had phoned just hours before she was scheduled to arrive to reserve a table for two for 6:00 p.m. in her name, so there wasn't much time to prepare.

Knowing Dante and Nino would be out front to greet Julia and James when they arrived put me at ease. We had already decided to seat the two of them at Table 5, which, back then, was our best table. It was against the brick wall we had treated to resemble a Roman ruin, just beneath a large framed mirror. Table 5 was a big table, but we expected they would need it, because Julia was a very tall

Dante and Nino Laurenti

woman, and they'd likely be ordering an assortment of dishes.

As the time for Julia's reservation drew near, I started poking my head out the kitchen door, which had an unobstructed view of the restaurant's entrance, hoping to catch a glimpse of her. Julia stood six feet two inches tall, so she was easy to spot wherever she went. I couldn't believe my eyes when I finally saw her silhouette, along with that of an equally tall gentleman, in the window behind them. The way the lighting was in the restaurant, I couldn't see their faces, only their shadows against the window.

"Oh my God," I murmured under my breath. "It's her!"

James Beard, an inch taller than Julia, had on his signature bow tie, with a patterned shirt and a cardigan hanging loosely around his shoulders. Thank goodness we had assigned them to Table 5, I thought. They were going to need the extra room.

I lingered in the doorway long enough to watch as Dante led them to their table, noting the awkward smiles and stares from some of the other diners as they passed. Julia looked stylish in her loose-fitting sweater and calf-length floral skirt, which made her appear even taller.

I was bursting with excitement when I returned to the kitchen to report their arrival. Most of the workers had heard of Julia Child and James Beard, but even those who had not must still remember my description of their importance, I'm sure. They were the mother and father of the American food renaissance. Yes, James Beard was strictly red, white, and blue American. He was all about the food products of the American land and its cuisine, the food that reflected the flavors of America. Julia, on the other hand, was all about bringing the delights of the French cuisine to the American people. She had gone to France with her husband, Paul, who was employed by the U.S. State Department and, from what I understood, was in charge of dispelling the myth of the "ugly American" in France after World War II. Julia enrolled at the renowned Cordon Bleu cooking school and fell head over heels for the French way of cooking. She was determined to teach it to Americans, feeling so vehemently that America must eat well.

Throughout the evening, I peeked out to see how things at Table 5 were going. The two appeared to be enjoying themselves. They had sampled a lot of different dishes, and I was eager to hear their feedback. As they lingered over coffee and dessert, I made my way to the table to introduce myself. Julia was someone I greatly admired; her passion for food, and her desire to share that passion with others, were very much in line with the way I felt as a chef. More important, as a woman, she had risen and succeeded in an industry that was dominated by men. I hadn't realized how rare it was for a woman to find work as a chef until I began networking and became more involved in New York's food industry.

I was immediately disarmed by Julia's warmth and modesty. She spoke with the same warbled voice I had heard on television, but she was without airs. There was no pretense with Julia. She was direct, open, and extremely curious. She wanted to know more about me, and she and James had lots of questions about the meal they had just consumed, with Julia especially focused on the wild mushroom risotto. I was happy to answer all of their questions, although I could hardly believe that these icons were so interested in hearing what I had to say. Our conversation was easy and relaxed, and recalling it delights me to this day.

→·←

It was 1983, and I had found my dream house, a turn-of-the-century Arts and Crafts–style home in Douglaston Manor. We weren't in the market for a home when the house came to my attention, but I had told my real-estate broker—who was also a neighbor in Bayside—of my interest in finding a home on the water after a day of walking the Cross Island Trail. The trail hugs the shore of the Long Island Sound and stretches for 3.1 miles along the Cross Island Parkway. I spent a lot of my downtime there, staring out at the water, and walking along the dock of the Bayside Marina at the trail's eastern end. One afternoon, while standing on the dock, I noticed these gorgeous waterfront houses across the way and realized how much I wanted to live by the water. I still had cherished childhood memories of relaxing at the water's edge with my friends near Busoler, and I yearned to experience that again. Being near the sea liberates me from negativity and tension and enlightens me when I am feeling lost or confused. I feel a certain freedom when I am close to the water.

I had made clear to the broker that the house needed to be affordable, then quickly put the whole idea out of my mind. I was convinced that such a home would never come on the market in this part of New York.

Nearly two years passed before she finally called me to say there was a house I might be interested in in Douglaston, with a gorgeous view of Little Neck Bay. It was an estate sale, so the price was right. The problem was, everything else was wrong.

The home had not been updated in years, and it had tiny little windows from which you could barely see out. At the time of its construction, there had been no central heating, so the house had eight fireplaces. The plumbing and electricity also needed updating, and the list went on. Still, standing on the front lawn and looking out at the bay transported me back to my childhood days of frolicking in the Adriatic Sea.

The house had unparalleled views of Little Neck Bay and the imposing Throgs Neck Bridge; it also had much of the original woodwork, parquet floors, and a coffered ceiling made of oak. It reminded me of Europe. I was not unhappy living in Bayside. We had a lovely home there, the kids had their friends, and my mother had her own separate living space. We had a German shepherd mix named Gypsy, a couple of gerbils, a big nasty parrot that Joe and I had found on the street in Manhattan that loved me, hated Felice, and could only say "Puerto Rico," and a gray cat with white paws that Tanya named Appy, because the friend who gave it to her was having her appendix out that very day. Still, there

was so much to like about this waterfront house—
"waterfront" being the key word.

Felice was not against the purchase, but he was
apprehensive about setting us back into a financial
hole. We still had plenty of loans to pay on the
restaurant, and the house needed extensive updates
and renovations.

My mother did not hold back her disapproval.
"What are you getting into now?" she railed. "Don't
you have enough?" A part of me knew she was probably right. But in my life I have always been very
enthusiastic. When I see an opportunity, I like to
go for it. I tell myself, **I can do this,** only later questioning if perhaps I might have pushed too hard.
I have learned to come to terms with my choices,
and that means asking myself the tough questions.
**Okay, you are in it now, so how are you going to
finish it? How are you going to get to the end of
this?** I have always had the support of my family.
And by then, Felice and I had a good rapport with
the bankers.

We agreed that we would remain in the Bayside
house until all of the renovation work was complete, and we would take our time, doing only what
we could afford. It sounded like a good, solid plan.
Felidia was doing well, and we were making great
strides in paying off our debts. Still, before long I
started asking myself, **Why did you do this?**

We hired Studio MORSA, the same design firm
we had used for Felidia, to help us with our vision

for this house. I wanted to build an apartment for my mother in our home, to ensure that she had a place of her own and could maintain her privacy and independence. The functionality and design of the kitchen were particularly important to me, and I planned it so that while cooking I could look out to the bay and see the sailboats passing by. Everything had to be done to my exact specifications, and I was very particular when it came to choosing the appliances—especially my beloved range, which I lovingly call "my Ferrari." I couldn't know it then, but for fifteen years my cooking show **Lidia's Italian Table** would be filmed in this kitchen.

Before any work began, I removed all the old, beautiful woodwork and put it into storage. We then proceeded to gut the house, and slowly added new electric, plumbing, the works. All of the original windows were removed and replaced by bigger, more functional ones, to insulate the house better and maximize the view. We also closed up three of the eight fireplaces. The project took nearly two years and required a hell of a lot of work.

As with Felidia, all kinds of unforeseen problems surfaced once construction got under way, and the costs continued to climb. We reached a point where we ran out of money, and we needed to sell the house in Bayside in order to finish the work. I completed my mother's kitchen first, and we moved into a half-finished house.

By then, Joe had graduated from Fordham Preparatory School, a private all-male Jesuit high school in the Bronx, and was off to his freshman year at Boston College, so it was just Felice, Tanya, my mother, and me.

Tanya had just started high school at Loyola, an independent Jesuit school on Park Avenue. It was at Joe's suggestion that we decided to send her there. His experience at Fordham Prep had been so wonderful that he advocated for Tanya to attend a Jesuit school. Most of them (Regis, Xavier, and Fordham Prep) were for boys only, so Loyola was the only option, being coed. Joe had skipped eighth grade, and he suggested that Tanya do the same. I liked Loyola because of its unique philosophy of educating its students to become good people with a strong moral fiber. Visiting the campus elicited memories of being with the nuns at the Scuola Canossiana, and how much comfort they had brought me. I felt the Jesuits were going to help me raise my children, and that gave me a sense of security.

Tanya and my mother had been riding together to Manhattan in the mornings. One of our neighbors in Bayside drove a taxi and agreed to bring the two of them into the city with him in the mornings for a small fee, dropping Tanya at school and my mother at Felidia, where she would do everything from answering phones to checking inventory. The beauty in this arrangement was that Tanya was able to grab a nap during the hour-long drives in and out of city—precious sleeping time for a weary teenager. I loved this schedule, because it gave me a chance to spend time with my mother and daughter and, at the same time, continue to do what I loved.

On most days, Tanya would stay after school for sports practices or games, and our neighbor with the taxi would pick her up there. Other days, she would walk or take the subway down to the restaurant to join us for an early dinner before she and my mother headed home. She'd often bring her friends with her to the restaurant. They'd sit and do homework together, and of course we would feed them all. There really was no place in Manhattan for teenagers to go, and no parent wanted ten of them hanging around in a New York City apartment; this was the perfect solution. We'd let the kids congregate in the private upstairs dining room if the space was not in use; it was a great place for them to be, especially on cold winter days. We'd serve them cake and hot chocolate, and they'd gab the hours away.

Our taxi driver neighbor agreed to continue working with us to get Tanya and my mother back and forth to the city from Douglaston.

So there we were—Tanya, Felice, and I—squeezed in with my mother in her newly completed one-bedroom apartment as the construction continued around us. Even Appy the cat was with us.

To furnish our new house, we took a huge trip to Italy and bought furniture, rugs, and materials to make the drapes and bedcovers. I also bought Italian linens. I love the slightly scratchy feel of linen sheets. It reminds me of my childhood: I recall the sheets in Nonna Rosa's bed were a bit rough and scratchy.

At that time, we were also purchasing wines for Felidia's wine list, so the trip was intense. Our trips to Italy allowed the restaurant to develop an amazing wine list. Producers were eager to give me an allocation of their wines. The industry in Italy was just warming up. It was not the huge machine it is today, so the producers were thrilled to get distribution in the United States, at a restaurant with excellent food that would be paired with their wines.

When the work on our home was finished, we were finally able to spread out and give my mother back her space. Soon we would add Chi Cha to the family. She was a Chow Chow, and she looked like a lion with a beautiful blue tongue. Though she needed a lot of attention, she was a good guard dog. We all loved her, but she was really my dog, and she was with me until she passed at the ripe old age of eighteen.

The new house became a landing pad for Joe and his college friends. In 1989, Joe was a senior at Boston College. He would bring a carload of his buddies to New York for the weekend, and of course our house was where they crashed. On Sunday mornings, they would slowly crawl out of Joe's attic residence, which could hold fifteen to twenty of them. The Sunday sauce would be perking on the stove, the salted water boiling; all I needed was to know how many were eating. Should I cook three, four, or five pounds of pasta? To this day, adult men tap me on the shoulder at Felidia and say, "Mrs. Bastianich, you might not remember me, but you cooked for me when I was young." One of Joe's friends once jokingly remarked that every meal I served to him was so elaborate that it was like the Last Supper. It gives me great pleasure to know that I have touched these young lives.

❧ ❦

Five years after we moved into the Douglaston house, I published my first cookbook, written with the food critic Jay Jacobs. Jay and I had become good friends. Since his article appeared in **Gourmet** magazine back in 1984, Jay had become a fixture at Felidia. Sometimes he would sit with me after the dinner rush and bombard me with questions about the Istrian cuisine. I'd fix him a little appetizer or some other sample to try, and he'd quiz me about the ingredients or the origins of the dish.

"Write a cookbook," he'd say. "You need to write a cookbook."

I'm not a writer, I'd tell him. "I can cook, and I can explain to you what I am doing, but I have never written a book."

"Let's do it together," he suggested. And so we did. I wrote the recipes for some of the most memorable foods from my childhood, from antipasti to pasta and rice dishes to entrées. Included were my recipes for Polenta with Fontina and Mushrooms, Shrimp and Mixed Bean Salad, Plum Gnocchi, Risotto with Squash Blossoms, Zucchini and Tagliatelle with Leek Sauce, Swordfish in Sweet and Sour Sauce, Roast Chicken with Rosemary and Oranges, Stuffed Breast of Veal, and Duck Roasted with Sauerkraut. Of course, I also shared many of my favorite dessert recipes from Chocolate Zabaglione Cake to Apple-Custard Tart. What was special about this book was that, along with the recipes, I included stories, memories, and even photographs from my childhood growing up in Istria.

I was very proud the day **La Cucina di Lidia: Recipes and Memories from Italy's Adriatic Coast** hit the bookstores in 1990, and I was grateful to Doubleday for making it happen. Seeing these beloved family recipes in print made me realize how important it was to record and document them. Even better was that I was sharing them with others who could now enjoy them, too. The book's publication brought even more attention to Felidia—and me. It was so popular that it was reprinted in 2003 with a new subtitle, **Distinctive Regional Cuisine from the North of Italy**, and it continues to sell even today.

Over the years, I got to know both Julia Child and James Beard well, and Julia and I developed a solid friendship. She was so much fun to be around, and I admired her frankness. If she had something on her mind, she did not hold back. I was surprised to learn that, as accomplished as she was in the kitchen, she did not consider herself a chef. She thought of herself more as a cook; she was someone who found a deep passion for French cooking and wanted to share it with the women of America.

At a Williams-Sonoma book signing
with Julia Child and Chuck Williams

In time, she invited me to dine with her at her home in Cambridge, and, on subsequent visits, to cook with her in her iconic kitchen. And I had her to my home in Douglaston. By then, our friendship was going into its eighth year, and Julia had tried my wild mushroom risotto and was desperate to learn how to prepare it.

Joe did not have the good fortune of joining us on the night Julia came for her risotto lesson. But my mother, Felice, Tanya, and my mother's new friend, Giovanni, were there.

Ten years after my father's passing, my mother had met someone new. His name was Giovanni Bencina, and he was widowed, just like her. The two had met at the Magnanini Winery in Wallkill, New York, where we had gone one Sunday for an Italian farmhouse meal and some **balera** music and dancing.

Giovanni invited my mother to dance, and at the end of the event, he expressed interest in seeing her again. When my mother put him off, I pulled him aside and slipped him the phone number and address of Felidia, telling him, "She is there almost every morning."

Sure enough, the following day, Giovanni appeared at the restaurant to see my mother. He continued to pursue her until she finally gave in. With Felice's and my blessing, Giovanni eventually moved in with us, into my mother's upstairs apartment. They planted a garden together every year.

He pruned the grape trestle and replanted the fig tree whenever the cold winter got to it. He took my mother shopping and to visit friends, and on some Sundays they returned to Magnanini's to dance.

Julia was excited to meet everyone, and settled in at my kitchen counter as I fired up the stove in preparation for our risotto lesson, which was great fun. I wanted her to really feel at home and to experience an Italian family. After the meal, Felice pulled out his accordion. He always played it at holiday time, and we would end up singing along, which is exactly what happened the night Julia came to dinner. We cooked, we ate, we sang, we even danced. It was a magical evening.

The next time Julia came to Douglaston, she was with a camera crew. It was 1993, and she wanted me to appear as a guest chef on her **Master Chefs** series, which aired on Public Television. The premise of the series was for America's master chefs to show Julia their best recipes. I would be cooking two dishes, Risotto ai Funghi Selvatici, risotto with wild mushrooms, and Orecchiette con Broccoli di Rape e Salsicce, orecchiette ("little ears," a pasta shape) with broccoli rabe and sweet sausage. And I would be doing the preparation right in my own kitchen.

Watching the crew set up in my kitchen had me feeling a little nervous. But the jitters quickly passed once I began demonstrating my first recipe.

"When one talks about the Italian table, pasta always comes to mind," I began. "But rice is always a second runner-up, and today we are going to do a risotto, a risotto with mushrooms. . . ." Now I was off, cutting the mushrooms, preparing the pots, and explaining my techniques to the viewers. Every now and again, I'd catch a glimpse of the camera out of the corner of my eye, but for the most part, I tried to stay in the moment and focus on what I was doing in the kitchen.

It was a lot of fun, and being in my own kitchen made it that much easier. At the end of the segment, everyone gathered around my kitchen table to enjoy the fruits of my labor. This time, Joe was with us, along with my mother and Giovanni, but Tanya was not. She was now a senior at Georgetown University in Washington, D.C., and we missed her.

We all had fun celebrating what would turn out to be my debut on Public Television. Once again, Felice pulled out his accordion and played some tunes for the camera, while Julia and the rest of us feasted on the risotto and the pasta. The episode was even nominated for an Emmy Award in 1994. It would be another four years before I came back to Public Television, this time with my own show, **Lidia's Italian Table.**

23

Feeding Others = Feeding Me

I certainly acknowledge and enjoy my success now, but my first years as a woman chef in New York were full of a lot of hard work and almost as many trepidations. Would I make it among all of the male chefs, who were towering above me with their toques—those tall, white chef's hats? I never was comfortable with those hats. But to be part of the restaurant scene you had to participate at events and fund-raisers, as well as teach, sharing your art and meeting a lot of great professionals; I could always learn something from them. And so I did, doing cooking demos and schlepping pots, pans, pasta, and sauce all over New York, and across America, too. In those early days, I had to get our name out there and move the business along. I did whatever it took to let people know about and taste my regional Italian food.

At that time, a line of mostly French chefs dominated New York's restaurant scene. My presence was questioned in the beginning, but once they saw me in action and tasted my food, the doors opened for me, and I became part of the gang—Daniel Boulud, Jean-Georges, André Soltner, Éric Ripert, Jacques Pépin, Thomas Keller, and more. It hadn't been quite so challenging to fall in with the contingency of American women chefs, including the likes of Alice Waters, Mary Sue Milliken, Tracy de Jardin, Susan Feniger, Barbara Lynch, Gale Gand, Nancy Silverton, and Emily Luchetti. But with the male chefs there seemed to be a sense of competition. Among the female chefs, there was more camaraderie. We needed to stick together; we needed to showcase the strengths of women in the kitchen.

I hadn't realized, when I first opened Felidia, just how unusual it was for a woman to be at the helm. In Italy, it was the women who mostly cooked at home and in the restaurants. Cooking was always a family affair, so being in the kitchen was not a big issue. But as I began to get involved in the different culinary and restaurant organizations, and as I started attending conferences, I realized that women had been largely marginalized. Being a chef was a man's profession.

In Felidia's early days, no one ever believed I was the chef. I had to assert myself, and I did that by being a professional, being prepared and passionate, being the best at whatever I did, even at the events with the big chefs in the starchy white toques. In my heart, I knew that the food I was cooking was real, the story of the Italian people at the table.

Physically, women have some challenges in the kitchen, like lifting heavy pots on and off the stove. You learn to adapt, you learn to find a way. But the biggest challenge for women in this industry is how to balance a family with such a demanding career. A chef's career starts young, with school, training, and apprenticeships. And just as a woman is getting ready to build a family, there's the inevitable next step up the career ladder.

In our industry, the hours are the worst. Most of the hardest-working hours are when everybody else is off. There is the lunch shift, but also dinners, weekends, and holidays. So how do you make up to your family for not being there when they want you most?

With our two restaurants in Queens, Felice and I always had Mondays off. We would take the kids and my mother out for dinner to an elegant restaurant, or even for a drive to the ocean. Dinner was shorter because the kids had school the next day. Oftentimes we'd eat at seaside places in Long Island (Bayville) or in the restaurants of other Istrians in Astoria. And we always closed for three weeks in the summer; this was our vacation, our time to spend with family. Yes, we dragged our children all over

Italy during those summer respites, sometimes to the point of exhaustion, but we were together, and that counted for something.

Joe and Tanya knew that this was our passion, that we had to do this. It was what kept the family going, what paid for that new bicycle, the sneakers, and the latest style of clothes they wanted. Felice and I were okay with their knowing that it takes hard work and dedication to make things happen. Once we opened Felidia, we closed on Sundays, and for the family that was an improvement.

Not that it didn't tug at my heartstrings when I heard Tanya or Joe ask, "Where were you?" for that important school event. If I couldn't cheer them on from the sidelines of a big game, they would moan, "All the parents were there except for you."

I knew that plenty of other parents had to work. I needed to make my kids realize that this was a choice, and a choice for the whole family, so we could all live better and take vacations, and they could go to the colleges of their choice. I continue to remind my children, and now my grandchildren, that our family success in the restaurant business is just that: the family, all together, made it happen, and they were a big part of that success.

As much as I loved what I did, I never really wanted my children to follow me into the restaurant business. I wanted them to have an American education and find an "American" job, whatever that meant.

✦✦

More than a decade had passed since we first opened Felidia, and we were starting to see more black on our financial statements than red—and far fewer outstanding loans and debts. We could finally breathe, and I was looking beyond our Manhattan restaurant business, with an eye to supporting charitable causes that I had never had been able to give as much support as I wanted in the past. Over time, I had really begun to understand the power of food, and how I could use my skills as a chef and restaurateur to benefit charities and help people in need. I wasn't just a chef; I had a prominent brand now that could be used for doing good in the community, and country, that I loved.

I remembered the many people who helped us on our trip to America, to furnish our first home, to fill our cupboard and refrigerator with food, who took the time to show us how to become Americans. I could not forget that kindness, and I wanted to give back in kind, to share with others in need.

One of the first big fund-raising events I took part in was on behalf of Share Our Strength (SOS), a national organization working to end childhood hunger in the United States. Founded by the brother-sister team of Billy and Debbie Shore, the organization was soliciting chefs to participate. My friend Angelo Vivolo and I thought it was a worthwhile cause, and we signed on to organize and manage the event for the Shores. This was the first major event for SOS. The fund-raiser was being held at Lincoln Center, in the first-floor foyer of Avery Fischer Hall. Angelo and I had attended a planning meeting with Billy and Debbie, and we decided we would call some of the best chefs in New York and ask them to prepare one of their signature recipes.

Each chef would have his or her own long table with burner equipment, and we would prepare our recipes as the guests floated from table to table. To ensure there was no duplication between the chefs participating, we spent the next half hour figuring out who would demonstrate what. As Angelo and I were talking it through, an idea emerged: **Why don't we do a little performance?** After all, we **were** holding the event in a performance hall. We cleared it with Billy and Debbie, but now we had to convince our fellow chefs to perform.

Henny Santo, the wife of one of the owners of Sign of the Dove, then one of Manhattan's most beloved restaurants, grew excited and volunteered to let us use their restaurant in off hours to rehearse. We decided we would all sing Édith Piaf's "La Vie en Rose," and one other melody, "Chitarra Romana" ("Roman Guitar"), an undisputed classic Italian song, written by Eldo di Lazzaro in 1934, and put on a kind of chorus-line show. We all had our lyrics, and we rehearsed them as best we could. It was so silly, which made it even more enjoyable.

We could hardly get through a rehearsal without somebody's breaking down in laughter.

I was really looking forward to the audience's reaction. We had rented a stagelike platform, which we set up toward the wall near the entrance to the building. The hall was full of guests when, on cue, we all started to walk from our assigned tables, made our way to the platform stage, got ourselves into formation, and began to belt out the lyrics to "La Vie en Rose," as we, in our crisp white jackets, kicked our legs high in the air and in unison. We were channeling the Rockettes, and it was hilarious. Our show garnered the event a lot of attention, and really put Share Our Strength on people's radar.

I enjoyed the feeling I got when I was helping others, and continued to participate in events and fund-raisers to benefit organizations such as C-CAP, the Careers Through Culinary Arts Program, which provides underprivileged students with scholarships to pursue careers in the restaurant and hospitality industries.

I also joined the National Organization of Italian American Women, and became a founding member of Women Chefs & Restaurateurs, along with Barbara Tropp, Barbara Lazaroff, Elka Gilmore, Johanne Killeen, Joyce Goldstein, Mary Sue Milliken, and Anne Rosenzweig. Our first meeting was held over coffee at Sarabeth's Kitchen on the Upper East Side, and our goal was to host events and conferences that would help connect women in the food industry with information that could help them succeed and thrive.

One of the biggest difficulties for women in our profession—back then and today—is obtaining access to financing. I had encountered this firsthand when I went to the bank looking to secure funds, back when we were buying the brownstone to build Felidia. I wasn't able to get approval until I brought Felice into the deal as a cosigner. No matter that he wasn't feeling well that day; he had to come with me to the bank to legitimize the transaction.

At the heart of this was the basic issue of empowering women and giving them the same opportunities in the workplace that men had long enjoyed. As far as I was concerned, the need to have a man as a cosigner on a loan was something that had to change.

One of the ideas that we explored as a group was to help bring women and big corporations together; we wanted to teach women how to be their own bosses, how to apply and obtain loans, and perhaps even to secure corporate sponsorships.

In 1973, the grande dame Carol Brock received a charter from the esteemed all-male organization Les Amis d'Escoffier to start Les Dames d'Escoffier, a society of professional women involved in the food, wine, and hospitality industries. Les Amis d'Escoffier had been established to pay homage to legendary chef Auguste Escoffier.

Brock's Les Dames d'Escoffier was officially

launched in 1976 at the French Consulate with fifty highly regarded women involved in the culinary arts in and around New York City. Carol was my friend and neighbor in Douglaston, and a few years after launching the organization she came to invite me to join. Membership is limited, and by invitation only.

This organization interested me because its members were such a diversified group of women, and they were promoting the education and advancement of women in careers related to the food industry, providing scholarships for women in the field. In 1985, Les Dames became an international organization. I am still involved.

To my delightful surprise, I learned that the organization had chosen to honor me with the Grand Dame Award of 2017. This award, given on alternating years, recognizes an "exceptional woman" who has made extraordinary contributions within the industry. Past recipients include Marcella Hazan, Julia Child, Marion Cunningham, Edna Lewis, Alice Waters, and more, so this was quite a mark of distinction. I was thrilled when, that same year, Tanya was extended an invitation to join the organization.

➤◄

Joe and Tanya were both maturing into young adults with focus and drive. Education had always been important to me, and I was pleased to see both of them doing well in school. I was proud when my son was accepted into Boston College, where he majored in philosophy with a minor in theology. After he graduated, I was over the moon with joy when he landed a job as a bond trader with Merrill Lynch in New York's financial district, where he went to work daily in a suit and tie and made big money decisions.

In 1989, we had marked Joe's graduation from Boston College and Tanya's concurrent graduation from Loyola School with a huge party at the house in Douglaston. We gave it a Roaring Twenties theme, and the guest list topped two hundred. For the young crowd, I had the driveway tented with a dance floor and DJ, and for the parents and grandparents a string quartet on the front patio, with tables set up on the stairs leading down toward the water. These educational milestones were cause for celebration, and Felice and I were ever so proud of both our children.

I was floored the day Joe showed up at Felidia, after two years working on Wall Street, and told me he'd quit.

"What do you mean, you quit? You just don't quit a job," I said, trying to avoid the urge to shout.

Joe explained that he was miserable in his job, and that he wanted to do something with food. Maybe he could hang around Felidia and help us out?

I didn't know how to respond. As a mother, I was always concerned with my children's education and pushed for them to study hard and continue to college and beyond. Of course, I shared the desire that every parent has, to see his or her children go further and live better lives than we did. But I was also driven in part by my humble beginnings as an immigrant. My background made it all the more important for me (and Felice) to see our children blossom and secure white-collar jobs.

The start of my career had involved many years of cooking and sweating in a kitchen, and those years were certainly not glamorous. I loved what I was doing, but there was no question it was hard work. The reality was that I did not want my children to pursue a career in the food business, mostly because of the long hours and the extended periods away from family. Yet, at some level, I realized that Felice and I had unintentionally infused them with a love, knowledge, and passion for the business. The more I thought about it, the more I realized that they had been in training for the restaurant business since they were born.

I didn't give my son an immediate answer that day. I wanted to think about what he had said, and I wanted to talk it over with Felice.

Since opening Felidia, Felice and I had been slowly growing apart. Building the restaurant had really exhausted him, and his passion for the industry seemed to be waning. He was seven years older than I, and he was starting to look forward to slowing down and enjoying a more leisurely pace.

He preferred spending time with his friends in Astoria, while I was working hard to keep Felidia busy—and profitable. I was invigorated by our success and eager to grow and expand as a businesswoman and a chef. I had begun making many important connections within the food industry as a result of all the fund-raising and charitable events I was attending, and I imagine that my newfound popularity was adding to our marital tension. Felice was a European man, and unaccustomed to seeing a woman be out front. I wasn't sure I wanted Joe to be in the middle of the growing tension between us.

I did a little research and learned that statistics showed that young adults were likely to change jobs up to three times before finding a profession they really connected with. I knew about passion and the meaning of what it was to connect. I just needed some more time to think—and discuss the matter with Felice. A few days passed before I spoke to my son again.

Finally, I sat down with Joe and told him that his father and I had agreed that he could start at Felidia, but we needed to be realistic. All three of us had strong personalities, and that brought with it the occasional clash. With tension between Felice and me already present, we came up with a plan to guard against parent-child problems at work.

We gave our son two thousand dollars and a list of wine producers, restaurant owners, prosciutto producers, and various friends we had made over the years all across Italy. He was to spend one year abroad, traveling to the various regions of the country and learning all he could about the Italian culture and its cuisine. We would call our friends to let them know that he would be making the trip, but it would be up to him to make arrangements, either to work with them, to serve as an apprentice, or simply to visit and get familiar with their products. Joe and Tanya spoke Italian with us at home, especially with my mother, so language would not be a barrier.

To my surprise, Joe readily embraced the assignment. We bought him a car to use in Italy, a very old Volkswagen Golf, and he had some money of his own, and he jumped in full-throttle. Traveling up and down Italy, he really got a feel for the culture. He came back with much more of an understanding of Italian food, as well as some funny stories. When he visited the Lungarotti family in Umbria, he was given an opportunity to work as an assistant chef in their small restaurant, Le Tre Vaselle. He was told to report to the kitchen at a given hour, unaware that a new chef was coming to start work there that same day. Joe arrived at the kitchen first and greeted the staff, and believing Joe was the new chef, they replied in unison, "**Buon giorno**, Chef." Joe liked the way the title sounded, but he was far from ready for that position. Everybody had a good laugh when he explained who he was, then quickly joined the others to peel the mounds of potatoes on the table in front of them.

Often he'd end up sleeping in his car. He learned that toilet paper was the one essential he didn't want to be without, so he kept a small stash in the back window of the vehicle.

When Joe came back to New York, he was enthusiastic, full of information, and ready to begin work at Felidia. He was with us about two months when he started growing restless. He wanted to know how he could expand—he didn't want to stay with Mom and Dad, he wanted to do something on his own. We encouraged him to begin looking at real estate with an eye toward opening his own restaurant.

"Go out there and find some deals," I told him.

My son hooked up with a commercial-real-estate agent and looked at a number of locations. He found a viable option at 355 West Forty-sixth Street, the site of a restaurant called Carolina, which had closed. The area was ideal. It was in Restaurant Row, near the theater district, and the landlord was quite reasonable. He offered Joe a twenty-five-year lease at a decent rent, and my son put his business skills to work, preparing an elaborate business plan.

He had chosen a high-traffic location with a lot of turnover, so his concept was to create a comfortable place that served really good Italian food at affordable prices. He envisioned a mix of traditional Italian and Italian American options. We worked on the menu and came up with the idea of offering diners three different pastas, which would be continuously served to them at the table by waiters who kept making the rounds with the steaming-hot pots. A salad was included with the unlimited pasta entrée, for one fixed price. The pasta sauces would vary according to the season, and the pastas themselves would vary—some fresh, such as ravioli and pappardelle, and some dry. The plan sounded like a winner. In fact, this concept is still in full force at Becco—Joe's first restaurant—where it is loved so much that we brought the same winning concept to our customers at Lidia's Kansas City, with the executive chef Dan Swinney in the kitchen, and to Lidia's Pittsburgh, as well.

To start, Felice and I agreed to give Joe $250,000 to spend on the building renovations. My mother chipped in a little bit, too.

The next step was to find a chef. Joe chose Giuseppe Vitale, an Italian immigrant who had a good Italian and Italian American palate. He named the restaurant Becco, derived from the Italian verb **beccare,** which means to peck, nibble, or savor in a discriminating way. Becco took off like a rocket, and it has not stopped since. Giuseppe in the kitchen and Joe in the dining room were a winning combination; they made a great team, and diners loved them both. But after three years, Giuseppe fell ill, and he decided to look for a less demanding job at another establishment.

William Gallagher, who certainly was not Italian, but had worked in Italian restaurants, took over the reins. Billy's knowledge, coupled with some time he spent in the kitchen with me, earned us a top-notch chef; he is still in the kitchen at Becco today.

Joe's restaurant came to life in somewhat the same way that Felidia had; it was a family effort. Basically, Joe rolled up his sleeves, got in there, and worked, physically renovating the place and making it happen. From the outside, the restaurant looks like a hip, recently renovated farmhouse. Inside, the ambience is more like that of a well-worn family trattoria, with wooden beams and decorative chickens and roosters.

In keeping with his "affordable" theme, Joe made a list of fifty different wines at eighteen dollars a bottle (now a bit more expensive), and his collection continued to grow. Becco took off like mad when it opened its doors in 1993, with business booming from day one. It was a huge success, and we were all thrilled.

That same year, Tanya graduated from Georgetown University, where she had majored in art history. She had actually completed her studies one semester early and then spent six months in Italy, meeting artists and going to museums. It didn't hurt that her love interest, Corrado Manuali, lived in Italy as well.

Tanya met Corrado in 1989, when he stayed with us that summer at our home in Douglaston while attending an English-language course in Manhattan. Felice and I had met his father at a hospitality convention in California the summer before, so, when he called from Italy to let me know his son was going to be in town, I invited Corrado to stay with us. Tanya was away in Normandy, France, on a summer-abroad program, when he arrived, so she met him for the first time at JFK Airport when he and I came to meet her flight. His expression told me everything I needed to know. But, even though Corrado clearly fancied my daughter, she found him a nuisance at first and was annoyed when I asked her to let him tag along with her and her friends.

➤•◄

In the fall of 1993, Tanya began her master's program at Syracuse University, as a fellow on full scholarship in Italian Renaissance art. She spent one semester there, and the last three semesters of the program in Florence, Italy. Corrado was an officer with the Guardia di Finanza, an Italian militarized law-enforcement agency under the authority of the Ministry of Economy and Finance. By this time, Tanya's annoyance had fallen by the wayside; they moved in together in Prato, a small town about twenty-five minutes outside of Florence.

The master's program combined research and serving as a student teacher of undergraduates doing a semester abroad through Syracuse University's program in Florence, a role that Tanya enjoyed immensely. She completed her degree in the spring of 1995, and that September started her Ph.D. in Italian Renaissance art history at Oxford University. She spent her first year in England, and the remainder of her research in the archives in Italy. We knew something was happening between her and Corrado, but we got very little in the way of information from our daughter.

Then, in June 1994, the two were engaged. I actually got to play a big part in the engagement. Diamond engagement rings are not customary in Italy, so providing one was foreign to Corrado. But, understanding its importance to Tanya, he went with his father to a jewelry store in Italy and purchased a ring. The two were in the car and halfway home when he instructed his father to turn around and take him back to the store. He was convinced Tanya would not like the ring he had selected, so he returned it.

Meanwhile, Tanya was window-shopping for engagement rings in New York City while visiting home. She loves estate rings and fell in love with one at Marcus Estate Jewelry, which was located inside Bloomingdale's. Over the next two days, she returned to the store to "visit" the ring; she even brought me along to see it. On the third day, when she went once again to admire it, she learned from the salesperson that it had been sold.

What Tanya didn't know was that I was the one who had purchased it. After my visit to the store, I called Corrado to tell him about the ring. It turned out that my cousin Marie Matticchio, whose husband, Louis, had helped us move to Astoria when we first came to America, worked at Bloomingdale's, and she used her discount to help me buy the ring for Corrado, to make it affordable for my future son-in-law. Tanya knew none of this and was quite upset that her dream ring was gone.

On June 24, 1994, Tanya and I were together at Felidia. We had come into the city from Douglaston in two separate cars; when it was time to leave, I told her she needed to rush home in hers because I had loaded ice cream into the backseat and I didn't want it to melt. I said I had a stop to make—I was giving a lecture on food—and would meet her back in Douglaston in a few hours. I was really heading to JFK Airport to pick up Corrado, who was flying in from Italy to propose to my daughter.

There was police activity on the road as we neared my house, and when we got closer, I saw Tanya standing outside of her vehicle, speaking with a uniformed officer. She had been in a minor accident, and I quickly pulled over to make sure she was okay. When she saw that Corrado was in the car, she became curious. She'd had no idea he was coming into town.

I told her to finish up with the police and come straight home. When she arrived at the house, she found me in the kitchen and began talking about the accident. I immediately interrupted her. "Why aren't you going upstairs to see Corrado?" I asked.

When she got to the bedroom where he was staying, she found him down on one knee, her beloved ring in hand, and a proposal on his lips.

Joe had also met someone special. A young woman named Deanna Damiano had captured his attention. They had been introduced by a mutual friend. One year younger than Joe, she was interested in merchandising and started as an associate buyer for Bloomingdale's in the training program. Both sides of her family were second-generation Italian American, so she was comfortable in our very Italian family. I found her to be a deliciously quiet girl, and we loved her at first sight. Most important, Joe was in love and very happy around her.

Joe and Deanna were married on February 19, 1995, at the Church of St. Ignatius Loyola, a parish church administered by the Society of Jesus, on the Upper East Side. Four hundred and fifty guests crowded the pews to witness the exchanging of their vows. Father Frank T. Kennedy from Boston College presided over the service. Father Kennedy was an internationally recognized scholar of the Jesuit music tradition and a founding member of the college's music department. He became a confidant for Joe; they met many times for dinner after he graduated. It meant a lot to him that Father Kennedy could be there to officiate.

We held the reception at the Plaza, the regal, turn-of-the century hotel on Fifth Avenue. The Plaza for me was the perfect fairy-tale wedding venue; it was elegant and grand at the same time. I knew the chef, Joe Friel, having worked with him on benefits for various organizations. I also knew Paul Nicaj, one of the catering managers there. Paul had worked for us at Felidia, and now runs restaurants and catering halls of his own. My friendship with these two men enabled me to go into the kitchen and work alongside them to prepare my son's menu. I saw no better way to welcome Deanna into the family than actually be a part of the flavor of the event.

I spent the better part of the week preceding the wedding cooking my Istrian specialties. The cocktail-hour buffet included everything from sauerkraut to **baccalà** to foie gras to a whole suckling pig. This was an Istrian-Italian wedding, and being in the kitchen gave me the opportunity to express our ethnicity.

Among the more traditional offerings was my homemade **krafi**, the Istrian wedding pasta similar to ravioli and stuffed with various cheeses, plus raisins, cloves, cinnamon, and orange rind—all the seasonings once considered by the Venetians to be elitist. We dressed the pasta with the sauce from the roast. **Krafi** was something that we served at Felidia, and I was happy to prepare them for Joseph and Deanna's wedding. We stuffed more than one thousand ravioli—each person typically eats three or four, and 450 guests attended the wedding.

After the wedding, Joe and Deanna moved into the apartment above Becco. At the time, Restaurant Row was not as glamorous as it is now. It was still a bit Hell's Kitchen–esque, and there were some shady people out there late at night. Deanna knew what she was getting into when she married my son, and she was okay with it all.

The following September, Tanya and Corrado had their wedding reception at the Plaza, too. We served the same spread of food as at Joe's wedding, and, once again, I worked in the kitchen with the chefs to prepare it all.

Tanya was more than happy to have an affair similar to her brother's. She loved the venue, and her only request to separate the two evenings was that there be white flowers on all the tables. Her main concern was her wedding gown, a dress made of silk and hand-pieced lace with short sleeves and an open neckline, which she had custom-made in Rome and carried on the plane from Italy. Part of Corrado's formal military attire, which he would wear for the big day, was a sword, which he had to check with the pilot of the plane, as is required of all weapons. In keeping with Italian tradition,

Corrado paid for the dress. They were a beautiful couple. Between them, they invited twenty-five guests, fifteen of their joint friends and ten of Corrado's family members from Italy. The remaining two hundred were my and Felice's guests.

Once again, we held the ceremony at St. Ignatius Loyola on Park Avenue. Father Eugene Prior presided over the nuptials. He was the dean of students while Tanya was at Loyola, and would later baptize both of her children. A charismatic spiritual leader, he bore a striking resemblance to my father, with his chiseled features, gray hair, and piercing blue eyes. Sometimes, when I was around him, I felt as if my father were there with me.

Tanya and Corrado also had a second ceremony and reception in Italy, for Corrado's family and friends. They held the event at the American Academy in Rome, a research-and-arts institution that offers opportunities for American artists, thinkers, writers, architects, and musicians to spend some time in Rome.

Tanya's beautiful and elegant Italian wedding took place at the academy's Villa Aurelia, on the Janiculum, one of Rome's famed "seven hills." Mrs. Clara Jessup Heyland, an American heiress from Philadelphia, had bequeathed the villa to the Academy in 1909. We had that event catered, and some of our friends traveled from America to attend.

I was on the board of the American Academy, and continued my involvement with them even after the big event. I embraced the opportunity to help the then president and CEO, Adele Chatfield-Taylor, brainstorm ways in which visiting Americans in Italy could get more involved in the Italian culture. Of course, food was the idea I put on the table. We redesigned the whole kitchen, and began hiring chefs to do the cooking. Dinner was something the fellows all had to take together, and I enjoyed participating in some of the nightly meals, a heady brew of intellectualism and food. I liked just sitting back and listening as the parties shared their thoughts and ideas.

Making things happen at an institution such as this is a long, bureaucratic process, but we persevered, and we made some very positive changes. We also started developing a garden there. Alice Waters got involved, too. She also brought young American chefs to Rome. Under her guidance, the program has really evolved.

Tanya and Corrado remained in Prato, a half-hour northwest of Florence, after their Italian wedding. Tanya continued student teaching while working on her Ph.D. thesis, and Corrado returned to his full-time post as an officer with the Guardia di Finanza while completing his law degree at La Sapienza, University of Pisa.

I was so pleased that I had been able to give my children these special wedding celebrations. Many a night, lying on my cot at the San Sabba refugee camp, imagining my future, I had promised myself that when I had children I was going to give them the best that I could; with these elaborate and elegant affairs, I felt I had fulfilled that pledge.

→·←

Unfortunately, my relationship with Felice continued to deteriorate. We wanted and needed different things, and he was beginning to look elsewhere. After thirty-one years of marriage, we amicably divorced in 1997. The children were both married by this point and beginning their own lives and families, which made things less complicated. We agreed that I would buy the business from him. I needed to close the door to that chapter of my life and move on. As with any breakup, there were some hurt feelings. I focused on forgiveness, which is such a potent medicine. In forgiving, you liberate yourself, and I was ready to be liberated. We continued to celebrate family holidays together. I wanted our children and grandchildren to know us both separately and together.

Felice spent the remainder of his years going back and forth between Istria and the United States. On December 12, 2010, at the age of seventy, he passed away from complications of diabetes. We held a funeral mass at the Most Precious Blood Roman Catholic Church in Astoria, the church where we were married, and he was laid to rest at St. Michael's Cemetery in Flushing.

With the divorce final, now on my own, I saw—
and pursued—a variety of opportunities. There
was nothing, and no one, holding me back, and
newfound energy and enthusiasm propelled me
forward. The sadness associated with the divorce
passed quickly, and I threw myself into a variety of
projects, including educational efforts, mentoring
up-and-coming chefs and restaurateurs, and doing
more television. I could embrace my children's entrée into the restaurant business much more freely;
feeling good about myself, I could support whatever they wanted to do, emotionally as well as financially.

24

Nonna Lidia

One of my biggest joys in life is being a grandmother. In the past, when friends who were grandparents would share their joy—countless pictures, and stories of milestones in their grandchildren's lives—I would smile enthusiastically, but I could not help marveling at how exaggerated their sentiments seemed. Now that I have five delicious grandchildren, I know better. It is extraordinarily fulfilling.

There is something about grandchildren that is almost intangible, unexplainable. They are part of you, your very body and soul. The eyes are the same color, the nose resembles the family nose, and as they grow older their mannerisms, their talents, likes, and dislikes fit in with the family gene pool. And yet you bore none of the effort and pain involved in birthing these children. They are yours just to enjoy.

I recall meeting each one of them after they were

born, starting with Olivia, Deanna and Joe's daughter, my first grandchild. Olivia arrived on December 27, 1997. As soon as I saw her, I picked her up in the nursery, brought her close to my chest, and rested her little head on my shoulder. I felt the bonding instantly. That is how it was with the other four, too: Lorenzo, Miles, Ethan, and Julia. I would literally smell them, drawing deep breaths, not unlike the way a mother dog smells her puppies. I wanted to recognize their scent forever. I cuddled their cheeks against mine, felt the warmth of a new life, and held them tight. I wanted them to sense my heartbeat, the beat of a heart that would love them unconditionally and forevermore.

As they have grown, I have loved being a guide, a crutch, from their first crawl to their first step, to their first grade, to the hard choice of high schools, to the competitive world of colleges and universities. In a way, I am there to help my children raise their children, just as my mother helped with mine. Somehow, I feel that I am an extension of their parents and share the parental duties. But I also want to be there for them when they invariably confront life's challenges—a refuge, a safe and secure port, when life throws them a storm. I want them to have complete trust in Nonna Lidia and confide all their pains and joys in me. And as I share with them my life experiences, I hope and know they will take some of those experiences and use them to build their own lives.

What is important is that they learn how to love, that they have respect always for themselves and for the people around them, and that they strive, to their full potential, to embrace the gifts God bestowed on them, and do this with passion in their hearts.

Dear Olivia, Lorenzo, Miles, Ethan, and Julia, this book is for you.

I am writing it so that each one of my beloved grandchildren will know the courage their great-grandparents Erminia and Vittorio had in leaving their homeland to search for freedom and a safer place to raise their children. And so that they may know of the struggles of their grandparents Lidia and Felice as they sought to find a place in this great new land. It is my hope that they, and all who read this story, better understand the hardships and the successes of America's immigrants.

Tanya and Corrado chose to return to New York in 1998. Corrado wanted to start a family, and he knew that, as a new mother Tanya needed to be close to her own family. I was ecstatic when I learned the news. And of course I offered to help them find a house. A friend suggested a small Tudor in my neighborhood that was in their price range, and soon we were neighbors. Corrado enrolled at Fordham University School of Law to earn a master's degree in law, which, in addition to his Italian law degree, would enable him to practice in the United States.

My mother, me, and my five grandchildren—
Miles, Julia, Lorenzo, Ethan, and Olivia—in my
backyard

Joe and Deanna were already living in Douglaston when Tanya and Corrado arrived. They had
purchased a small home not too far from me. And,
with the return of Tanya and Corrado, I had everybody close. In a way, it was reminiscent of how we
had once lived in Busoler, able to walk from house
to house and share that deep sense of family.

It was great while it lasted. Eventually, Joe and
Deanna sold their house in Douglaston and bought
a home in Connecticut. Still, I have Tanya and two
of my grandchildren, Lorenzo and Julia, just a few
blocks away. And now Joe and Deanna and their
children live in Manhattan.

Over the years, my grandchildren have brought

me unfettered joy: our time in the kitchen and the garden, our time traveling and getting to discover the world together, our time for storytelling in Nonna Lidia's bed. We would snuggle together under the covers, and in unison they would ask, "Nonna, tell us a story from when you were a little girl." Nothing has brought me greater pleasure than to share memories of times spent in my own grandmother's courtyard.

>»-«<

After seventeen years of working in the Felidia kitchen, I began having problems with my knees. I realized the time had come to bring in an executive chef. The restaurant was running like a fine-tuned machine, and I needed someone who would continue to nurture and love my baby.

I tried two chefs, one Italian, the other American, but neither of them felt like a good fit. So I called my friend Chef Luigi Caputo in Torino. Luigi had a delicious restaurant, Ristorante Balbo di Torino, and I trusted his judgment.

"Let me think about it," he said.

A few days later, Luigi phoned me back. "I think I have somebody, Lidia. He is a young man, a great talent, and I think that you would get along."

"Okay, let me talk to him."

The young man's name was Fortunato Nicotra. He was born in Sicily, and his parents migrated to

Torino, in the heart of northern Italy's Piemonte region, to work in the factories there. He attended culinary school in Torino, and went on to work in restaurants in Germany and France before returning to Sicily, where he was running two restaurants, both with a Michelin star, when Luigi reached out to him.

After several long-distance calls, we arranged to meet at Felidia in New York. When we got into the kitchen together, Fortunato wanted to show me all the fancy foods he knew how to prepare. I tasted his dishes, and I liked what I saw. But it wasn't quite what I was seeking for Felidia. I knew his mother had cooked for him in Sicily, and I asked him if he could prepare some of the dishes she had served. It was then I knew I had a winner. He agreed to come to New York for two years, and I set about securing his paperwork.

Turning over my position in the kitchen was not an easy process. But I needed his expertise, and we found a way to collaborate. He was not resistant to my kind of protectiveness of the restaurant and my food, and he had what it took to run the kitchen. Slowly, he took over, dish by dish. After producing my dishes elegantly and with comfort, he added his own flavors.

We still sit down and talk about recipes. We send food and wine professionals to Italy to learn, and he and I go together, sometimes with Billy Gallagher from Becco. Some of our other chefs, such as

Dan Sweeney and Cody Hogan of Lidia's Kansas City and Del Posto's Melissa Rodriguez, now also join us.

Fortunato was in the kitchen with us for only a few months when Ruth Reichl of **The New York Times** gave Felidia three stars. A few years later, in 1998, **Wine Spectator** named Felidia "One of the Top Ten Italian Restaurants in the U.S."

By then, Fortunato was happy in his position at Felidia, and he agreed to stay on with us here in America. To my surprise, he ended up marrying my director of public relations, Shelly Burgess, who is also an executive producer of my TV show. Shelly, a bright young woman from West Virginia, was a graduate of Vanderbilt University and met Tanya when she, too, was in Florence earning her master's through Syracuse University. The two became friends, and when Shelly decided to return home to the States, Tanya recommended I interview her. She has been with me ever since.

It was not love at first sight for Fortunato and Shelly, at least not for Shelly. She was working as my assistant at Felidia when Fortunato first arrived, and she questioned whether I really wanted him at the restaurant with us; she found him arrogant and forward and had serious reservations about my choice. Eventually, he wore her down, and the two are now happily married with three beautiful children, Alex, Julia, and Luca, and a lovely home in New Jersey.

Having Fortunato at Felidia was a godsend. Knowing my baby was in good hands made it a lot easier to say yes when the producer of Julia Child's **Master Chefs** series came a-courting. Both he, Geoffrey Drummond, and the show's director, Nat Katzman, called me at my home that day, full of compliments about my performance on Julia's show back in 1993. I was poised to extend my gratitude when suddenly one of them asked, "How about a cooking show of your own?"

I was flattered and flabbergasted all at once. After my visit to Julia's home in Cambridge some years back, when I had sat in the very kitchen where she had filmed her show, I had briefly envisioned what it might be like to host a show from my kitchen. Now, with Julia's encouragement and her blessing, I was about to find out.

The two men felt I had the potential to host an Italian cooking show and teach America how to cook Italian as Julia had done for French cuisine. I was ready to give it a shot. A La Carte Communications was the name of their production company.

Taking Julia's example, I proposed we tape the show in my kitchen and air it on Public Television. I had and have a great admiration for Public Television. It had started in 1970, about twelve years after we arrived in America. I loved watching its classical programs. And I felt good having my children watch these educational programs, too. Public Television was a platform offering intelligent shows and information, and it was where I wanted to share my knowledge about the Italian culinary culture.

I might have been expressive and a good teacher of what I loved—cooking—but I was not a trained actress. There was a lot to learn along the way. I must say, the A La Carte team, coupled with Julia's example and encouragement, is what shaped me into the TV chef I am today. I underwent no official TV training, just learned on the set as we went along.

Then there was the whole challenge of sponsorship, as well as fund-raising, both of which A La Carte took care of. I was not at all aware of the hard work it takes to make a good television show, or the complexities. Once taping began, my whole house was overrun by the production team; the three cameras and various lights had cables running all over the downstairs, into the cellar and the garage. All of the windows and doors had to be covered with tape to prevent any natural light from entering the kitchen. My living room, with all the furniture piled high in one corner, became the control room, and Tanya's old bedroom became the makeup-and-wardrobe department. The garage was filled with refrigerators, and the kitchen and living room in my mother's upstairs apartment became the food-prep area.

Starting in 1998 and for the next fifteen years, **Lidia's Italian Table, Lidia's Italian-American Kitchen, Lidia's Family Table,** and **Lidia's Italy** were filmed in my house in Douglaston. My mother, whom everyone has come to know as "Grandma," the children, the grandchildren—whoever was in the house—would make guest appearances on the show.

A La Carte had a business and creative plan. Each new set of shows was accompanied by a matching cookbook, used as the basis for the season. The advance money on the books helped to fund production of the shows.

We began the series with scripts culled from my first cookbook, **La Cucina di Lidia,** and a second, **Lidia's Italian Table,** which I published in 1998 with William Morrow.

Working in front of the camera was not difficult at all. As long as there was a stove between the camera and me, and I had a pot and a mixing spoon in my hands, all went **a gonfie vele,** full-sail. I was looking beyond my kitchen to share my passion now with millions of people over the "tube," but I felt that my viewer was right there with me in my kitchen. I was teaching a friend.

In 2001, **Lidia's Italian-American Kitchen,** published by Knopf, provided material for our shows. This was the first book we published with Knopf, and we have continued our relationship with them ever since. In 2004, **Lidia's Family Table** provided us with more new material. Viewers especially loved the episodes my mother appeared in, and we received a tremendous outpouring of support from our audience.

My mother enjoyed being a part of the programming, and she continued to assist me in other areas of the business. Back when I was still in the kitchen at Felidia, she insisted on working in the coat-check room, checking people's coats, umbrellas, briefcases, and other belongings as they arrived for dinner. Having her in that role made me feel awkward, but she loved the job, and loved having friendly interactions with our clientele. Frankly, there was no way she was going to give it up—no matter what I had to say. My mother also got involved with some of our charitable works. One year, on Christmas Day, we opened Becco only for families with children undergoing treatment for cancer and living at the Ronald McDonald House in New York City. She dressed up as Mrs. Claus and spent the evening entertaining all the kids, putting smiles on their faces as well as the faces of their parents.

After six years of filming, I separated from A La Carte Productions in 2004 to form a production company, Tavola Productions, with my director of publicity, Shelly Burgess, and my daughter, Tanya, at the helm.

No doubt, Tanya and I shared a few traits, including a drive to succeed and a passion for life—both inside and outside the kitchen. But Tanya's extensive schooling had also empowered her with sharp business skills and an ability to research and evaluate complex proposals. After returning from Italy, my daughter had wisely taken some time to settle into motherhood after giving birth to her first son, Lorenzo. But I knew it wouldn't be long before she started to yearn for more and pursue her career anew. By then, my business was expanding and I realized I needed the assistance of a skilled businessperson to help grow the business. There were cookbooks to be written, TV shows to be produced, and a growing number of opportunities to expand the business with new products and ventures. I approached Tanya and asked her if she'd be interested. To my delight, she said yes.

Almost overnight, Tanya became one of the managers of our new production company, negotiating sponsorships and raising funds. In 2005, we released our first set of shows and have continued to produce them ever since. Happily, Shelly has continued with us as an integral part of the team.

The filming of **Lidia's Italy** continued with scripts based on two companion cookbooks published by Knopf in 2007 and 2009, **Lida's Italy** and **Lidia Cooks from the Heart of Italy**. The latter was the first book I co-wrote with Tanya, and I really enjoyed the collaboration. We each had our strengths; Tanya is a great researcher, organizer, and storyteller. I am a good recipe writer and tester, with endless enthusiasm to teach and feed people. We were a perfect team.

It works this way: We come up with an idea for a book together, and also talk to Shelly about what it would look like on TV. Then it is pitched to the publisher, Knopf in our case. If it is a go, Tanya makes a rough list of recipes, trying to arrive at the right combination of courses or sections of the book. Then she and I talk with Amy Stevenson, the culinary producer, who tests the recipes with us. We decide what ingredients to add in, and which ones to take out. At that point, Tanya pulls together a rough outline for each recipe and creates a huge document, before Amy, Tanya, and I begin testing.

We usually do the testing in blocks of four to five days—more than that is too much, because it is an exhausting process. We cook about fifteen things a day. Tanya cuts, preps, shops, and chops, and Amy and I cook, with Amy writing it all down on the recipe drafts. Tanya snaps pictures as the food is being completed. We then taste it to see if we like it or need to make any changes. We test every single recipe. It takes about two years to prepare a cookbook from start to finish.

In 2010, I also wrote a children's book, **Nonna Tell Me a Story: Lidia's Christmas Kitchen,** released by Running Press Kids. This book had nothing to do with my show and everything to do with sharing my childhood stories, from growing up on the farm in Busoler with Nonna Rosa. I was thrilled when it was published, for I was able to share a little piece of Grandma Rosa with children everywhere. An added benefit was that now my grandchildren would be able to share Nonna's stories with their children someday. Two more children's books, **Lidia's Egg-Citing Farm Adventure** and **Nonna's Birthday Surprise,** came later.

Lidia's Italy and **Lidia Cooks from the Heart of Italy,** published in 2007 and 2009, continued to give us plenty of material for our upcoming shows. These two cookbooks together cover all the regions of Italy, plus Istria. We had quite the challenge raising funds for the companion shows, because we had big ideas of filming lots of field footage in Italy. We did it, and got some gorgeous footage. We did loads of traveling and spent hours on the road, capturing video of me with cows grazing high up in the mountains, me out on boats with local fishermen. We had a crew of about ten people, among them two cameramen. Tanya was usually out with half of the crew in one place while I was filming parts of the show with the other half. There were some good laughs, lots of card playing on the bus, but loads of work, too. After traveling to all the different regions of Italy for **Lidia's Italy** and all the Italian American communities for two seasons of **Lidia's Italy in America,** I returned to the studio and focused on cooking, tips, and interviews. My material was developed from recipes from my cookbooks **Lidia's Favorite Recipes, Lidia's Commonsense Italian Cooking, Lidia's Mastering the Art of Italian Cuisine,** and **Lidia's Celebrate Like an Italian.**

In 2013, after fifteen years of filming in my kitchen, we ceased production at my house in Douglaston.

The productions were getting too complicated for the modest space, and I was afraid Grandma would trip on the matrix of cables and wires there. We moved the show's production to the Clarke Kitchen showroom in Norwalk, Connecticut. Tom Clarke, the owner and CEO, was very receptive to having us film on the premises. In addition to the filming, we did several fund-raising events for local schools in the space.

I am fortunate to see the recognition **Lidia's Italy** has received since it was launched. The James Beard Foundation awarded us the distinction of their award for Television Food Show, National or Local in 2009. We had also been nominated for Best National Television Cooking Show or Special in 2002, and Television Food Show, National, in 2007. In 2008, **Lidia's Italy** was nominated for an Emmy, and in 2013 I won the Emmy Award in the category of "Outstanding Culinary Host."

In addition to my series, we began filming a number of television specials for Public Television. **Lidia Celebrates America: Holiday for Heroes** premiered on Public Television in December 2016. The episode introduced viewers to seven military veterans who shared their incredibly inspiring stories with me. A quest for freedom is what had brought me to America, so it was important for me to pay homage to the men and women of our armed services and to highlight the lifesaving sacrifices they make daily for our freedom. In 2017, **Lidia Celebrates**

America received the award for Best Special from the James Beard Foundation. The previous year, the foundation had recognized another one of our special programs, **Lidia Celebrates America: Home for the Holidays,** in this same category.

❧ ❦

Fortunately, my restaurant business has continued to flourish. Felidia, under the direction of Fortunato Nicotra, hasn't missed a beat. And we have expanded Becco three times.

Joe's early success as a restaurateur emboldened him to seek out other opportunities. One year, I was asked by the James Beard Foundation to spearhead the press dinner that takes place on the eve of the big award event. For restaurateurs, these awards are the equivalent of the Academy Awards. I decided to gather all the young chefs who were doing Italian food and doing it well.

One of the people I invited was Mario Batali, an up-and-coming chef at the time, who had his own place, Pó, in the West Village.

Of course, I also invited young sommeliers, and Joe was among them. That night, Joe and Mario met for the first time, and soon they were talking about going into business together.

Mario sold Pó, and the two opened Babbo on Waverly Place in 1998. The restaurant featured fine Italian food served to a rock-and-roll soundtrack.

The menu, written in "goofily charming menu language," as **New York** magazine described it, featured classic Italian recipes using seasonal, local ingredients. Spicy Two-Minute Calamari Sicilian Lifeguard Style, Mint Love Letters, and wine by the **quartino** were just some of the offerings. Reviewers and foodies loved the place.

Their second joint venture was Lupa, a Roman trattoria, and then came Del Posto, with a menu of updated Italian classics served in glorious surroundings, which Mario, Joe, and I opened together on Tenth Avenue in 2005. In 2010, **The New York Times** gave Del Posto, with Executive Chef Mark Ladner at the helm, a glowing four-star review, making us the first Italian restaurant in forty years to receive such a distinction. Del Posto was also awarded a Michelin star, as well as the coveted Relais & Châteaux distinction, a Five Diamond Award from AAA, and the Grand Award from **Wine Spectator.** Melissa Rodriquez, a woman with much talent, is now our chef at Del Posto, and we are so proud of her.

Esca, a southern-Italian trattoria celebrating the fruits of the sea, with David Pasternack as a partner chef, took the place of a previous restaurant Joe and I had, Frico Bar. Joe and I opened Lidia's Kansas City in 1998, followed by Lidia's Pittsburgh in the Pittsburgh Strip District in 2001, which we opened in a former railroad house just north of the city's historic Union Station. Tanya eventually took over

the ownership and management of those two restaurants, as well as the management of Felidia.

❧❧

Periodically, our yearly vacations, family visits, and
research trips to Italy would take us back to Trieste.
Rabuiese is the "**posto di blocco**," the border crossing between Italy and Istria—in Yugoslavia under
Tito, in Slovenia now.

Pre-1990, Yugoslavia was composed of six
"republics"—Croatia, Slovenia, Serbia, Bosnia-
Herzegovina, Macedonia, and Montenegro—which
were ethnically similar but had different heritages.
After Tito's death, in 1980, Yugoslavia fractured into
independent countries. Croatia fought a bitter war
with Serbia; Bosnia-Herzegovina suffered a civil war
among Orthodox Serbs, Catholic Croats, and Muslim Bosniaks. Most of what was northern Istria is in
Slovenia, and the southern part is in Croatia. Now,
when we come from Trieste, we have to cross Slovenia to get into the Croatian part of Istria. It is a
question of only twenty-some miles, but nonetheless two border crossings.

Trieste was our depot before going to visit family
over the border. There we would buy coffee, rice,
fruits, and chocolates to bring as gifts to the family and kids in Istria. I loved the city, because it
brought back so many memories. Usually, we visited with friends and any relatives we had left.

Before we left Trieste, I would pack the backseat of the car with cheese, salami, coffee, and other foodstuffs that we'd purchased, and then have Tanya and Joe sit on top of it. I'd cover the children with blankets and tell them to close their eyes and go to sleep. Getting those things over the border was tough in those days, and so making the food "disappear" under the blankets and kids was an efficient way of getting needed things to our relatives.

Over the years, we forged friendships with several restaurateurs in Trieste. One of them is Bruno Vesnaver. His family had the famous and still-operating Buffet da Pepi, on Via della Cassa di Risparmio, next to the Church of Sant'Antonio Nuovo, where Franco and I had our Confirmations. Bruno now has a second restaurant, Antica Ghiacceretta, on Via dei Fornelli, which serves up great pasta and fish.

We always tried to spend a few days in Trieste visiting with our friends before continuing on to the Collio wine region of Friuli, about thirty miles northwest of the city. It is considered the best white-wine-producing region of Italy, although now it makes some great red wines as well. We would visit this region on every trip, always in search of good wines to bring back to the States. We had made many friends in the area, and with all these trips, we had considered getting a little place there.

Joe's love affair with wine was in full bloom when Bruno introduced us to Valter Scarbolo, a young producer in Friuli who knew of a small winery on twenty acres with a house that was for sale. It was in Buttrio, Collio Orientali. The winery was only partly planted with vines, and the house was in need of major repairs.

In 1997, we bought it and renamed the winery the Azienda Agricola Bastianich. That year, in Valter Scarbolo's wine cellar, and with his help, my son began making wines. Two years later, another opportunity came and we bought a winery in nearby Gagliano, in Cividale del Friuli. This one had a cellar and a **foresteria**, a small country home, just what we wanted.

The headquarters of the Azienda Agricola Bastianich is now at 44 Via Darnazzacco, Gagliano, Cividale del Friuli, and we have added a bed-and-

Our vineyard in Gagliano

breakfast along with a quaint restaurant called Orsone, meaning "big bear," like the name of the mountain it faces. We have made this our Italian home, and spend time there in the summer with the family. The backdrop from our **terrazza** is the peaks of the Julian Alps, and if we turn 180 degrees and continue straight down the road, in forty minutes we are in Grado, a beautiful summer resort on the Adriatic coast, or in an hour in Venice. Cividale del Friuli is itself a quaint and beautiful medieval town, perched on the high banks of the Natisone River.

En route to my courtyard in Busoler each year, I make my stop at Gagliano, Cividale del Friuli. I especially love it here in the fall, at harvest time, when the air is filled with the excitement of a new vintage. Friuli has a hearty cuisine, especially polenta cooked on the **fogoler,** an open-fire hearth. But in the springtime, the focus is on foraging for the young shoots of the wild **sclopit (Silene vulgaris)**, **tarrassaco** (wild dandelion), **ortiche** (nettles), and **luppolo** (hops), which are made into stuffing for pastas, soups, risottos, and frittatas.

The highlands of the Julian Alps are great pastures for the herds of cows that yield the milk that makes the delicious local cheese Montasio, used in the Friulian cuisine, and the best cheese for making **frico.** The area of San Daniele del Friuli is also well known for some of Italy's best prosciutto. Wash it all down with a glass of the local white Friulano, and you are in Friuli.

25

Reflections

Every night, when I lie down to sleep, I spend a few minutes reflecting on my day and have a conversation with God. I thank Him for all the good things that happened on this day and ask Him for direction on the things that I missed or that went wrong. And I ask Him to stay with me tomorrow and the days that follow and guide me.

I thank God for all the gifts He has given me in life—my two beautiful children, my five extraordinary grandchildren, and their families—and I ask Him to keep them healthy. I ask Him to guide them and give them strength through their lives, for life is not easy today for young people.

I thank Him for giving me the gift of having my mother with me at the age of ninety-seven. Yes, our life as immigrants and refugees, moving from communism in a corner of Europe to democracy in America, was emotionally wrenching, difficult, and sometimes sorrowful, especially for my mother. She now has the blessing and enjoys the love, warmth, and fullness of four generations of family.

I thank God for the personal gifts He has given me, starting as a child. I value and deeply appreciate the comforts my profession has given me—and the gift of being able to share my work and the love of food with others. But although I have been given all these gifts, I know they are not mine to keep. I know He has a mission for me, and I ask Him every single night to show me the way and direct me how I should share these gifts in His name.

I have a special affection for the Holy Mother, especially the Mother of the Miraculous Medal. Somehow, because I am a mother as well, I feel she understands me, especially when I am in spiritual need. I talk to her long after the sun has set. But I especially feel the connection when I am in front of her icon in church, or when I pull out the Miraculous Medal I always carry with me.

I pray as well, sometimes when I am in church, sometimes at home, and sometimes when I am on the road. I say the Hail Mary and Our Father as prayers, but I like talking to God. He listens.

No matter what God you talk to or pray to, God is there for everyone.

❧·❧

In 2008, I was invited to cook for Pope Benedict XVI during his visit to New York. The invitation came about through my work over the years with various charitable organizations. One of the first big fund-raisers I had done was in collaboration with Angelo Vivolo; since then, we have done many benefits and events together. One of the organizations that we gravitated to was UNICEF. At the time, Audrey Hepburn was the spokesperson, and I emerged from my first meeting there full of excitement, brimming with ideas on how I was going to help the needy children of the world. Of course, the cooking of food would be my way.

I called Angelo, and over coffee we came up with an idea, a **Roman Holiday**–themed dinner. I could certainly cook Roman food, and if Audrey Hepburn would make an appearance, we could fill the hall. Not only did Audrey attend; so did Gregory Peck and Isabella Rossellini. A plate of **bucatini all'amatriciana** was our offering to them.

Through my work with UNICEF, I got to learn about UNIFEM, an NGO whose focus was on helping women, particularly mothers in third-world countries, to feed their families. Angelo and I got on board, and for the next six years we organized fund-raisers for the organization, which we held in the Delegates Dining Room of the United Nations building in New York City.

Through my work with the United Nations, I had met Italian Archbishop Celestino Migliore, then the Permanent Observer of the Holy See to the United Nations. He had seen me at several of the fund-raisers we did at the UN. During one event he walked over and asked, "Would you like to cook for the Pope?"

"Would I!" I replied.

Pope Benedict was coming to New York in the spring of 2008, and I was charged with organizing, overseeing, and executing the food preparation at the Papal Residence in Manhattan during his visit. The Pope would be in New York from April 18 to April 20, and his first stop was the UN Headquarters to address the General Assembly. He was also scheduled to visit Yankee Stadium, St. Patrick's Cathedral, Ground Zero, and a Jewish synagogue—the first time a pope made a visit to a synagogue on U.S. soil.

Angelo Vivolo and I started to plan and prepare how to execute his meals. During our first meeting with the Archbishop Migliore, he described the events he wanted us to host and explained whether it would be official church business or more relaxed in nature. Angelo and I were to come up with a menu for each occasion, which would be sent to the Vatican for approval. The first thing we needed to do was find out about the Pope's likes and dislikes, and if he had any food allergies. We communicated our questions to the nuncio, and then set about brainstorming the menus. I always try to learn a little about the person I want to feed. Pope Benedict was a very open, very present cardinal; he was known as a theologian, deep and conservative.

When he was elected, it was a bit of a surprise to everyone. He was born in Bavaria, and his mother had been a chef in one of the hotels there, so I was sure he had some great food memories. I wanted to evoke those memories in him, to bring in elements that he would recognize, so I identified spätzle, sauerkraut, goulash, and strudel as items for his menu. And I did capon soup, because when you are traveling, soup is a restorative meal.

Once Angelo and I had settled on the menu, we gave it to the nuncio, who sent it on to the Vatican for approval. When we heard back, the only "no-no" was cinnamon. Oddly enough, it wasn't the Pope who couldn't eat or didn't like cinnamon; it was one of the people traveling with him. The group didn't want to miss out on the strudel, so they made sure I eliminated the cinnamon.

With the menu accepted by the Vatican, I began to assemble my team. I chose as chefs Billy Gallagher (Becco), Fortunato Nicotra (Felidia), and Mark Ladner (Del Posto). Joe was one of the sommeliers, and we picked some of the Bastianich wines to pair with the meals. Angelo organized the service staff and all the logistics of serving the food. He also had to get security clearance for all of our staff members!

Pope Benedict had invited fifty cardinals for the evening of the first dinner, so we would be cooking for a large group. He was staying at the Papal Residence at the nuncio's house, a town house on East

Seventy-second Street between Fifth and Madison Avenues. The residence is like two town houses combined to create one large home. It is a gorgeous old building originally owned by the Grant family. (Hugh J. Grant served as mayor of New York from 1889 to 1892.) The Grants were strongly faithful to the Jesuits, so much so that Mrs. Grant paid for the entire building of Regis High School, a private Jesuit prep school for Catholic young men on East Eighty-fourth Street.

As you enter, there is a big reception area and foyer. One flight up is the official dining room and living room. Above that, on the third level, is the room for the Pope and a beautiful private chapel, the Chapel of the Holy Spirit, which boasts magnificent Tiffany windows.

We were stationed in the kitchen, which was off the reception area and down a few steps. The day of Pope Benedict's arrival, we had arrived early to unload all our goods and get set up. We were all in the kitchen, busy preparing his first meal, when somebody anxiously announced, "The Pope is coming!" A large team of bodyguards began pouring into the residence. I had never experienced anything like it. There were two sets of security personnel, those from the Vatican in Italy and another group consisting of American agents. The inside of the town house is considered to be the soil of the Vatican, much like the inside of a consulate or embassy, so only the bodyguards from the Vatican were permitted inside the house; the team of American security personnel were posted just outside the building. I was surprised by the tension that flared between the two groups—those inside and those outside—each time the Pope entered or exited. Everybody was just trying to keep him safe.

When the Pope arrived, we all ran into the hallway and peered into the reception area, eager to get a glimpse of His Holiness. The foyer was brimming with suitcases, the old Queen of the Nile kind of luggage. I couldn't believe how many there were. Pope Benedict was in his white cassock and zucchetto, or skullcap, with strands of his white hair falling onto his forehead. He seemed tired, and rested in the foyer for a few moments before meeting the waiting dignitaries and the nuns who resided in the house, all of whom got the chance to be blessed by him. I sensed a powerful energy all around us. The spirituality and belief of an individual can have an effect on one's own body chemistry. I have read articles about this phenomenon, the effect deep prayer and belief can have on our brains.

The nuns in the kitchen had been so busy getting the house ready for his arrival that they had been delayed in preparing his lunch. Nothing was ready, and here he was—and they were nervous.

"What were you planning to serve?" I asked.

Fillet of flounder and an antipasto were on the menu; I jumped in and executed the meal.

When the Pope was "in," the house was full of

members of the Vatican's security team. Perhaps not surprisingly, the guys quickly found their way to the kitchen. They were constantly visiting us for espresso and cookies.

Friday night's meal, a formal occasion for his first night, went off without a hitch. Saturday night's meal was going to be a little more relaxed. April 16 had been the Pope's birthday; the anniversary of his papacy was the nineteenth. He had celebrated both events on the sixteenth in Washington, D.C., and we marked them again that Saturday night, April 19. Even though we had all that strudel, we also had a big, beautiful cake made by Biagio and Salvatore Settepani, two brothers who owned Bruno's Bakery, topped with an edible "mitre," the ceremonial headdress, a tall white peaked cap.

Angelo and I brought the cake out together and carefully placed it on the table in front of Pope Benedict. He admired it as we all sang "Happy Birthday" in English and Italian. At the end of the song, Angelo handed the Pope the cake knife. We all watched and waited as the Pope stood frozen in front of the cake. Nothing was happening, so I gently took his hand with the knife, and together we cut the first piece.

My God, I thought to myself, **what did you just do?**

The Pope looked at me, though not with a stern expression; it was more of an appreciative gaze, or so I wish to believe.

I noticed one or two raised eyebrows from those present, but no one—including the Vatican bodyguards—said or did anything. Later that evening, I reflected on that moment for a bit. I wondered how many others had taken it upon themselves simply to grab the Pope's hand. I just assumed his hesitation was because he didn't know the cake-cutting protocol here in the States, and my instincts had me grabbing his hand to guide him along. In life, you can't plan for every moment; some things just happen.

Everybody in the town house wanted to see the Pope, from the nuns who watched over and cleaned the house to all the members of the kitchen crew. On the last night of his stay, we arranged a meeting in the lobby of the residence, where everybody got a chance to be blessed by His Holiness. We were allowed to bring members of our family, and I invited my mother, Franco, and his wife, Margaret, to join me there.

One by one, we stepped forward to receive our blessing and pose for a picture with His Holiness. When it was Billy Gallagher's turn, I noticed him reaching around in his pocket, and wondered what he was doing. Billy is a big, burly guy. He is a fisherman at heart, so I was surprised when he pulled a handful of rosaries from his pocket. Tears formed in his eyes as he explained that his whole family had given him the beads, hoping to have them blessed by Benedict. It was such a moving moment, and the Pope happily obliged. After the blessings, we all went to the official living room, where one of the visiting dignitaries played a piece for us on the violin.

❧ ❧

I was also fortunate enough to be invited to feed Pope Francis when he visited New York in September 2015. The nuncio had been succeeded by Archbishop Bernardito Auza. Angelo and I had kept in touch, and if there was a cocktail party or other event, we were always invited to take charge of the food. Pope Francis would be at the Papal Residence in New York for two dinners, two lunches, and all of his breakfasts. Unlike Benedict, who was reserved and introspective, Pope Francis was the people's Pope. He was from Argentina, so I was thinking big pieces of meat would elicit a positive response in him. When we sent the menu to the Vatican, however, we learned that he was watching what he ate, and he wanted lighter options. Since we couldn't build on the Argentinian theme, I had to dig deeper.

I learned that his family was from Piemonte, at the foot of the Alps in Italy, and not far from the Ligurian Sea, a source for fresh fish. So, for one of his meals, we did whole bass freshly caught on Long Island, and risotto, the preferred starch of the Piemontesi, and finished with a warm peach

tart. Again, we did soup for its restorative quali-
ties, choosing a capon soup with **agnolotti** for His
Holiness. I also made risotto two times during his
visit, for Pope Francis loved risotto. He wasn't a big
breakfast eater: tea, fresh orange juice, and toast.

Unlike during Benedict's visit, when there were
people coming to the residence for official meetings, this Pope had no business scheduled to occur
at the town house, so, for us, his visit was much
more relaxed. He would have breakfast, go out
for his morning appointments, come back to have
lunch, take a rest, and then come back for dinner.
One afternoon, while he was having his rest, we
were all relaxing in the kitchen, having our coffee and discussing our preparations for dinner that
evening. All of a sudden, somebody began shout-
ing, "The Pope is coming! The Pope is coming!"
And before we could even get out of our seats, there
he was. He walked right into the kitchen, dressed
in his cassock and zucchetto.

"May I have coffee with you?" he asked in Italian.

We didn't know what to do. Tanya was working
with Angelo and the service staff this time, and she
flew out of the room and raced up the stairs to the
service kitchen, where the Lavazza espresso machine was located.

In this old house, the service staircase from the
main kitchen in the basement is a tight wooden
spiral. Tanya was wearing all black—for service, of

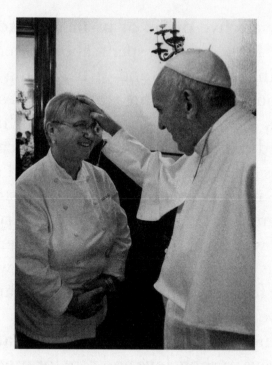

A blessing from Pope Francis after
cooking for him in New York, 2015

course—and her jacket pocket got hooked on the
bottom of the wooden railing as she sprinted up
the stairs to make the coffee. She didn't want to
miss a second of being in his presence, so she was
moving as fast as she could, completely unaware
(or ignoring) the fact that the pocket had ripped
off her jacket. I guess she wanted the coffee to be
perfectly hot for him. She was so elated to know he
was coming to the kitchen, someone could've torn
her whole jacket and she still would have showed
up to serve him an espresso.

There were five or six of us in the kitchen that day, and Pope Francis spent about twenty minutes talking with each one of us, asking us questions about our lives and work. He blessed each one of us individually, then went into his pocket and pulled out rosaries. He gave one to each of us. As he was leaving the kitchen, he turned and said, "Pray for me." Even now, retelling the story, I get goose bumps. It felt very comfortable, very natural. His aura was mixed with our auras. There was an incredible energy. For me, it was such a wonderful feeling. I feel very connected to Pope Francis now, as if he were family.

Preparing, cooking, and sharing food are fundamental ways to show love and care for others; when you share food, you share life. When I cooked first for Pope Benedict and then for Pope Francis during their visits to New York, I was paralyzed at the thought of being in their holy presence. But then something special happened that I could never have anticipated. When I cooked and served them my food, the food was the equalizer, a gift they accepted humbly and with gratefulness. In the sharing of the food that I had prepared, a closeness of spirit happened between us. I felt as if we were part of one family. I felt a tangible closeness to both Pope Benedict and Pope Francis, and one that cannot adequately be explained.

⇒·⇐

Through my work with food, I have been fortunate enough to meet many incredible people. In October 2008, I was invited to the White House to attend the official dinner in honor of Silvio Berlusconi, then prime minister of Italy. When I received the invitation, I remember thinking, **Do they have the right number? Am I here by mistake somehow?** I had done the visitor tours of the White House when I was in school, but now I was being invited to sit in a room with the presidents of the United States and Italy.

I wanted to be proper, to fit in, just as I had in my early days as a schoolgirl. Those insecurities always resurface, no matter how old you are and how far you have come. But I did feel comfortable and very much part of the evening. Being there reaffirmed that I really was an American.

In a way, I still feel like Giuliana and Lidia: I am a part of two of the greatest cultures in the world, Italian and American. The Italians have a long history, art, a love of life, and food. As an American, part of a new country, rich and shiny, I learned how to think like a businesswoman and to reach for the stars.

The White House was beautiful—the setting, the protocol, the gowns, the way I was escorted to my table. The experience was unforgettable.

We were a small group, ten tables of ten. At the front of the dining room was a podium, with a table set up on either side. Seated at the one on the left were George W. Bush and a few other guests. I was at the table on the right, seated next to First Lady Laura Bush. Also at my table was the guest of honor, Silvio Berlusconi.

Other prominent people in attendance that evening were former New York mayor Rudy Giuliani and his wife, Judith; Speaker of the House Nancy Pelosi and her husband, Paul; U.S. Supreme Court Justice Antonin Scalia and his wife, Maureen; Secretary of State Condoleezza Rice; and the musician Frankie Valli and his son Francesco.

Laura Bush invited me to visit the White House a second time. The mayor of Milan, Letizia Moratti, was pitching to have Expo 2015, the Universal Exposition, in her city, and I was invited to a breakfast at which she would present her proposal to the First Lady. Laura Bush and her daughters since have been to Felidia, and we are still in touch. Having a toe in both cultures has made me a sort of cultural "ambassador" between the two countries. In 1996, the Italian government recognized me with the Cavaliere della Repubblica award for "Outstanding contribution and dedicated service to the Italian-American Community." This was a huge honor. In 2008, I was bestowed the distinguished title of "Commendatore della Repubblica Italiana," Commander of the Republic of Italy, by the president of the Italian Republic, Giorgio Napolitano, for my "commitment to the Italian heritage and the Italian Food." "Commendatore" is a lifelong title and the highest award an Italian can receive from the government. It still amazes me that I am a member of that exclusive club.

When the Obamas moved into the White House in 2009, First Lady Michelle Obama invited a number of chefs to visit her White House Kitchen Garden, and I was among that illustrious group, which included Daniel Boulud, Joan Nathan, and Dan Barber. Mrs. Obama was into healthful eating and understood the importance of teaching children good eating habits, sentiments I share wholeheartedly. I was happy to see that she was raising awareness of the importance of farm-to-table food, eating fresh, local, and seasonal food. I believe the government needs to create a business climate that allows small farmers to compete against far larger industrial operations.

In many ways, members of the food industry are now listening to consumers, planting, harvesting, and preparing foods with an awareness of flavor and nutrition. There seems to be a real respect for our environment, the earth, and the husbandry of the animals that we eat. The consumer can be— and needs to be—the most effective advocate for this much-needed shift. Let's evermore respect the men and women who work the land to produce honest food for our nutrition. When you are shopping, support and buy from small farmers and honest producers. As they say, put your money where your mouth is, and the wheels of change will keep churning.

With the unveiling of the fifty-thousand-square-foot Eataly in the Toy Center Building in New York City on August 21, 2010, we have become very much a part of that effort. I had read about Oscar Farinetti's Eataly, the largest Italian market in the world, which he opened in 2007 in a former vermouth factory in Torino, Italy. **The New York Times** called it a "megastore . . . that combines elements of a bustling European open market, a Whole-Foods–style supermarket, a high-end food court and a New Age learning center." At that time, I was also following Carlo Petrini's Slow Food movement, the idea of going back to the actual producer of food, appreciating the traditional ways of making cheese, making everything organic, the way real farmers would do.

The Slow Food movement strives to educate consumers about food tastes, improve biodiversity, and encourage more interaction between consumers and food producers. The Slow Food Foundation for Biodiversity, a nonprofit organization started by Slow Food International and Slow Food Italy, helps organize and fund worthwhile projects across the United States.

The Slow Food movement has a big fair every second year in Torino at the Lingotto Center, the old Fiat production plant, and the first Eataly to open was in Torino. I also knew that Farinetti had worked with Petrini and was a fan of his Slow Food movement, and he applied the Slow Food philosophy in selecting the foods and other products for Eataly.

I went to check out this new store, and the next day I called Farinetti and told him I would like to meet with him and learn more about how he had come to this idea, since he was neither a chef nor a farmer. He was a charming man, with sparkling eyes and a warm smile under his boxy mustache. As I toured Eataly with him, I was fascinated by the layout of the store. It had all the counters of a great food store with really wonderful Italian food products on the shelves. There was also a fresh fish counter, a butcher shop, an endless display of seasonal fruits and vegetables, a bakery in which fresh bread was baked all day long, and an extraordinary spectrum of traditional Italian desserts. Plus a gelato station!

Next to each food category there was a restaurant to match, which would cook the specific products on sale. There was, of course, a coffee bar, a **scuola di cucina** (cooking school), and an extensive selection of cookbooks for sale.

I just loved it, and I returned several times during that trip to Italy. When I arrived back in New York, I told everyone that this man Oscar Farinetti was a genius with food. We kept in touch, and he invited me to take part in two food events, where I cooked and gave a cooking class.

It didn't take Oscar long to decide to bring his concept to America. But he needed partners. At that time, our group consisted of Mario Batali, my son, Joe, and me. I was excited just thinking about the possibility of partnering with Oscar, but this would be a mega-undertaking, and we would need more partners on board.

We found them. And we moved quickly. In 2010, Joe, Mario, and I, the Italian partners, and Alex and Adam Saper, two American brothers who love Italy and Italian food, opened Eataly at Twenty-fifth Street and Fifth Avenue. The Saper brothers knew Oscar and had worked with him in opening Eataly Torino, so they were the perfect partners to help us launch the store here in New York.

New Yorkers reacted well, and the business quickly took off, prompting us to open a second location, at 4 World Trade Center/101 Liberty Street in 2016. In 2013, we had opened a location in Chicago, and then one in São Paulo, Brazil, in 2015, followed by Boston in 2016, Los Angeles in 2017, and Las Vegas in the plan for 2018. The enthusiasm has prompted us to continue to grow; we also have plans to open in Toronto.

Stepping inside Eataly is like coming to Italy—an open square filled with food, with prosciutto being sliced, mozzarella being pulled, a bounty of fruits and vegetables, and a rainbow of colors, textures, tastes, aromas, and sights. Just as in Torino, we have a butcher and a meat restaurant; we have the vegetables and someone who can clean the vegetables for you, and then we have a vegetable restaurant. We stock top-quality fish from local fishermen, and we can cook it for you, too. In La Scuola, Eataly's cooking school, where I am the dean, customers can learn about the products and how to prepare them.

Perhaps one of the first stops for a new visitor to Eataly is the Piazza, modeled after the piazzas or squares of Italy. The Piazza is the hub, the heartbeat of Eataly. It is kind of a social epicenter, where friends come to meet friends, and strangers as well. It is like one big family table, where everyone is welcomed to enjoy assorted meats, cheese, fish, antipasto, and a glass or two of wine.

The second stop is our pizza-and-pasta restaurant, which serves a traditional Neapolitan pizza and a continuous flow of house-made fresh and dry pastas with traditional seasonal recipes.

My hope is that Eataly brings a slice of Italy to Manhattan, to America, and opens the door to a delightful culinary journey.

26

Striking the Balance

Usually when February 21, my birthday, nears, I take off and get lost somewhere in the world. Celebrating my birthday as the numbers climb, and making it into a big to-do, is not what I love to do. I prefer spending my birthday with a few intimate friends or with family. Even putting a few friends and family together is a big deal for me.

As the big seven-oh was nearing, in February 2017, my daughter, Tanya, and my daughter-in-law, Deanna, told me that they were planning something, and that no one but their families and I were invited. There would be ten of us in all. They decided we should go to the CuisinArt Resort on the Caribbean Island of Anguilla, a short ferry ride away from the popular St. Martin. (Little did we know how terribly, tragically damaged both islands would be seven months later, when Hurricane Irma swept ashore.) Much to my delight, the celebration they planned turned out to be the perfect way for me to spend my "big" birthday.

I was so excited: it had been a few years since all ten of us had vacationed together, mostly because of conflicts in the school schedules for all my grandchildren. The one good thing is that my birthday falls around the Presidents' Day celebration, which gives the kids a long weekend off. This year, my birthday fell on a Tuesday—the day after Presidents' Day, when all the schools were closed.

During our first few days on the island, we enjoyed breakfast, lunch, and dinner together as a family. We hopped around the island, trying different restaurants every night for dinner, and ended each evening with a competitive game of **bocce** back at the resort. The CuisinArt Golf Resort & Spa actually has a **bocci** court; it's a game Istrians love to play. Indeed, Felice and I won the Istria Club tournament one year.

My Tuesday-night birthday celebration was going to be at the resort. Tanya and Deanna had it all planned, and I'd been told to relax and dress casually, in an island style. Other than that, the two wouldn't give me more than a clue or two about their plans. The only thing I was told was that our close family friend Father Stephen Katsouros, a Jesuit priest, would come and wish me a happy birthday. Tanya had arranged to fly him down. His brother has a house on Anguilla, so he would visit him and come celebrate my birthday with us.

In 2015, Father Katsouros was instrumental in

launching Arrupe College, and he is now the dean and director of the college, which offers a two-year associate degree to motivated students with limited financial resources. Arrupe is part of Loyola University Chicago, and many of its students are the first in their families to pursue higher education.

Father Katsouros asked me to be on the board of Arrupe College, and, understanding the dedication he has to educating young men and woman, and especially those in need, I knew this would be a fulfilling experience for me. I believe that educating young men and women and giving them the tools to live a better, more rewarding life is the key to making America a better place for all.

The plan was for me to meet everybody at the lobby bar for a drink to start my birthday celebration. We had connecting rooms. The grandkids were split: three boys in one room, and my two granddaughters and I in the other. As we got ready for dinner, my room was humming with activity, as one person showered while another got dressed. Since it was my birthday, I had called first dibs on the shower. There were the usual cries as the girls demanded to know who had left a bathing suit on the floor, who had left a trail of sand behind, where was a dry towel?

I had my outfit planned, with black pedal pushers and a flowingly loose, long white chiffon top whose black chiffon cuffs were embroidered with shining black glass beads. I slipped on black sandals, and I was set. The girls were dressed and ready.

My seventieth birthday celebration,
with the grandchildren

The boys and the adults were already waiting for us
in the lounge, as was Father Katsouros.

It was great to see him, a bit out of context—
in his summer wear rather than his usual clerical
collar. We had our drinks, toasted, and chatted. At
some point, Father Katsouros stood up and said he
would see us in a few minutes.

After we had our drinks, Tanya and Deanna got
up and summoned us to follow. We ended up on
an open grassy plateau facing the ocean. In the distance, there was the silhouette of a man in the setting sun; it was Father Katsouros, wearing his stole
on top of his summery party wear. There was a little
table in front of him, spread with a simple cloth;
on it he had his missal for the liturgy and all the

gifts for the Eucharist. He was offering mass for the family in the most beautiful setting. The sky was fuchsia pink; the soft sound of the waves breaking on the shore and the murmur of the palm leaves swaying in the breeze made the setting celestial.

There were ten chairs in a line facing him. I was so moved my eyes filled with tears, but this was no time to cry; this was a time to be ever so happy and ever so grateful. The mass was beautiful and quick, with a personal eulogy to the family. He then posed a question to each one of us: "What does family mean to you?"

Each one of us gave an impromptu, honest answer from the heart. For me, this reaffirmed that my family members, big and small, understood in their own ways that family is something very special, a place of love, a place of safety, a bond to keep always. We received Communion and a blessing; I felt so gratified, happy, and honored.

As we were getting up, I noticed in the corner of my eye a white tent on the beach. I suspected that was our dinner destination. And so it was: under the tent a beautiful long table had been set, adorned with white and orange flowers and votive candles.

As we arrived at the landing leading down to the sand, waiters started popping the champagne, and a four-piece calypso band started to play. Champagne in hand, we kicked off our sandals, jumped onto the beach, and started to dance barefoot in the cool sand. With all my family dancing around me, and my white chiffon shirt flowing in the warm breeze, I felt as light and happy as a bird.

Surf-and-turf was the theme. With the champagne we had some fried conch, grilled local barbecue-flavored shrimp, and oysters; then dinner began with a delicious fresh tuna ceviche with mango and pineapple, after which we had half of a two-pound spiny lobster each, grilled and served with drawn butter, followed by a whole tenderloin filet seasoned with local rub, grilled, sliced, and served with grilled vegetables. Bowls of green salad including delicious tomatoes from the resort's hydroponic farm were set in a line down the center of the table, between the votive candles. The adults put away a few magnums of well-chilled Bastianich Vespa Bianco. The kids ran and played and danced on the beach between courses, coaxing me to join, which I did from time to time.

"Happy Birthday, Grandma" was sung in unison when the birthday cake came out, followed by a spread of desserts. I was full and content. The only person missing was my mother; at her age, this trip would have been too hard for her.

Slowly, we shifted from the table to the beach chairs, to sip some grappa and Cognac. The moon was casting her silver streak, shimmering on the now dark-blue water; the sky was full of stars like I had never seen before. It was one of the happiest moments in my life.

Getting to be seventy is not that bad after all.

Epilogue

—

Return to Campo San Sabba

I found the courage to return to Campo San Sabba on my fourth trip back to Istria, in 1973. The big iron gate was closed, locked tight with a chain and padlock and topped with rusty barbed wire. When I peeked in between the bars, I saw the big empty courtyard that had once been such a hub of activity. Painful, difficult memories of our months there flooded back. I could hear the refugees' laments floating in the air, haunting sounds that I can never forget.

I looked up at the empty windows of the gloomy, silent building where we had lived and thought about the darkness of the lives that had passed through the camp so many years ago. In 1975, San Sabba became a **museo civico**, a civic museum; on subsequent trips, I found the courage to go inside. By then, the entrance to the complex had changed,

It took me many years to return to the
San Sabba refugee camp in Trieste.

and there was a new gate. The dirt in the courtyard
had been covered by concrete, and the inside of the
brick building where we'd lived had been charred
by a fire that occurred several years after authorities
had stopped using San Sabba as a refugee camp. As
I got closer to the structure, a big lump grew in my
throat. My eyes filled with tears, and I bit my lip
hard so I would not cry. There were other visitors
there, and I realized that, for some reason, I felt
ashamed that I had once lived here with my family.
It felt so real to me again—all the people huddled
together, waiting on line for food, trying to find
a place to sit at one of the long wooden tables. I
could see the cramped spaces where we had lived,
taken showers, washed clothes. I recalled the plea-

sure I felt when I left the camp to go to school, and the sadness when I came back every night.

I wondered what happened to all the other refugees we'd lived with. Where had they all gone? Had they found good homes, as we had in America, been welcomed by authorities, and able to find opportunities to build new lives and be educated? Or had they been shunned in their "new world"?

Every so often, I get an e-mail from someone who remembers me or my family from San Sabba. Sometimes the writer has seen my cooking show, and recalls my name or has a vague memory of our meeting. Sometimes I receive photos of women who were in the camp at the same time I was, asking if I remember them. Often I just can't, no matter how hard I try. The reality was that I didn't have any close friends inside the camp; I tended to stay with my parents and Franco and didn't spend much time on my own.

I still go back to San Sabba periodically. It was so important for me to take Joseph and Tanya in their teens, so I could share with them that part of our history, and they could appreciate and cherish what Grandma Erminia and Grandpa Vittorio did for our family to bring us to freedom. I have now taken my grandchildren there, too, for it is part of their story as well.

On a more recent trip to Trieste, I visited the warehouse at Magazzino 18, in the Porto Vecchio, where there are storerooms full of the belongings the **optanti** brought with them to Trieste. They had hoped to find new homes and settle in, either in Trieste or at someplace nearby, but it was not to be. The **optanti** found that there weren't any places for them to settle, and no place for them to put their furniture. With no other options, they put their treasured personal pieces in a warehouse, fully intending to retrieve them once they had new homes. Eventually, the **optanti** did find new homes, scattered across Italy in places as remote as Calabria and Sicily. Others continued their journeys and eventually settled in Canada, America, Australia, and elsewhere across the globe. Many of them were never able to reclaim their furniture, and so it sat in this warehouse for decades, unused and gathering dust.

In Magazzino 18, the chairs are piled high, the tables stacked on top of one another, the beds dismantled. In one room, pots and pans, silverware, and table linens are still waiting for their owners to return and claim them. There are walls lined with books and notebooks and photos, all covered with dust and cobwebs. As I carefully examined these items, my throat tightened and my eyes filled with tears. My thoughts went to my father's trip, with all our belongings, to Brescia where my mother had found work as a teacher, and to all of those hopeful families who had also made the journey, expecting to find peace and prosperity in Italy. I hope they all found a peaceful and happy place to continue their lives. I hope they all have homes full of furniture.

Forging a new life in a foreign land is daunting. It requires sacrifice and hard work and, most of all, staying true to your values. So many people ask me how I have managed to attain such success and yet remain in a stable place. The luxury of age and hindsight enables me to provide an answer. It doesn't just happen; you have to work at it. Self-control, meditation, spirituality, religion, and family are all key components. As you grow, you need to stay connected to the source. It is like a stairway: you have to keep the steps intact so you can get back to your safe place. You need to have a kind of home port where you put down anchor when the hurricane comes; you must stay connected to your roots. That helps you to have humility and an understanding of your true self. But how do you balance it all? You cannot keep all these elements as separate islands; you need to weave everything together, to intertwine your job and your family.

For me, my friends feed my soul. So do the sea, art, and classical music.

Every summer for the past ten years, my old friend Wanda Radetti—whom I first met at the five-and-dime store in Astoria—and two or three other women and I hire a sailboat with a skipper, and we sail with abandon in the Dalmatian archipelago. We love our time on board—sailing, swim-

All the heartbreaking possessions left behind by
Istrian refugees, stored for decades in the
warehouse Magazzino 18 in Trieste

ming in the crystal-clear pale blue-green waters for
hours at a time, relaxing in the cockpit with a glass
of wine, and doing some cooking. There's a bit of
retail therapy for us when we're in port, but our
focus is on the time we spend on the water.

In my travels around the world, especially those
with my children, visiting museums and art galleries is always part of the schedule. Our latest treasure was visiting the Orangerie in Paris, a small but
important museum that houses some of Claude
Monet's **Nymphéas** works. In that beautiful set-

ting, we sat in peace, admiring his paintings without uttering a word to each other.

As a child, I would hear classical music flowing out of the arched windows of the Roman arena, but now I go looking for it. Over the years, I have heard Pavarotti, Beverly Sills, Renée Fleming, Leontyne Price, Franco Corelli, and Joyce DiDonato, under the baton of such greats as Valery Gergiev, Leonard Bernstein, James Levine, Gianandrea Noseda—way too many to mention. But I loved them all. I always feel as if the singers are singing directly to me.

My mother is an extraordinary anchor for me. In this fast-paced and hectic new world, so many people are liberating themselves from their families, putting their loved ones in old people's homes. This is tragic, to me. Parents and grandparents are a precious commodity. You must not waste them. Make sure your children have time with them. They, too, can gain strength from them.

To recharge, I continue to visit my courtyard in Busoler at least twice a year: in March into early April for the wild asparagus, and in July into August for the sea. As time has passed, our immediate relatives have become too few, and the next generation is too spread out. But my cousin Sonia Fonio Perdija and her family still live there.

Sonia is my first cousin and the daughter of my aunt Lidia, my mother's only sister. She is eight years younger than I am; she was two when I left Istria, and I got to know her only when I returned as a bride. She recently retired from the Scuola Sijana, a grammar school in Pola, as assistant director, and her husband, Zlatko Perdija, is a retired naval engineer who worked at Uljanik, the big shipyard in Pola. They returned to live across the street from Nonna Rosa's courtyard, where Zia Lidia and Emilio built a house. They have one son, Dinko (Domenico). Sonia's father was Emilio, my beloved uncle who took me fishing in the evenings, so Sonia, too, loves fishing and the sea.

We refurbished Nonna Rosa's courtyard and maintain it as close to its original condition as possible,

Celebrating my mother's
eightieth birthday at Del Posto

with no modern remodeling or building. Now and then, we do add a coat of fresh paint, new shutters on the windows when needed, and some equipment for convenience and comfort, such as a washer, a refrigerator, and a gas stove.

For me, the courtyard is still a sacred place, a sanctuary of sorts that holds some of my most precious memories. Those memories are brought to life by the minty smell of the pine trees and the sound of the owl—yes, the owl of my childhood is still there, and I still hear his hooting. Sometimes, when I close my eyes, I can see Grandma Rosa in her black dress, apron, and kerchief, sweeping the figs that have fallen from the tree that serves as a centerpiece to the courtyard.

Returning to that courtyard is my way of staying connected; it's also a way for me to instill in my children and grandchildren the need to stay connected to something important to them, to build roots and security that will sustain them through the years.

There are still three big umbrella fig trees providing shade and juicy figs in the summer. We planted one olive tree in the center of the courtyard, and 375 olive trees on the land that Nonna Rosa and Grandpa Giovanni worked so hard in order to feed us. The shimmering silver-leaved trees sway in the Istrian breeze in their honor. The trees now produce olive oil, and we ship it to the States and share it with the family. We still enjoy and appreciate the fruits of the

Nonna Rosa,
tying vines in her favorite place,
the fields in Busoler, c. 1960

soil of the place where we have our roots; we stay connected.

Sonia and I live oceans apart, and yet, when I am there with her, I feel at home, and so connected to her that I relive my story, my family, my childhood. We go foraging for asparagus in the spring, and all we eat for lunch and dinner for a few days is wild asparagus frittata. She has a little fishing boat, and sometimes we go fishing together, just as I did with her father, who passed away on May 18, 1982.

When we go to the beach, we get there early in the morning. Since Pola has so many beaches, the decision is not an easy one. I have my favorites—Verudela, Stoja, and Kamenjak—and she has hers as well. On the way back, we stop at the **mercato** in Pola, now Pula, where I used to go to sell vegetables with Grandma. We stop for an espresso at the Caffe Milan, in the square adjacent to the market, and then return home to the courtyard to cook our lunch. Sonia is a great artist, and she captures the local scenery in beautiful colors. I especially love her paintings of the fields, full of golden wheat and dotted with explosive red poppies, my favorite flowers. These are the fields I used to run through. We often talk of who will carry on the courtyard tradition. For now, it is the two of us who keep it alive.

Will someone carry on after us?

Acknowledgments

Having written many cookbooks, I was encouraged to write about a new and different subject—myself. Well, not totally new. I have always been happy to talk about my childhood and share my story of coming to the United States as a refugee and to talk about my experiences in the food industry. But I have always shared these memories in snippets in interviews and throughout my other books. It is a much more difficult (and much odder) task to talk about yourself enough to fill a whole book, especially one that others will, I hope, enjoy reading. I have many people to thank for making this new experience so gratifying. I truly appreciate all of their attention and efforts.

A book like this does not happen without the support of a fabulous publishing house, Knopf, and a strong publishing team. Many thanks to my editor, Peter Gethers, for his constant guidance and hard work. And thank you to Janna Devinsky for keeping everything organized and flowing. Looks count, too, so thank you to Kristen Bearse, who designed the pages you're reading, and to Kelly Blair (and Carol Carson, the art director) for the jacket. It looks just how I had hoped it would. Thanks, too, to my dear friend Paul Bogaards for always supporting my publishing endeavors and for his unending enthusiasm. To our Knopf promotional mavens, Jessica Purcell and Sara Eagle, thank you for all your hard work. And thank you to Melanie Dunea for capturing, in the cover photo, the joy and spirit—and food!—this book embodies. And a special thanks to Lisa Pulitzer, without whom this book would not have come to fruition.

To all the friends and colleagues who have been a part of my life, please know that each one of you has shaped who I am. Thank you for that.

My family has always supported my choices, no matter how extreme they may have seemed. I can barely express my appreciation for that. In particular, I must thank my mother, who made a very brave decision sixty years ago to leave behind most of her family and the life she knew in search of a better life for her children. Mom, I am forever grateful. I love you.

Joseph, you too have added much to my life and our business from when you were the joyous, mischievous boy who would do his homework on the tomato boxes in the restaurant cellar to the achieving businessman, restaurateur, and winemaker you've become. You contributed much to the expansion of our then-young business, and found your passion in the vineyards of Friuli. A toast to you, for this is your story as well.

My daughter, Tanya, encouraged me to take this project on and has been by my side the entire journey. Very little happens in my life without her presence and input. She is the businesswoman behind me, always thinking of new projects and extensions of what I am already doing. I can always count on her for strength, support, and so much more.

My dearest Tanya, your name and presence are scattered throughout this book and you certainly are a cherished and loved daughter, but for me you have been and are much more. With your love for history and storytelling and your consummate dedication to research you have helped me tremendously in putting this memoir together. Not only did your academic strength and wisdom help me in weaving together my life story, but this story is for you to continue. Family history, traditions, and roots need to be remembered, celebrated, and continued, and I know that our family torch, our family story, will continue to be nourished by your passion and dedication to our family and its history.

You possess both a creativity and a business acumen that fuel me and give me energy and strength to confront new challenges. You are there to manage and oversee Felidia and Lidia's in Kansas City and Pittsburgh but also to coauthor my books, produce my television shows, and oversee a multitude of projects—newsletters, websites, social media, television distribution, speaking opportunities, and so much more. You are always up to the challenge of a new project or business, and I am extremely blessed to have you by my side to help make these important decisions regarding the future of what your father and I started several decades ago.

Life has its stages, and as my mother and grandmother took care of my upbringing and nurturing in preparing me for my future, so did I and Grandma Erminia love you and nurture you, but life has its turns, and I am the caretaker of Grandma Erminia now, in which you have selflessly joined me, making sure that Grandma Erminia's remaining life has in it all the gratitude and love she deserves. For that I thank you. I can somehow see myself in you, for I know that you will carry on and teach my grandchildren our family's traditions, values, and memories.

Mille grazie from a grateful and very proud mom and partner.